)H

Check
or to re
www.bir
www.birm

56567

LENNY HENRY

ALSO BY JONATHAN MARGOLIS

Cleese Encounters
The Big Yin

LENNY HENRY

A BIOGRAPHY

Jonathan Margolis

Copyright © 1995 by Jonathan Margolis

All rights reserved

The right of Jonathan Margolis to be identified as
the author of this work has been asserted
by him in accordance with the
Copyright, Designs and Patents Act 1988.

First published in Great Britain in 1995 by
Orion
An imprint of Orion Books Ltd
Orion House, 5 Upper St Martin's Lane, London WC2H 9EA

A CIP catalogue record for this book is available
from the British Library

ISBN: 0 75280 087 6

Printed in Great Britain by
Butler & Tanner Ltd, Frome and London

PREFACE

'I have to believe in what I do because I can't plumb and I can't mend cars.'

Lenny Henry

Lenny Henry, it has been said, is the sort of black person that racists make exception for. Britain's only successful black mainstream comic, he is the Frank Bruno of the comedy circuit. Humour crosses many divides, and Lenny has the rare ability to walk the tightrope between cultures.

Only he could make a comment about police harassment of blacks and be intently listened to by both the establishment and alienated young blacks. Only he can say, as he has done, something as flip as, 'The English legal system works on the basis of guilty until proven black', and not just get away with it, but have even establishment types nodding in recognition of his wisdom.

The fact that Lenny is of Jamaican origin, via Dudley in the West Midlands, is more an afterthought for his fans. He firstly registers as being an immensely funny, talented man, impressionist, stand-up, singer, serious actor and director. Yet his ethnic background has proved to be the motor force behind his entire career. His developing humour over the last two decades almost charts the shift in the cultural climate in this country.

Lenny's comical streak developed at an early age, spurred on by his own desire for acceptance. As a child, he was unable to ignore that he was black. One of his early memories is of the little boy next door, who would one day be his friend and the next would open the letterbox to spit through it and shout, 'Blackie.'

One of only six black boys in his year at Blue Coat Secondary Modern School in Dudley, Henry became a legend in his own playtime for a series of uncanny impressions. This classroom act would develop into a class act which would win the him the hearts and laughter of the nation. Later he would say: 'I don't think I consciously wanted to be accepted by the white kids, but the reasons my impersonations were funny were definitely that here was this black guy doing impressions of white people.'

This was a sentiment to be echoed by one of the judges on the TV show *New Faces*, which would eventually unleash Lenny onto a wholly unsuspecting public.

New Faces was the 1970s sharp-edged springboard for young talent. It could be a merciless blooding ground. In 1975 this young steel-industry engineering apprentice from Dudley stood with his back to the audience to commence his bid for stardom with an impersonation of Michael Crawford's Frank Spencer in *Some Mothers Do 'Ave 'Em*.

Years later, when Henry was trying to establish himself as an inter-national star, it was his impression of Steve Martin in his concert film, *Live and Unleashed*, that sparked American curiosity about the star, and eventually landed him with his first (and only) Disney lead in the film *True Identity*. One studio bigwig was quoted as saying: 'Lenny did Steve Martin so well, we had no idea that he was black.' Even in this oddly inverted way, the race issue has never been far behind Lenny Henry's career.

He recalls the 'darkie jokes' that he told to his predominantly white audiences as part of his routines in the early stand-up days: gags such as wiping the sweat off his face and saying it tasted of chocolate, and the put-down he used with hecklers – threatening to move in next door to them if they didn't shut up. But that part of his career was preceded by a long period doing an even odder routine for a man later to become an icon of anti-racism.

After winning *New Faces*, Lenny linked up with Robert Luff, the impresario behind the *Black and White Minstrel Show*. As the only black Black and White Minstrel, he did a five-year toil of endless summer shows in hotspots like Great Yarmouth, before admitting to Luff that he 'didn't feel quite right with these people blacking up'. In fact he admitted: 'I'd like to do anything else rather than that.'

'Anything else' turned out to be a TV spot with fellow comedians Tracey Ullman and David Copperfield on *Three of a Kind*.

In the era of political 'right-on'-ism, Henry has been expected to figurehead the anti-racism cause through his humour. Such a responsibility has sometimes proved irksome – he is, after all, a funny man and not a politician. Lenny has complained about this expectation: 'Nobody goes up to Bernard Manning to ask him how we get out of the recession – but I am always asked about racism and famine in Africa.'

However, as Lenny's career grew, so did his confidence to use his status to champion the rights of ethnic minorities.

There has, all the same, been some debate about Lenny's most successful characters. His famous sex beast Theophilus P. Wildebeeste, for example, has raised the question of whether Lenny was rubbishing the notion of black sexual heroism – or merely reinforcing it.

Yet his unique position as cultural go-between allows him to make insightful comment without offending either side or ghettoising himself. This ability was seen at its best during the Brixton riots, when Lenny's South London wideboy character, the big-mouthed Delbert Wilkins, proved an unexpectedly articulate commentator on the troubles.

Several years ago with the support of the then controller of BBC1, Jonathan Powell, Lenny launched *Step Forward*, a series of workshops for young and predominantly black comedy writers.

'Comedy,' he said, 'is a very Oxbridge thing – black kids with a sense of humour are more likely to make a rap record than apply to the BBC for a job.'

Today, Henry reckons that between a third and a half of his time is spent trying to kick-start the careers of youngsters from ethnic communities through his production company Crucial Films. Is this sheer altruism, or the knowing loneliness of someone who is isolated while at the top of his profession?

More recently on his current TV series, *Chef!*, Lenny told his producers that it would be nice, as he put it, 'to see a few brothers and sisters around the place'. As a result *Chef!* was made with a black sound recordist, black associate producer, black director of photography and several young black trainees and assistants.

To add to his now impressive political credentials, Lenny has been a leading light in Comic Relief, and in 1993, despite his earlier lament about being required to have views on famine and Africa, wrote a very serious letter to *The Times* protesting against Government cuts in foreign aid.

This swing in his attitude – from Black and White Minstrel to black Pied Piper – is a result not only of his growing confidence, but also of advice from alternative comics like Rik Mayall and Ade Edmondson and, more especially, his wife Dawn French, of the comedy duo French and Saunders. She suggested that Lenny finally drop his self-deprecatory jokes and try material which was simply funny instead. 'It planted a seed which led to me changing my act,' he admits. In a comedy climate where the up and coming were all very much Oxbridge educated, right-on politicos, Lenny has managed not merely to hold his own, but in the end to excel over almost every other new-wave comedian.

The marriage to Dawn has spanned a successful and happy thirteen years, and led three years ago to them adopting a young, mixed-race baby girl named Billie.

Yet even being an adored professional comedian and national institution, as Lenny Henry is, has failed to prevent the personal racist attacks that the couple have been subjected to. Dawn admits that being the target of racial abuse due to their mixed marriage – hate mail and excrement being lavished on their front door in Hammersmith, West London – led to them moving out to Shinfield, Berkshire.

'I won't say anything,' says Lenny tersely, 'because I don't want to encourage them. I wrote a sketch about it which I did on stage to get it out of my system.'

So where to now? The move several years ago by Disney to export

Lenny to the States was a flop. Lenny was signed for a £1.75 million, three-film deal which was terminated after *True Identity* bombed at the box office.

The central theme of the film was for Lenny a well-worn one – him disguising himself as a white man to escape from the Mafia. Lenny's sister, who visited him on the set, cried because she couldn't recognise him. 'The only way you'd know it was me was that I bounced when I walked,' Lenny says.

Although he was upset by the precipitate end to his Hollywood career, he rejected the idea that he was ever destined, as the *Los Angeles Times* suggested, to be the next Eddie Murphy or the new Bill Cosby. Instead he said: 'I'm from Dudley in the West Midlands. Hollywood's a completely different world.'

The essence of Henry is his ability to be all things to all people. 'His talent seems limitless,' wrote the *Daily Telegraph* recently. 'He is a comedian, impressionist, singer and now serious actor.

'His appeal is classless and ageless. He is as popular with the over-60s as with the under-20s. He is equally at home doing stand-up routines in northern clubs or working with the alternative comedians who graduated from the Comedy Store. He seems incapable of giving offence ... Six-foot-two of baggy-suited sunshine and good humour – there is apparently no one immune to his charm.'

He is, nevertheless, not an easy man to get to know. TV and show-business associates who think they have got extremely close to him have often realised at some stage that they still do not understand the man. One TV producer who worked closely with Henry over a long period was almost embarrassed, when interviewed for this biography, at how much he had never discussed with him.

Similarly, lifelong friends from Dudley, with whom he has maintained contact, admit that they know little of his professional life. He has one life in London, breezing from smart restaurant to fashionable bar, and another back home; on his frequent visits to Dudley, even as a major star, he still hangs out in the same pubs and haunts he did as a teenager. He is renowned in the town for not having lost his roots. But the two worlds do not converge.

'The real Lenny Henry is difficult to find,' wrote Adam Sweeting of the *Guardian*, 'which isn't altogether unexpected in an impressionist. His characters flock through his conversation as though their host is some kind of airport lounge – a bit of Delbert, a quick howdy from Theophilus P. Wildebeeste, a flash of Groucho Marx and lumps of dialogue between black kids called Poitier or Claudette jostle rudely for space.'

A small côterie of Dudley friends – a social worker and a Naval officer among them – know Lenny Henry quite well. His wife, Dawn French, knows him best of all.

'Everything Lenny does,' she says, 'comes from within him. He has had his eyes open all the time. He's a very honest man. And there's no side to him, there really isn't. What he wants is to avoid being put in a category like any other black actor. He doesn't want to be England's version of Richard Pryor or England's version of Eddie Murphy. He wants to be England's version of Lenny Henry.'

CHAPTER I

THE BLACK COUNTRY

'Me, get repatriated? To Dudley?'

Lenny Henry

On Friday, 29 August 1958, the following story blazed across the top of the front page of the *Dudley Herald*, the principal weekly newspaper of the time in the small, metalworking and mining town ten miles to the west of Birmingham.

JAMAICAN BIT DETECTIVE'S HAND TO MAKE GETAWAY, the headline howled. 'A Jamaican, twice caught driving after being disqualified,' the text read, 'bit a Dudley detective constable's hand and drove off when an attempt was made to arrest him.' William Alfred Richards, aged nineteen and born in Kingston, the reader learned, had been seated in a Ford Zephyr car with a sixteen-year-old girl, Lilian Doris Morris – no racial definition of whom was provided – when the detective tried to question him. Richards said, 'Excuse me,' pushed the girl out, and tried to drive away, taking a nibble at the policeman as he did so.

Mr Richards, a motor mechanic, tried to explain to the court that he did not believe the plain clothes man was a police officer. 'I am sorry because he is a nice man,' he said. Richards added that he had been in England for two years and not got into trouble. 'Then I started to mix with some wrong ones amongst my countrymen, who taught me wrong things. I am very sorry. If I get a chance, this won't happen to me any more.'

Sentencing Richards to three months' imprisonment, Mr Hooper, the presiding magistrate, said, 'You are not a fit person to drive in this country. If you come to this country you must behave yourself.'

This was the world, and the Dudley, that Lenworth George Henry, whose parents were also from Jamaica, was born into on 29 August, the same day the story of William Alfred Richards appeared. It was a society where racial prejudice was legal and above board, where it was perfectly OK for a newspaper to refer to a minor miscreant as 'a Jamaican' if an editor felt like it, and where 'the colour bar' was in everyday operation. In Dudley, as in most British towns in 1958, it was perfectly clear to black people that they were here on sufferance. Winston and Winifred Henry would no more have dreamed of announcing baby Lenworth's birth in the classified columns of the *Herald* than have imagined that their newborn son would one day be a loved and respected figure, both locally and nationally.

Lenworth was the fifth of seven children, and was soon given the inevitable nickname Henry the Fifth. There may, possibly, have been something auspicious in the stars that day for a poor black child born into a large family – Michael Jackson, the seventh of nine, was born on the same day. But, somehow, even humdrum Gary, Indiana, where Jackson was born, has more cachet, more possibility, to it than Dudley, West Midlands. Even Dudley-ites who are loyal to their town, and none has been more consistently so than Lenny Henry, have to admit that Dudley is not an exciting or romantic place. It has an average, down-to-Earthness that Lenny often uses in his comedy – without a trace of the disdain that commonly tinges comedians' comments about their home town.

The official guide to the town and its surrounds, published in 1994, does its best, nevertheless to represent Dudley as some kind of Florence of the Black Country, and there is no doubt that there is more to the place than its downbeat reputation promises. The town has a very fine ruined castle on a hill in its centre – Elizabeth I stayed there in 1575 – some attractive suburbs and far more pretty countryside, being on the edge of Worcestershire, than the phrase Black Country immediately suggests. (For students of the daft anomalies of English local government, Dudley Castle was a treat; before the council boundaries were reorganised in 1974, the castle was officially part of Staffordshire, while the town that surrounds it was Worcestershire.)

Dudley, although an industrial town that still shakes all day to the rattle and roar of lorries carrying huge loads of iron and steel through it, is also an old settlement, already established in Norman times. The marketplace is still a marketplace as it was then, and there is a whiff almost of Camelot, something quite mythical, in the description of Dudley's coat of arms in the guidebook. 'Per chevron Or and Gules,' it reads in what appears to be either an attempt to render in print the Black Country accent, or a stab at a script for the master of gobbledegook, Stanley Unwin. 'A Chevron Azure between in chief two lions rampant per pale Gules et Vert each supporting a Beacon fitted proper and in base a Salamander reguardant fitted proper on the Chevron between two pieces of Chain each in chevron Or a Roundle barry wavy Argent and Azure between two Pears slipped and leaved Or.'

All this was written, a little disappointingly, not in the age of jousts and courtly love, but in 1976, when Dudley Metropolitan Borough, which includes the towns of Stourbridge, Kingswinford, Brierley Hill and Halesowen, was set up. By that time, when Lenny was eighteen, his own description of Dudley as 'Worcestershire's "Little Harlem"' resonated a great deal more with the truth than the small town pomp of the council's foray into heraldry. Dudley was, from the mid-1950s onward, when Winifred Henry arrived from Kingston, Jamaica, a notably black town, and a proportion of white West Midlanders were not best pleased by this development.

On 31 July 1962, as Sir Oswald Mosley, the 1930s British fascist leader, marched again in London, 400 white Mosley-ite youths from the West Midlands converged on North Street in Dudley and rioted. A few miles to the east, in Smethwick, a decade after William Richards took his ill-advised nibble at a plain clothes policeman and was told in effect by the magistrate to behave or go home to Jamaica, a Tory candidate at a by-election defeated the Labour cabinet minister Patrick Gordon Walker with the unofficial campaign slogan, 'If you want a nigger for a neighbour, vote Labour.'

A couple of years later, Enoch Powell, one of the MPs for Wolverhampton, to the north of Dudley, made his notorious 'Rivers of Blood' speech, promising a future of civil violence if black immigrants were not repatriated. Powell was a Birmingham man, and having put Wolverhampton thus on the map, it fell in the Seventies to a virulent local brand of skinheads to try to put his predictions into effect. For a while, Birmingham and the West Midlands became, thanks to the feelings of a vocal white minority, the racist heartland of Britain, a worthy counterpart to the other Brum, in Alabama. Growing up as a black man in Dudley was not, it need hardly be added, the easiest of tasks.

Today, Dudley is a little on the bland side, if anything. 'It's a funny place, a bit of a nothing town, really,' says one long term resident. 'It's not a suburb, so you can't say it's part of a greater conurbation, because it is not. It's the place that Midlands comedians love to take apart. That's one of the reasons I've got a lot of admiration for Lenny Henry – because he has come from Dudley and made it.' (Lenny is not the only Dudley-ite to have made it. A few months before he was born, one of the town's previous favourite sons, the Manchester United footballer Duncan Edwards, was killed in the Munich air disaster. Sue Lawley, the television personality, is another Dudley great.)

Dudley's worst housing has been razed; it was once among the most insanitary and disease-ridden in Europe. There were streets where, in the 1840s, the average age of death (the figure tinged by a huge infant mortality rate) was 16.7 years. Dudley's people are known for being friendly and unexcitable. Its most famous features, Lenny Henry aside (and he lives in Berkshire), are a delightful, slightly dilapidated zoo in the castle grounds, the Black Country Museum (which contains Lenny Henry's infant school, St James's, pulled down and rebuilt brick by brick, although not particularly as a tribute to Lenny), and an enormous shopping mall, Merry Hill, which is attached by a monorail to an impressive canalside arrangement of restaurants, offices and a hotel at Brierley Hill. In the many ethnic eating places at these new developments, there is every probability that the children of the violent racists of the early Sixties today enjoy a spot of foreign food; neither Dudley nor the rest of the country ever lived up to the xenophobic hopes of the white no-hopers.

Despite the gruesome fact that Dudley was once the world's leader in the manufacture of the iron neck collars used to shackle slaves, it has since the Fifties had a strong Afro-Caribbean culture and an equally deep-rooted Asian tradition. But what is most obvious in the town today, the odd curry house excepted, is a stubbornly non-cosmopolitan Englishness, a remnant of its days as an uncompromisingly tough place, where education was regarded as a positive disadvantage in life. Dudley's native cuisine, for example, is reputed to be cow pies in the Desperate Dan tradition; there was once said to be a café called the Pie Factory, just outside Dudley, where in the unlikely event that a customer ate a whole pie, he got a second free. There is today a restaurant in the town's indoor shopping arcade, the Churchill Centre, called Dutch Delights, complete with every visual evocation of old Amsterdam – windmill logos, clogs and the rest of it. What particular Low Country cuisine does Dutch Delights specialise in? Herrings? Rijsttafel? Pancakes? Well, not as such. On a typical day, the menu features Cod, Chips and Peas, Sausages, Bean and Chips, and Pie, Mushy Peas and Gravy, a delightfully Dudley version of exotic eating.

Although Lenny Henry has done more than any other British show-business personality to bring a black perspective into his comedy, it has been by sticking for, perhaps, eighty per cent of the time in his work to a strictly Pie, Peas and Gravy, Dudley world view (as well he might, since it is where he is from) that he has become the most successful *English* comedian of his generation.

Lenny Henry's mother, Winifred, or Big Winnie as she is still known in Dudley today, was born in 1925. She arrived in Britain from Jamaica alone in 1957, leaving her husband Winston and children Hylton, Seymour, Kay and Beverley in Kingston. Word had it at home that Dudley offered jobs and a friendly welcome; the chilling expressions 'No Coloureds' and 'Coloureds need not apply' had already become popular additions to the local dialect.

'Dear Mum – she was one of those Fifties Jamaicans who'd read in the Commonwealth papers about all the jobs in Beautiful Britain,' says

Henry. 'It never struck Mum that she was going to be the cheap labour, doing all the jobs nobody else would do. She just thought as they all did then, "Woweee, England looks like the easy life, it's going to be great. We'll meet the Queen personally." So off she sets and then comes back to Jamaica to fetch Dad and the rest of the family. She was very brave. It was terrible when they first came over. People were so ignorant. A lot of black people knew all about Britain and Britain's history, and a lot of the English people at the time thought they would have tails. My mum told me all about that.'

Winnie worked as a hospital cook until she could afford to send for Winston, and the four West Indies-born children. The eldest, Hylton, was ten when the Henrys were finally reunited in a rented flat in a now demolished area of Dudley. Lenny was the first Henry child to be born in Britain. Winnie would go on to have two more children in Dudley, Paul, and the youngest, Sharon, who was born in 1968, when Lenny was ten and Winnie forty-three. Although Winston Henry was small and wiry ('like a walnut with legs', according to Lenny), the Henry children were mostly big like Winifred. Lenny's six foot two loping presence, so striking to people who meet him, especially when so many performers are physically small, is the family norm.

A degree of poverty was also the norm, as it was for all recently arrived Anglo-Jamaicans. The Henrys' was a working-class and a hard-working home. Both Winifred and Winston had jobs, Winston in the foundry at Beans Industries in nearby Cosley, making parts for British Leyland, Winifred in various factories such as that of Dudley Drop Forgings. No one went hungry, but there was little spare money, and there were certainly no holidays or day trips to Blackpool, even though things in England seemed remarkably cheap to Winnie and Winston. For the Henry parents, these were unquestionably good days, better, as Winnie now says, than today.

By the early 1960s, Winnie and Winston were able to provide a very decent and spacious house, in Douglass Road, off Buffery Park, a ten-minute walk from the town centre. The semi-detached, on the corner of Douglass and Rollason Road, seemed huge to other children who would visit. It had three downstairs living rooms, one with a picture of

Jesus hanging on the wall, besides the un-enterable inner sanctum of the Best Room. Winston grew enormous cabbages and potatoes in the garden. A family treat at 15 Douglass Road might be the laying of a new carpet, provided by Winnie's latest bingo win. But there was no official pocket money for the children. Clothes were handed down and shoes endlessly mended. 'Posh kids could afford to have parents,' Lenny has said, 'but we just had a mum and dad.'

Lenny's father was an aloof, slightly forbidding figure, whom his fifth child never really got to know. He played dominoes and drank Jamaican rum. Winston died in hospital aged seventy-two, of kidney failure and associated problems, when Lenny was nineteen and already an established show-business star. Lenny was devastated by the loss although, to his own surprise, he did not cry at the time. (His grief came out instead in dramatic and unexpected fashion at the wake, when he 'went loopy' and asked the friends and neighbours crowding into the house to leave because they did not seem to be suitably miserable.) 'My dad was one of those remote dads who was at work all day, came home, sat and read the paper and then went to bed,' according to Lenny. 'He was quite dour although he liked a bit of a song.' Sadly, it was at Winston's deathbed that Lenny spent the most time with his father. 'I didn't really talk to him very much until he was dying. Then I asked him lots of questions, it was like *Mastermind*,' he says. 'I wanted to know everything. I was asking him where he met my mum, the whole story. It was all very sad. It's something you always regret, not really talking to your parents until it is too late.'

Winifred was left, aged fifty-two, to look after the younger children and earn a living. It was a job she pulled off with aplomb and, by Lenny's account, with as firm a hand as when he was very young. Even now, he raises an eyebrow at the severity of the physical punishment that occasionally went on at 15 Douglass Road. It was, he says, 'a typical West Indian upbringing. Getting hit was an important factor in it, which was horrible, but gave me a healthy respect for right and wrong. Mum did most of the hitting and the telling off. She could put together some curses and threats that would frighten a docker.' His father had only hit him once, when he was caught torturing his little sister Sharon with a pair of nutcrackers, but he certainly bears his mother no grudge for having beaten him, even if it did hurt at the time. A rare thing among creative people, perhaps, he says he and his siblings had a 'wonderful' and 'lovely' childhood, and generously credits Winnie with having made it possible. 'Mum was – and still is – fabulous,' he avers. In 1982, Lenny bought Winifred a two-bedroom bungalow in posh Kingswinford, where she hung a picture of Lenny meeting the Queen on the wall as soon as she moved in. He also bought his mother a car and sent her on holiday to Jamaica once a year until she became seriously ill with diabetes in her sixties.

There was, of course, far more to life at the Henry home than hitting. 'Mum was very strict and clouted us occasionally, but she's always been very loving and caring. The house was always full of people,' Lenny enthuses. 'I remember sleeping in beds with my cousins and nephews, but we were never hungry or anything – and we're a very close family.' Eating was another central activity in the home. Lenny and visitors remember plates piled so high with Jamaican special-ities that a small child could barely see over the mound.

The Henrys were also a strong Pentecostalist family, which required Lenny to go to church and Sunday school until he was fifteen. Although his mother has said she doubts that Lenny is a Christian after all that, he admits to having been very good in Bible class. 'I believe there's a God,' he says. 'And I think He's like everyone's psychiatrist. For most people, God's someone you talk to when you're in the crap ... I say to him, "Please make this gag work."'

Physically, Lenny's family inheritance was his strapping figure and a marked athletic inability that would turn into a lack of interest in sport, and later into a healthy antipathy towards it. But Winnie Henry was responsible for two essential and priceless emotional qualities in Lenny. The first of these was a steely ambition and dynamism. As Lenny says, 'Our family have always been triers. Mum always said: "Work hard and you'll get there." She's very strong and, like most women, was always the driving force. I admire my mother more than anyone else in the world. With seven of us kids, it can't have been easy for her: she had great tenacity and a real pioneering spirit. When I found things hard through being thrown into show-business at the deep end and was thinking of jacking it in, she was the one who kept saying: "Keep going. Keep your feet on the ground and work hard." ' Winnie would also advise him from time to time, 'Son, it's time you found yourself a nice girl with plenty of brains.'

The other trait Big Winnie would instil in young Lenworth was one that would also, from an early age, serve him well. This was, of course, good humour, which at times showed itself simply as gregariousness and outgoingness, but equally often as the ability to be verbally funny, and never more so than when doing impressions of the show-business icons of the day. 'My mum said I was always funny, but it was unself-conscious. I was clumsy and asked dumb questions which she would find hilarious,' according to Lenny. 'Laughing,' he goes on, 'was always an important part of our life. My mum has an amazing gift for humour. If the oven burns up, she'll say: "Ooh, it's incriminated itself," when she means incinerated.'

What, one might well wonder, happened in the Henry household to the anger and sadness that is so often presumed to accompany such intense jolliness? Lenny Henry could boast of at least two reasons to justify having a miserable or bitter side to him. Being intelligent and sensitive is enough to make most comedians thoroughly depressive; Lenny had the added disadvantage of being a working-class black youth in a society which has still to make such lads feel wholly at home. Yet he was, by every account, happy to the point of unreasonableness, as he skilfully built instant bypasses around both the usual obstacles of teenage life, and the racism that you can find round any corner if you have an eye for it.

'Secure in his home life,' observed the *Guardian* writer Dave Hill of Lenny in 1993, 'he was never scarred by the harshness of the inner city or inculcated with the emerging black militancy. Lacking the knowledge to do differently, the young Lenny learned to fit in with what he found. His imitations were a passport to acceptance. "There was no hassle. There was no anger." '

Lenny Henry's cheerfulness was evident before his humour started to emerge. His first infant teacher at St James's School remembers him as 'a lovely lad, a very, very good little boy', but not notably funny or given to wonderful impressions. Another teacher there retains no outstanding impression of Lenny as a class comic, but as an equable, hard-working, controlled boy with beautifully rounded handwriting. Her overwhelming memory of having Lenny in her class for a year was not of him but of Winnie: 'She was a formidable lady, who would always come to pick little Lenny up wearing a lovely hat.'

Meg Newton, who lived opposite the Henrys in Douglass Road, remembers a subtly different after-school Lenny. 'He was a lovely little boy. They were always round with us, him and his little brother and sister, playing in the garden. I used to wonder what would become of Lenny. I quite worried about it, because he had absolutely no interest at all in his school work.

'My husband Eric was a lecturer,' continues Mrs Newton, 'and I think he saw a lot of potential in Lenny, because he started giving him some maths tuition. But then I used to peek at Lenny when he was doing the work Eric gave him, and he was looking up every answer in the back of the book. Actually, I couldn't bring myself to tell Eric.

'But the wonderful thing about Lenny was how happy he was. There was no trace of a serious side. It was almost as if he knew everything was going to turn out all right for him. It was only recently that I realised that in all the years I knew Lenny, I never saw him cry. Perhaps he did on his own somewhere, but it didn't seem as if anything could upset him.'

He was not incapable of being naughty, but such misdemeanours as he committed were always kind of appealing. He used to look after Paul, his younger brother, in the holidays when both parents were at work. Paul was always threatening to tell their mother about the things he got up to in the park. Once one of Lenny's friends accidentally let a swing hit Paul's face, taking one or two of the little boy's teeth out. Trying to get a gap-toothed brother, still tearful and considering telling on Lenny, past the observant Winifred taxed Lenny's never well-developed powers of deceit.

Another time, aged about nine, Lenny recalls nearly burning the house down while trying to read the dirty bits in his brother Seymour's cheap and nasty Western books. Because the bulb in the cellar wasn't working, Lenny tried to make himself a lamp from a milk bottle filled with paraffin with newspaper in the top. He lit this and placed it on the corner of a crate filled with books. After failing to put out the resultant fire with water, he had to ring the fire brigade from the public phone in the road. Terrified of the consequences when she got home, he hid in the park. When he finally came home, he says, far from beating him, Winifred gave him a hug and sent him to bed.

By the time he went to the Blue Coat Secondary Modern School, a very different boy, although still not in any sense a difficult one, was emerging from the diligent Bible scholar and junior school all-purpose angel. As Tony Wright, who taught PE and geography at Blue Coat, recalls: 'One day I was with a colleague, walking up the hill to the school's other site, and Lenny was walking down the hill. He would always pass the time of day and have a laugh, but this once, he had the most enormous sunglasses on, a really silly pair – it was a summer's day – and I always remember what he said when he went past. He said, "Sir, you think these are sunglasses, but they're not, they're my nostrils." That's the kind of thing he was always doing, this is the way he was. At that time I think life was just a joke for him.'

The question of how far he was by this time using humour to sidetrack racism is as difficult for Lenny himself to resolve as it is for an outsider. Not long after telling the late Jean Rook of the *Daily Express* in 1986 about 'our wonderful childhood in Dudley', he hinted, perhaps to be fashionable at a time when he was feeling particularly militant, that his comedy *was* a form of exorcism: 'Stuff that happened when you were a kid affected you; doing it on stage or writing about it gets it out. If I was doing welding or something I'd be very screwed up by now because I wouldn't have had a chance to get it out.' At other times, he gives every impression that, had show-business not happened to him, he could have settled happily into a black British working-class life.

It does not seem that Lenny was subjected to an enormous amount of racism in Douglass Road, but what there was hurt him, even if he gave nothing of this hurt away. Of one playmate, Donald, who lived a few yards away in Rollason Road, Lenny would later say, 'One day he'd be your friend and the next day you'd knock on his door, open the letterbox to look through and he'd gob at you and shout, "Blackie." Obviously his parents had said, "We don't want you playing with this kid next door." It was sad 'cos he had all these brilliant toys, the first Johnny 7 on the street.'

Another time, he recalls, 'I was playing toy cars with my friend and we needed a multi-storey garage. There was a grocery truck parked outside our house, and there was this empty Daz box. No one was using it, so *voilà*, we had our multi-storey garage. The guy said to my mum, "Your kids have got my Daz box," and she shouted at me and hit me. It wasn't because we'd taken it, because it was such a petty thing. It was because I'd embarrassed her in front of this white guy.' (Lenny went into this incident, complete with illustrations, in a sur-prisingly appealing – and revealing – 1991 graphic novel, *The Quest for the Big Woof*. He wrote, next to the cartoon: 'The van driver probably went home and said, "The darkies' kid lifted something out of my van. Another couple of years and he'll know how to hotwire the bloody thing!" That's the kind of thing people said, and still do. It was just an empty box.')

If Winnie had one lesson for Lenny it was the distinctly un-PC message that black people should 'fit in', whether that meant behaving better than the whites, or even accommodating raw and small-minded racism. 'I think that all those barriers that people put up to protect themselves, the restrictions they put on their kids, are to save face. It's saying to the public, "Hey look, we're trying our best to fit in." I had that drummed into me as a kid, and one of the reasons I wanted to be in show business is because I had this thing of, "Oh well, I've got to fit in and people have got to like me and I've got to aim to please."'

That desire to please, the product of Winnie's training, that Lenny first put into the public arena at St James's Mixed Infant and Junior School, is a theme that continues to run through Henry's life. For a long time in his career, he refused to be even remotely controversial, until this was overridden, seemingly, by a desire to please his wife, Dawn French and the very different social and intellectual milieu that she and her friends introduced him to. He claims that it was then that he decided to aim to please himself more, and please all of the people all of the time less; others might argue that he was simply 'fitting in' again, except with a new group of people.

As far as dealing with racial prejudice was concerned, as a boy, Lenny was shocked when a distant cousin advised him to hit with a brick anyone who called him a 'coon'; when he went to college to do a City & Guilds O.N.C. in engineering, he hit another youth after he accused him of putting his welding flame out and called him a black bastard. Lenny, who was squeamish about blood anyway, was terrified that he had killed the boy, and had also hurt his own hand so badly punching him that it throbbed for weeks. Although Lenny has never hit anyone since, it would not be beyond imagining that as an older man he might take a swing. He would be likely today, however, to use the truly devastating weapon of a killer joke, if one came to mind. (It cannot always be relied upon to do so; once in London, when asked by a troglodyte white multi-storey carpark attendant how a black man came to be driving such a nice Jaguar, Lenny considered a witty riposte, then roared out the more reliable, 'Fuck off.')

Lenny was not unique among the young Henrys in being funny, or in being successful in the world beyond Dudley. In 1990, Winnie confessed to a *News of the World* interviewer, 'Of my seven children, three are doing well and the rest are just trying to live like myself,' revealing with surprising candour the deep underlying structure of the family as adults. Effectively, the three British-born children, Lenny, Paul and Sharon, had raced ahead in life, while Hylton, now in his forties, Seymour, Beverley and Kay were leading regular lives in the Midlands, slightly in the shadow of their younger siblings.

This is not to say that the Henrys are not a close family; Hylton, a popular regular in Dudley's West Indian pubs, is a proud Lenny Henry loyalist, while Seymour, who works in electronics, follows and supports his famous little brother keenly. ('What you worrin' about, man – you performed LOADS of times, just stay cool,' Seymour advised Lenny before his first *Royal Variety Show* performance.) But it is Lenny, Paul and Sharon, who is still only in her mid-twenties, that most patently share the family's ambitious streak and the dry humour.

Paul has tried his hand as a dancer, and is considered to be a potential comedian – 'His friends keep telling him he should be a comedian, and I keep telling him he should get some material,' said Lenny in 1986. 'Course, then he writes it down and I steal the best bits.' In 1991, Paul became a scriptwriter, and remains a close professional colleague and critic of Lenny. The lack of taboo over openly criticising Lenny within the family started when he was first making his way in London, and returning to Dudley at least three or four times a month. 'If I go home and they don't like the new show there will be a deathly silence. That lot keep my feet on the ground,' he said at the time.

Sharon, the brightest of the seven Henry children – she was head girl of her year at school – is also, according to Lenny, 'an untapped reservoir of talent'. Sharon gets on especially well with Dawn, and they have appeared on TV together, modelling jumpers. Even today, the Henrys keep tabs on Lenny. 'Paul and Sharon watch everything again and again. If it wasn't funny, that's it. Their verdict is cold-blooded and I get very angry. "I saw you on telly," they'll say. "It was rubbish. Get some new material!" Sometimes they put the boot in but it's the best thing really 'cos nobody else would do it ... I hate people who give you the old mullarkey when they really think it wasn't very good. It must be awful to be so starry that nobody tells the truth,' Lenny has said. At the Henry home near Reading, a selection of his extended family of more than twenty nieces and nephews is usually to be found. 'His family,' Dawn French confirms, 'are the first to tell him if anything he does is rubbish. They tell him not once but twenty times.'

The Henrys were always, as Dawn learned early on in her relationship with Lenworth George Henry, both a perfectionist and an extremely intimate lot.

CHAPTER 2

PARADISE FOUND

'It is no longer important to be white — and it is devoutly to be hoped that it will soon no longer be important to be black.'

James Baldwin

Nobody could accuse our Victorian forebears of lacking a sense of humour when it came to matters of town planning. One of their favourite jokes was to take the most humdrum area of speculative housebuilding in a given city and call it Paradise. Not that the area of Dudley known as Paradise, and where Lenny Henry was brought up, was at all a bad one. Far from it, it is quite a pleasant part of town. There are a few questionable-looking houses around, the odd delinquent dog wandering the streets, but there are worse Paradises in British towns. Paradise Park, a few yards' walk from the Henry home — it is officially called Buffery Park — is large and flat and not particularly interesting, but it was the centre of the young Lenny Henry's life.

The park was a hanging-out place for boys at a time in the late Sixties and early Seventies when in bigger cities such an activity was already dangerous, with drugs and deviant behaviour on the increase. Safe in Dudley, Lenny and boys like him hung out, looking for games to play, stuff to do. Football, hide-and-seek and kick the can were all popular. Park football games would, according to both Lenny's and his friends' accounts, often have a very Lenny twist to them as, athletically untalented as he was, he sought to enjoy and make his mark on his world. 'We used to have a great game,' Lenny recalls. 'We used to set up our goal posts in front of the park bench where the old-age pensioners used to sit. It was brilliant. It was like skittles. You'd get ten points for each one.'

Another of the park gang tells a similar story. 'When he went over to the park to play football, Lenny used to go up to old people and ask them if they would stand a little apart from each other. Then he'd ask them to stand very still so he could use them as goalposts! It was all a joke but he used to get some of the old people very cross.' Some of these ancients both men refer to may have been slightly less old than childish memories imagine. As Lenny puts it, 'I used to play football all the time against these old crones. They were all like thirty years old, but we'd say, "We'll play the old men in the park. We'll put our jumpers down as goalposts and we'll stick ya!" And we used to kick them up in the air. They really enjoyed it. Got back to work on Monday going "bloody kids".'

A lot of what Lenny did in the park, however, was more serious in its purpose, although it is unlikely that either he or his friends quite grasped its significance at the time. Lenny's mimicry was becoming something of a local tradition. He started out with TV cartoon charac-ters – Fred Flintstone and Deputy Dawg, Top Cat, The Jetsens, Scooby Doo, and entertainers such as Max Bygraves, Mick Jagger and Elvis Presley. James Stewart, although a little old hat by this time, was a favourite, as was Lenny's Muhammad Ali, the only black character he 'did'. The novelty of a lanky black boy of eleven or twelve, with a booming and already quite deep voice and an uncanny presence, faultlessly taking off white celebrities, swiftly became legendary among the *cognoscenti* of Buffery Park. One of his finest impressions was of Tommy Cooper, which was a source of even more heightened hilarity; the effect of Lenny impersonating such an archetypal comic, and one who was not merely white, but white in a specifically English, pasty, sweaty way, was lost on no one.

'We used to have a lot of good times, and sometimes there'd be a command performance,' Lenny recounted on a 1988 *South Bank Show*. 'We'd finish playing three hours of kick the can or hide-and-seek, and then they'd sit around, and they'd make me do impressions, all kinds of things, and I'd be doing it for my mates. They'd demand things like, "Do Noddy Holder." And that's where I suppose I dipped my toe in the "pool of performance". This is where I actually tried things out, this is where I found out I could be funny and get away with it, because if you weren't funny, they'd take the piss out of you mercilessly. It was a good training ground.'

Lenny's rise to minor celebrity in the park came as a great wonder to himself. Despite the fine training for life he was getting at home, his self-image was not as healthy as it might be. 'Other kids were all good at sports,' he explains. 'Everybody except me was good at something – and I was no use at all, but I was starting to be good for a laugh. At first it was let's run off and leave Lenny, that's one way to be good for a laugh. But then I realised that I could also make them laugh by telling jokes and doing impressions. It was wonderful. I really surprised myself. I'd say: "Wow! I didn't know I could do that." Doing funny voices was a way of getting attention. It was something I could be good at. So I worked on my impressions.'

At home, where, with charming self-deprecation, he describes himself at this time of his life as, 'just Len who looked out of the window a lot', his real window on the world outside Douglass Road and Dudley was the television screen. Furthermore, even that somewhat restricted view tended to be pretty much dominated by ITV. More than any of the bookish middle-class youngsters who would become the 'alternative' comedians of the 1980s, Lenny Henry was a child of what the cartoonist Posy Simmonds once brilliantly described as 'telly-media-Jaffa Cake' – the loud, trashy, celebs-gameshows-and-adverts culture which the majority of British people began to live vicariously in the 1960s. The radio, which had been the dream machine of the previous generation of working-class comics (it was Music Hall before that) was no longer a cultural force of any potency. He would later come under the spell of comics and music, but when Lenny was eleven and twelve, in his milieu the telly was everything that mattered, and it was fitting that it was ITV that eventually discovered Lenny and gave him his big break.

'I watched Mike Yarwood especially. Whatever he did on his Saturday night TV show, I came in and did on Monday morning at school. I'd have a couple of new voices and a few jokes. Morecambe and Wise were also part of my childhood, very influential. You had to watch the *Morecambe and Wise Christmas Special*. If you went back to school and you hadn't watched it you were an outcast.'

Lenny watched TV avidly, all but taking notes. He would have great thoughts about the likes of Andy Pandy, Chigley, The Herbs and the Wooden Tops. 'I always thought Spotty Dog should have been put down, or at least dismantled. I didn't like the way he walked. I didn't trust him. I always thought the Wooden Tops was very, very weird. But all that stuff when I was growing up in the Sixties was very exciting . . . things like *Batman*, which was the most exciting programme for me as a young boy. I really wanted the cape and the cowl. When I saw it again when I was eighteen, I realised they were all playing it for laughs, and it was all high camp, but you just don't realise it when you're a kid.'

Deflect it as he might, the race issue sprang back every time for Lenny. Racial prejudice he encountered would rarely be spiteful, but it was ever present, even in those idyllic Buffery Park days. He was often called The Suntan Kid, not an example of viciousness by any means, but still a sign of racial consciousness. 'This is where I met all my friends, down here, all my very best friends from the Midlands,' Lenny explained on one TV show. 'Through them I learnt about myself. I learnt that I was black. I learnt that we were working-class, that we were quite poor. But the black thing wasn't really an issue. They made gentle jokes about it, but it was never really heavyweight, it was never malicious.'

Nevertheless, another major theme in Lenny Henry's life had emerged by now. This was that all his real friends were white. It is an aspect of Lenny that remains controversial for some black people even today. There is no question that Lenny is a hero in Dudley, but there is a subtle difference between the warmth he generates in the black and the white communities. There is no question of black people having disowned him; but at the same time, there is a strong sense of who *owns* him, and the consensus is that it is the white world. He moves in white circles, he succeeded in a white profession, he married a middle-class white girl and lives in a white town. The term 'coconut', spoken a little jealously, a little bitterly, will not infrequently arise when black Dudley people discuss Lenny. It means, black on the outside, white on the inside, and is not meant as a compliment but a complaint. It is felt by some that as long as successful black men continue to marry white women, the old inequalities will live on.

Back in the park, in the days of Oxford bags and tank tops, it would be unfair to suggest that the young Lenny deliberately chose white friends to better himself. It just happened that way; white lads, and very bright, pleasant white lads at that, were attracted to him because he was funny and good fun to be with. He was attracted to them because they were there, and the park, on Lenny's very doorstep, was more important to him than school; for some reason, he simply did not gel with black boys his own age.

'There were a few other black guys at school but they were only really acquaintances because we were all black. School was where most of my black friends were. Not in the park, where I used to do most of my hanging out in my early days. When I left school, the guys from the park were the enduring friends, and still are. Those were the ones I went to clubs and pubs with. They were my mates. Just me and a bunch of white guys. They were the ones who encouraged me to do voices. They used to dare me to make them laugh.'

A bunch of white guys they certainly were, but they were also rather special white guys. These were not the gormless National Front recruiting material Lenny's phrase might suggest; there was still a trace of social upwardness discernible in Lenny's choice of mates. While Lenny made no academic mark at all at school after impressing his infant teachers with his neat handwriting and tidy desk, his closest friends were distinctly A-stream, Dudley Grammar School types, and interesting characters with it. One, Greg Stokes, now a social worker in Walsall, went off to Sunderland Polytechnic to do a degree in psychology. Stokes, first known to Lenny as a skinny kid of twelve in Buffery Park, with straight-leg jeans, Chelsea boots, lank hair and a superannuated mongrel dog called Butch, is now a writer of some note in the West Midlands. Another of those park friends, Martin Thomas – known as Tommy – is in the Royal Navy. Thomas left school to do officer training, dropped out and came back in as a rating after doing a degree at Loughborough University. He rose to Chief Petty Officer, served with distinction in various postings around the world, and was Lenny's best man when he married. ('We still write, we still phone and we still meet up,' Lenny says of this inner core of mates. 'I believe in staying loyal to friends.')

Greg's was the first white household Lenny ever recalls being asked home to. Subsequently, he would often turn up at the Stokes home at or around teatime. A big boy with a vast appetite, Lenny was nicknamed 'holler legs' by Greg's father Doug, who worked for the Co-op in Dudley. Lenny was always a valued and welcome guest at the Stokes home; shortly before his fifteenth birthday, on the evening of Greg's sister's wedding, he was invited to the party, and kept the entire family entertained for hours with his impressions. (Lenny was, some years on, to play a crucial role in a horrifying disaster in the Stokes family; but that was much later.)

If Buffery Park was the womb of Lenny Henry's comedy career, the Blue Coat School, which in theory dated back to medieval times, but in reality was just another scruffy secondary modern, was its nursery. Despite friends like Greg Stokes passing the 11-plus and going to Dudley Grammar School, Lenny predictably failed the exam (although only its second part), and Blue Coat was a school with nothing discernibly traditional, let alone medieval, about it. Although the *Daily Express* once reported that Lenny, 'just escaped having to wear a traditional long dress as a school uniform, as they had phased them out before he got there', the traditional gear had, in fact disappeared from Dudley a full sixty-six years before Lenny was born. Academically, Lenny was a non-event, even though he tried; he once offered to clean his maths teacher's car if he would help Lenny gain some minimal insight into the mysteries of the subject.

He continued to be a dreamy kid. He had a paper round for a while, but got the sack for delivering the wrong papers to the wrong houses.

'I did tend to zone out sometimes, especially in school,' he once said on *Desert Island Discs*. 'I was a late developer really as far as academia was concerned because I just wasn't interested. There was nothing to inspire me at school.'

But in truth, there was. Lenny has often joked, 'I went to a mixed school – teachers and pupils,' and it was the teachers, inevitably more colourful than at junior school, who inspired him when he went to Blue Coat. They provided Lenny with an entire new spectrum of characters on whom to hone his ever-growing imitative powers; he also now had a captive and willing audience on whom to try out new impressions. On the showbiz side, the well-practised park routines could now be tried out afresh on his new colleagues, while the TV continued to inspire Lenny to update his playground act. Michael Crawford's Frank Spencer – another deeply white character like Tommy Cooper – came onto the scene during Lenny's time at Blue Coat, and his version of the Crawford character was an instant hit. Lenny was famous at school within weeks of the start of the first term in 1969; soon after he left school, he would be nationally famous.

He started at Blue Coat, he says, as 'a bit of a tag-along'. He would haunt the older boys asking for loans and whining, 'Ave you got any sweets?' That might have been terminal for a new boy at a relatively tough school, but Lenny softened the potential blows with his early series of successful impressions. These would often be in the form of practical jokes. 'One teacher had a hearing aid and Lenny was always messing him about,' says one ex-Blue Coat boy, Stephen Amos. 'He would talk to him in a normal voice, then gradually go quieter until no sound was coming out of his mouth and he was just miming. The teacher would always start twiddling the knob on his hearing aid because he thought the batteries were flat.'

But it was an English teacher, an aging, reputedly ex-military martinet called Ron Nash, who was the target for most of Lenny's jokes. Nash was given to ranting and raving at his formidable maximum volume in class – and occasionally in the staffroom, where he would regularly thump the table and rage. Nash's general truculence with colleagues as well as boys meant that Lenny's incessant teasing played as well with the staff as with his classmates.

'One of the famous stories,' says Bill Jones, Lenny's technical drawing teacher, 'was when Ron Nash used to have an English classroom which was the other side of the library and you could get into the back of it through the stockroom. The Head was supposed to be walking through this one day to talk to Ron Nash and as he got into the stockroom he heard this voice booming out in the classroom, and he thought that Ron was teaching, so he turned round and walked away. Then he actually met Ron outside his study. It had been Lenny doing his famous Ron Nash imitation. Lenny would have been about fifteen and a half at the time.'

Teaching Lenny, recalls maths master Brian Lindop, 'was interesting. He only had to listen to you for three or four weeks and he could pick up your local sayings which you didn't realise you said.' Another teacher, Gary King, remembers of Lenny's art lessons, 'To begin with he was just another lad in the class, but as he went along he made a considerable impression. He was great, he was always quipping and trying his best to impress us with his acting, and he did eventually. We used to finish early so that he could get on the tables and have a practice. I think we appreciated that he was trying his best to get on. I always thought he would make it. He was popular with the other kids, and I don't think he ever got on my nerves, although he did with some of the old hat teachers who just wanted a straight lesson.'

It was principally Mr Nash who would get irritated by Lenny, whom he would call 'Lenworth' when he was angry, and 'Henry' when he was merely a seething mass of fury. 'I can remember Lenny getting belted for doing a Ron Nash impression once,' says one class colleague. 'There were two entrances to the English room, and Bomber Nash walked in through the library entrance, where Lenny had his back to him. He got a clip round the earhole and a "Sit down Henry." But he didn't hit him hard and Lenny just smiled and sat down. I never saw him angry. He was very popular right from the start.'

Cornered by a *News of the World* reporter just before he died in 1994, Ron Nash himself finally had his retrospective say about Lenny: 'He was a handful. He was always up to something and it drove us mad. The trouble was he was a natural comic, and it was difficult to cope with him in a class full of lively youngsters. I never thought he'd get anywhere in life because he always played the fool. It was a relief when he went home at night!'

Any annoyance the teachers, even the irascible Mr Nash, seemed to display may well have been strictly within inverted commas. 'A lot of teenagers would have used humour such as Lenny's maliciously,' says one veteran of those days, 'and he could have driven a teacher up the wall. But I don't ever remember a teacher getting annoyed with him.'

Tony Wright, one of the Blue Coat PE staff, recognised that Lenny was not a potential sporting star, but liked him all the same. 'Physically he wasn't over-endowed with skills to say the least but he always gave it a fair crack. He wasn't the kind who forgot his kit and hid – he would give it a shot. I really liked the guy. I love kids with a lot of character and he had got an immense amount. I'm not sure that school had that much of an influence on Lenny. It may have taught him to read and write, and that was about it, but at least it didn't discourage him.

'I also taught his two sisters,' says Wright. 'Sharon was a lovely kid very much in the same mould as Lenny; Kay, well, Her Ladyship was the best way to describe Kay. She was very dignified and quite delightful. The mum was lovely, too, although I never knew anything about the dad. Lenny's mum worked phenomenally hard to keep the family together.'

'I know Lenny used to have a dislike of doing PE,' says a sporty ex-pupil, who does not quite remember Lenny as the ardent if untalented striver that Tony Wright recalls. 'I would say he basically tried – to avoid it. He would either use his humour do it, or a lot of the time just didn't bother bringing his kit. He would get punished for that, he'd probably be sent to some other class which I don't think bothered him very much.'

Lenny's version of school PE lessons does not clash with these observations. 'I was useless at sport. I was the one wobbling behind at cross country, trying to hide in the bushes. I never used to smoke, which was always the thing on cross country runs, you would stop in a bush and have a fag, but I used to be there anyway, choking with the smoke because I wanted to have a rest.' Fortunately for Lenny, the expectation that black children would be good at games had not yet fully developed in Britain in the early 1970s. 'We had quite a few black kids in the football team at school,' says this classmate, now an engineer, 'and they were very, very gifted footballers. But I would say there was less of a stereotype of the black athletic person then than there is now.'

But while other children at a secondary modern school would make their mark through sport, for Lenny, entertainment was more than a flip way of getting through the day and keeping friends. It was a mission. He often says that he settled on entertaining as his *modus operandi* solely as a way of attracting girls when he was lanky, tending towards being spotty, and hopeless at games. But at the same time, he had pretty well settled on being a comedian in some form as a career by the age of thirteen.

This early decisiveness was more than the ebbing and flowing children normally display in such matters, although Lenny had been through a few career options before his momentous choice at thirteen. When he was seven, he wanted to be a Beatle. At eight, inspired by Muhammad Ali, who had just emerged from his Cassius Clay days, Lenny wanted to be a boxer. (He says now that if Ali has taught him one thing, it is that he, unlike his hero, will get out of performing while he is ahead rather than go on past his peak.) At ten, Lenny was intent on being a fireman, at eleven a rock-and-roll star again. Perhaps because he possessed a particularly burning one himself, childhood ambitions continue to fascinate and amuse Lenny. 'It would be really weird if you became what you wanted to be as a kid, wouldn't it? The world would be filled with rock stars, ballerinas and firemen,' he observed recently in a *Radio Times* interview. He has analysed and re-analysed his decision to be a comedian; 'It was a big sense of power making people laugh. You could get away with things because you were funny and girls would be interested in you,' he concludes simply.

The Blue Coat teachers were extraordinarily indulgent towards Lenny's nascent desire. Sometimes this happened by default, because they could not think of anything else to do with him. 'I can remember I used to pick his group up round about the time that one of the then governments raised the school leaving age to sixteen,' says Tony Wright. 'Lenny was in the first group that copped for that. It was a case of the schools running around scratching their heads thinking of things for the kids to do for the last year. We called it the Rosla – Raising of the School Leaving Age – group. They were quite difficult to handle, so if you were a male PE teacher, you copped them. I seem to recall that I used to give them the last lesson on a Friday afternoon, which was not the best time, and we often used to have an impromptu performance by Lenny. I could sit back and let him entertain us for half an hour.'

At other times, he was more actively assisted in his career aims. His greatest ally in this was, surprisingly, since Lenny was even less successful in his academic subject than in almost any other on offer at Blue Coat, the science teacher, Jim Brookes. Mr Brookes, a wry and gently amusing man, now retired, jokingly claims a minor role in Lenny Henry's career, but it is probable that he played a greater part than he realised.

'Lenny wasn't particularly a great science student,' admits Mr Brookes. 'He was interested in the subject, and he got a grade 2 in the physics CSE, but we just seemed to get on well together. I think one of my good points as a teacher was that I've got a sense of humour, and I think he appreciated that. But the way we first had anything to do with the possibility of something coming from his ability was that I used to run a science club, an electronics club, after school on a Thursday evening.

'One evening, we were making radio sets and transmitters, and one or two of the lads had finished and we were testing them out with a boy, as it were, transmitting from one room into the laboratory. Lenny – he would have been about fifteen – came to the room because he'd come to pick up one of his mates. He was always joking, and I invited him to go into the prep room on his own with one of these transmitters to transmit to the lab and see how it worked – and to see how he got on. These were literally home-made transmitters – it was probably totally illegal. He was in the prep room speaking into a microphone which was connected to this little transmitter.

'There were about a dozen kids listening and Lenny was a matter of feet away in the prep room. He closed the door to be on his own. Now, the technical details are a little hazy, but the distinct part, the outstanding thing I have in my memory, is that he then regaled us for twenty minutes. He kept us all rolling in the aisles with his mimicry. It was extraordinary, an outstanding performance and, I like to say, the very first time he ever broadcast, because that's what it was, a broadcast performance to an audience he couldn't see.

'At the end of it, when he came out, I gave him half a crown and I said, "Lenny, when you reach the professional heights as a comedian, try and remember that Jim Brookes was the first person to pay you for your ability." '

(Interestingly for students of oral history, Stephen Amos, asked by a journalist for his Lenny Henry memories, gave the school folklore version. 'Lenny was always joking,' Amos, now an electrician, said. 'Once he rigged up a loudspeaker system in the science room. When the teacher came in, Lenny would be secretly speaking into a microphone from the back of the classroom. The poor guy went crazy trying to find out where the noise was coming from. He thought he was hearing voices in his head.')

'I knew Lenny at that stage only as a pupil,' Mr Brookes continues. 'I taught him in the fourth and fifth year, the pre-exam year, but I think it is true to say we always got on well with each other. I think occasionally I had to remind him he would be doing exams, but a lot of his concentration was going on his career. When homework was due or when pieces of work were needed they weren't always there on time, but they always came in eventually.

'Some pupils take to some teachers more than others, and it happened that Lenny took to me,' says Mr Brookes. 'It helped that I hadn't got annoyed with him as some teachers did, because his impersonations were uncanny. He could shout across the playground at the first-year children and make them think it was the teacher. But he always said he couldn't mimic me, which is odd because I'm from the Black Country. But obviously it is easier to mimic Yorkshire accents or Irish accents, and the staff were varied in their origin.'

Another important point of contact between Lenny and Mr Brookes – Mr Brookes thinks it was their first – was that the science teacher did the lighting and the stage management for the school Christmas concerts which, in his last couple of years, Lenny compered, by all accounts quite brilliantly.

'There was also the fact that his elder sister, Kay, was a year before him and I got on very well with her. She was good at science and was a very pleasant personality. She had a baby not too long after she left school and she used to bring the baby back to see me sometimes. Then his younger sister, Sharon, became head girl of the second year. Come to think of it, for some reason I think I seemed to get on very well with the whole Henry family.

'We've been to see Lenny a couple of times, and when we saw him at Oxford a couple of years ago, he invited us back stage and we had a chat and he hadn't forgotten me. But I would think that his memory of that particular incident is not as clear as mine, because such a lot has happened to him since then. But for me, well, some people say that it is my only claim to fame.'

Mr Brookes' only abiding sadness about Lenny is that 'Sometimes he goes rather blue, but that's the way of comedians depending on the audience they have in front of them. I am a Methodist and a church member, so it strikes me sometimes, but one cannot fault his ability and the entertainment he has given to people.'

The school Christmas concerts that Mr Brookes lit were Lenny's debut on-stage performances. Music was not exactly Lenny's first love, but a lifelong passion for the subject had already begun. He spent many lunchtimes scouring Dudley's second-hand record shops for 10p bargains. His tastes were properly esoteric for someone who would become an *aficionado*, his heroes obscure groups, such as the Ohio Players.

Lenny sang well, but he was in no respect a straight singer. Once, at a Christmas show, he stood with a begging bowl and a loin cloth and instead of singing 'Swing Low Sweet Chariot', belted out 'Jailhouse Rock'; it was not at all an unsophisticated musical joke. Another time, he appeared in a gorilla suit, which brought the house down. Lenny's desire to attract female interest by use of his comedy was apparently paying off. He credits a classmate, Alison Keeling, with giving him a shove in the direction of stardom at fifteen; 'When the music master asked if anyone could sing, she pushed me up on stage.'

He went further on the same theme in a TV interview with Nick Ross. 'There were many, many girls, Yvonne, Annette, they all know who they are. They all pushed me and said, "Go on, you've got to do it because you're gonna make it." They believed in my talent when I was wondering, "When is it all going to happen for me? When am I going to get out of this?" I just wanted to do something and impressions and jokes was all I'd got, so every opportunity I got from the fourth year onwards I was really pushing, getting up and saying, "Can I do this?" When I hit puberty, I think that's when it happened, because the interest from the girls was not forthcoming. I had to have some kind of hook to get them interested in me, so I started learning all these different voices and everything.'

Despite his self-deprecation, Lenny's project of attracting female attention by means of making them laugh seemed to go averagely well, although over the years he has extracted every drop of comedic juice out of the notion that he was a failure with women. 'In the Seventies I had absolutely everything,' he said on an Eighties edition of *Saturday Night Clive*. 'I had the platforms – I was six foot three in my stockinged feet. In my platforms I was eight foot tall and with an afro nine foot. I would go to discotheques and the only thing I would bloody snog was the mirror ball. It was pathetic.'

And possibly it was, but not quite as dreadfully so as he suggests. He was even briefly 'engaged' as a teenager – 'It was a teenage thing and not with a view to getting married,' he explains. His background was, as ever, constantly in the foreground, at this stage in his life at least; 'I had a very moral upbringing and never had time for girls who offered themselves for one-night stands,' he has said. As a teenager, Lenny nevertheless stayed out late a lot, partying, drinking, although not a great deal, and trying to impress women: 'I wasted a lot of time in discos chasing girls who didn't want to be chased,' he said in 1994. 'Now I think I could have put the time to much better use and been so much further on in my career. It's made me feel I have to catch up. There's not much time.'

If anything could better encapsulate the essence of Lenny Henry as a driven man, it would probably be this one statement. Few people, surely, would regard getting a career practically up and running by the age of fifteen as the mark of an aimless timewaster.

CHAPTER 3

THE SAUCIER APPRENTICE

'No one starts off wanting to be a comedian. The girls just laugh at you and walk off with someone better looking.'

Lenny Henry

Lenny left school with seven CSEs; he later called these 'toy qualifications'. In 1975, aged sixteen, he became a £21-a-week apprentice in electrical engineering at British Federal, a welding machinery factory just outside Dudley.

On the first day he was due at work, his father woke him up at 5 a.m. with the slightly cruel greeting, 'Time for the real world.' He realised very quickly that the kind of work his background and education had lined him up for was not what he wanted to do. 'It was so hard,' he says. 'It was awful. It was just so dull and boring and monotonous. I cut my hands every day and couldn't understand why.'

Not unexpectedly, he soon found the survival tactic that kept his head above water at school was effective at work too. 'I was always playing it for laughs in the factory,' he recalls. 'One day a screwdriver slipped and cut my hand. They all laughed but I couldn't see anything funny in it. So I went into my Max Bygraves routine ... "You Need Hands".'

Lenny's education had not strictly finished. He also began a three-year day release course at West Bromwich Technical College to do a City & Guilds Ordinary National Certificate in engineering. Terry

Mills used to teach Higher National Applied Maths at the college, but occasionally would take other courses, and in 1975 was asked to do some lectures to the Ordinary National Engineering students. Most of these young men made little lasting impression on Mr Mills, but one caught his eye, not for the quality of his sheet metal work – the course started with the study of conic sections – but initially for his dress. 'I always remember,' he says, 'this one big West Indian fella who was always better dressed than the others. He usually wore a suit, which was strange for sixteen- to seventeen-year-olds – the rest of them were in jeans and a sweater. The first time I saw him he had a grey suit and a tie on.

'I remember that he was very polite, which was unusual, and that his mind didn't seem to be really on what we were doing here, but the strange thing was that whatever he said, the rest of the class used to think he was hilarious. If he said, "Yes, Sir," they all used to fall about. It was like a mass hysteria thing. I couldn't understand this, so I happened to say something in the staff room to one of the senior lecturers and he said, "Oh yes, that's young Lenny Henry, he's just got to the stage where he has either got to go full time in the entertainment business or he has got to get down to his engineering.' I can remember saying, "Well, I hope he's a better comedian than he is a student." He was probably tired because he was doing late-night stands in clubs around the area.'

At as young as thirteen, Lenny was hanging out in Dudley's clubs and pubs. Lenny's way was always, it must be emphasised, hanging out as opposed to *around*, which implies aimlessness; most of what the young man was doing even now appeared to be career-oriented. 'I always stood by the decks and watched them play the records and sort of go "What's that?" and the DJ would go, "Get lost kid, will you, you're getting thumbprints over my records." I used to go to Graduate Records in Dudley and look for all the northern soul records that sounded like they'd been recorded in a garage somewhere in San Francisco.'

Lenny actually started performing locally while he was still at school. He first earned free bags of chips singing 'Jailhouse Rock' at an accommodating chippie. Then came Dudley Zoo. For a few summers, Lenny had worked as a bottle collector and washer in the bar there, which has attached to it a room called the Queen Mary Ballroom. Here, every Sunday night, a disco was held. His repertoire ever-developing – Donny Osmond and, an almost surreal touch, an impersonation of Mike Yarwood impersonating Telly Savalas playing Kojak, had joined the menagerie – Lenny's friends propelled him towards the stage. He did not take too much persuading.

The ballroom is a sweet little place that doubles as the Dudley Zoo restaurant. It is bright and light, although shaded all round by trees. It has a small dance floor and a capacity of a few hundred, making it a lot smaller than many school halls. At one end of the triangular room is a tiny stage, twelve feet across, with maroon velvet curtains and a tinsel backdrop. The ballroom is hung with twee light fittings, the dance floor itself by a tiny mirrored ball. The Queen Mary Ballroom is intimate enough to be small-town and comforting but still, when you stand on the purple carpet of the floor-level stage, quite big enough to be scary.

'It used to be glamorous, heaving with 600 kids at night,' Lenny recollects. 'You had to wear a gum shield to get in. We all went to this disco and my friends pushed me on to the stage when the DJ, Oscar Michael, asked for people to do a turn. I got this wonderful applause. It felt great. Wow! It was not just a few friends I'd made laugh, but 200 people, all those people who couldn't give a damn about me before, now they're really into me. Once I'd grabbed that, I didn't want to let go. I thought, "How can I exploit this?" '

An increasingly confident figure in the early 1970s uniform of Ben Sherman shirt, Levi's Sta-pressed trousers and Dr Martens, Lenny would first 'just mess about', doing turns such as dancing in Elvis Presley style. 'One night the guy in charge said: "I wonder if you can sing like Elvis as well?" I just got up and did it. That was the start. I must have been the only black Elvis anyone had ever seen.' Lenny won a bottle of whisky for his rendition of 'Jailhouse Rock', and shared it with the three mates who had urged him to go all the way and sing.

Soon the ballroom would pay him £1 a night, his first professional earnings if the science teacher Jim Brookes and his half crown is discounted, but they then sacked him for being persistently late. There was also a suggestion that the regulars at the ballroom were getting a little fed up with Lenny; 'I didn't realise that, if you played the same place a couple of times, you had to change your material.' He was sad about the initial enthusiasm at Dudley Zoo fading in this way, but it had really ceased to matter; Lenny Henry was, before his sixteenth birthday, known to the discerning from Stourbridge almost to Tipton. He was now sought after on the Dudley area night scene, where the audiences were older and cooler, and the fee could be as much as a fiver. Places like the Summerhill House Hotel in Kingswinford and four or five other pubs would stop the disco to let him perform.

'It got to the point where you would see Lenny come in and things would start to slow down a little bit and then, within a few minutes of him coming into the room, he would almost take over,' says Andy Harford, now in the music business in Birmingham, then a regular on the Dudley twenty-something scene. 'Imagine it, the DJ is there, playing his heart out and he has a floor full of people dancing away, then this guy comes strolling onto the stage. It didn't matter what the DJ did with the music, everything stopped because they were all going to listen to what Lenny was going to do. They knew his name.

'He was mostly incredibly funny. He did very few impersonations – it was almost like a stand-up comedy routine. He was certainly into doing his own background noises at that point in time, his hooter noise, his klaxon noise, I suppose you would call it. He would just stop the place dead. Imagine walking into a disco and having the power to stop the whole thing dead. It was awesome. He rarely got heckled; it was more on the lines of having the friendly punter in the audience sort of thing. It wasn't set up that way – it was just a two-way thing, really. I don't think he ever had a bad time.

'He is the kind of guy who is noticeable when he comes through the door because he is so tall,' Harford continues. 'Lenny didn't look much different from today. Because of his size, you couldn't tell how old he was, but he certainly didn't strike me as being a sixteen-year-old. He was, perhaps, a little bit more flamboyant than he is now. In those days, it was very much a white scene, so it was unusual to see a coloured guy in there. I think the only reason that the coloureds weren't in the scene at that time was because it just wasn't their scene – there was no colour bar as far as I was aware. I certainly recall having coloured doormen around, but there was a bigger difference in music then than there is today. It was before the high street importance of things like reggae.'

As the pub gigs continued through the summer and autumn of 1974, the summer that Lenny left Blue Coat School and started work, a process had already begun that would lead Lenny on to his biggest break of all – his appearance on the ATV Saturday night TV talent show, *New Faces*.

New Faces, which also discovered Showaddywaddy and Patti Boulaye, ran on ITV in the Seventies, and was required viewing for the hilarious savageness with which some of the acts were greeted by panellists such as Mickey Most and even gentle Ted Ray. The contestants were mostly working men's club-type entertainers rehashing old jokes and singing hackneyed songs like 'My Way'. Genuinely new faces did, however, beam out from the Saturday night prime time regularly; it was not a joke show. Knowing that it could be a platform for serious talent, and seeing Henry do Elvis singing 'Jailhouse Rock' on stage at the Queen Mary Ballroom late in 1973, a local DJ, Mike Hollis, who went on to become a Radio Luxembourg personality and is now a show host on Birmingham's BRMB station, wrote to *New Faces* to recommend Lenny.

Having heard nothing as a result of Hollis's letter, that January, while still a schoolboy, Lenny made his own way on the bus to a *New Faces* mass audition at the Dolce Vita, a night club in Birmingham. He impersonated John Wayne, Tommy Cooper and Muhammad Ali, and ended with Presley's 'Jailhouse Rock'. While other hopefuls were stopped almost as soon as they had opened their mouths, Lenny was allowed to carry on for a full mini set. The producer of the show, Les Cocks, and the pianist he travelled around the country with, were knocked out by Lenny. He was told immediately that he was practically certain to be on the show, and caught the bus back to Dudley half knowing that his professional career had already started. 'I wasn't scared,' Lenny said later of the audition. 'I should have been, but I didn't know enough to be scared ... It was just my party piece. I suppose I was showing off. If I'd known then what I know now, I'd never have done it. I just wasn't aware that I was going out to so many people with so many opinions.'

Lenny had not told his family that he had been to Birmingham for the ATV audition. These were dangerous days in British big city centres. A few weeks earlier, the IRA had bombed two pubs in the centre of Birmingham. 'When I came back, my mum said, "Where have you been, it's 6.30 p.m.?", and I said I'd been to an audition for *New Faces*. I hadn't told her that I had bunked off school. I still couldn't believe it. I'd done well and I was quite excited.'

His mother, with a selection of other Henrys in attendance, asked a little sceptically what Lenny had done at the audition. 'I told her it was, well, doing impressions. And, before I had a chance to eat or get changed, she made me give a performance in the hall of what I had done that day. There I was, going "One for the money ...", and they laughed. They thought it was funny. It made me wish I'd done it before, because maybe I would have got encouragement earlier on.'

Back in Birmingham, Cocks, the *New Faces* producer, was also delighted by Lenny's extraordinarily good performance. 'Don't forget there were a lot of other people going round doing the same as us, Cocks says twenty years on. '*Opportunity Knocks* was on the same kick, so if you really found something that you fancied, you said OK, I'll put you in the show. I thought he was a very funny kid. You have to realise that when you are sitting there at auditions, you see loads and loads of rubbish. I saw something like 35,000 acts to do the series, so you are watching and suddenly something happens and you think, yes, that is really good I like that, that has got something. I only remember the good things.'

The *New Faces* auditions, he explains, were curious occasions. The traditions of open auditions and, when the show was aired on TV, outspoken juries, came over from Australia with the programme concept. 'The first thing about the auditions,' says Cocks, 'is that you were usually in a night club during the day, when they look horrendous.

Night clubs look lovely at night when they are all swinging, but in the morning they're terrifying. You have also got to realise that at these auditions, all the other acts were sitting there waiting to go on, and quite often they would applaud the act that had just done whatever it did because they could see it was good, so you had got a strange sort of audience.

'People were driven by all kinds of things to do auditions. We were once at the Palladium – we used it for *New Faces* auditions in London because ATV owned it – and this guy walked on and did a very old joke, then got hold of the microphone and said, "Mr Cocks, I can't see you out there, but I know you're there. I must apologise. I'm not a comic, I'm an accountant, but I always wanted to tell the grandchildren that I played the Palladium," and with that he walked off. That's what helped me get through the day.

'In the case of that Birmingham audition, we had advertised that we were coming to town and they turned up in droves. I sat through so much rubbish, some of it was quite hysterical, though I wouldn't let the acts go on for more than a few seconds if they were rubbish. I would just say fine, thank you very much. You had so many people to get through and if the girl was singing out of tune or you just thought there's nothing I can do with this, you might as well say thank you very much and goodbye, rather than let them stagger through and waste your time and theirs. It sounds hard, but you have got a lot of things to get through.

'But the second Lenny Henry walked on, you knew you had something. It was like that with Jim Davidson, Roger de Courcy, Victoria Wood and Marti Caine, all the great *New Faces* successes. Lenny did about three minutes, which was the most anybody ever got. When I saw him do his Tommy Cooper it was very, very funny – perhaps not very PC today, but there you go.'

Lenny was told immediately that, subject to the usual official confirmation, he would be appearing on *New Faces*. 'He was amazed. Absolutely dumbstruck that he was going to be on the telly,' says Cocks. 'They always were. I said to Jim Davidson, "Can you make March 21st?" and he actually wanted to call his book *Can You Make March*

21st, but the publisher didn't think it was a good enough title.'

The full confirmation from ATV took an age coming, and Lenny was left for a good couple of weeks in the limbo of believing he was going to be on TV but, for the lack of anything in writing, in the meanwhile, being a schoolboy in Dudley with a sideline in doing shows at pubs he could not yet buy a drink in. The great phone call came on a significant, and in many respects very unpleasant, day for Lenny. With his friend Greg Stokes, Greg's father, Doug and his mother, he had gone to Goodison Park in Liverpool to watch West Bromwich Albion play a fourth round FA Cup match against Everton. Mr and Mrs Stokes watched the game from the stands while Greg and Lenny stood on the terraces. Lenny, who weeks earlier had been fêted on his triumphant day at the Dolce Vita, was the subject of a tirade of racist abuse and physically chased by what Greg describes as, 'raving fascist Scousers'. The boys slept in the car on the way home from Liverpool. When they arrived back at Douglass Road, Lenny learned that he had officially passed his audition.

Lenny's first appearance on the show later in the year, when he had already started his apprenticeship, was enhanced by a trick invented on the hoof by Cocks and the director, although often attributed by others to Lenny's genius. 'When we got into the studio, we decided that it would be a nice idea if Lenny started off as Tommy Cooper with his back to the audience, and then turned around so the audience could find out he was black. I told Lenny that that was what I wanted him to do. I said, "Look, you're a black Tommy Cooper, and it's a funny idea because he's white", and, to be fair, he was a young kid and absolutely delighted to be on *New Faces*, so whatever we wanted him to do he was quite willing. Bearing in mind that he left us and went to the *Black and White Minstrels*, I can't believe that it worried him too much. And he got it right first time. Everybody fell about. It got an absolute wow of an applause. It was as silly as a Chinaman coming on doing a Chinese Tommy Cooper. After the show was recorded, I phoned Tommy up, because I knew him very well, and I said you have to watch the show this week, you'll find it interesting. He did and rang back and he was over the moon as well.'

Lenny, with the conic sections of his working life decidedly not on his mind, adapted to TV with astonishing ease. He even subtly worked on the back-to-the-audience start to his act to keep it fresh even on those like Cocks who were getting used to the Tommy Cooper opening lines. Lenny was introduced with the words, 'This boy is only sixteen years of age, talented, house trained and very, very funny. Ladies and gentlemen, it's gotta be ... Lenny Henry.' One of Lenny's first lines made it plain that not only was he black, but he *knew* he was black; 'Betty got me this job as an Ambre Solaire salesman and it won't come off,' he said, adding a line which would become one of his catchphrases, 'You may have seen some of these impressions before, but not in colour.'

'It was the break of a lifetime,' Lenny enthused years later. 'I had no experience, and this director was just saying, "Just treat the TV like a box of groceries," and there I was on the television in front of millions saying hello to me mum. That's why I was so confident. I'm much less confident than that now. It was a wonderful experience. I will always be grateful to *New Faces*.'

Not only was Lenny suddenly catapulted from limited local fame to a mass – and appreciative – national audience on TV, but on the same day he also got his first ever press interview, and not with any old local paper, but the mighty *Daily Mail*. The paper's TV Editor, Martin Jackson, was a member of the *New Faces* panel, and judged this act worthy not only of top marks but also an instant star interview.

'I vividly recall his first appearance at the Birmingham ATV studios because it was such a sensation,' says Jackson, who went on to become a senior figure in the television industry. 'Of all the *New Faces* I did, and I must have done fifty or sixty of them, that was the one, the memory of him suddenly turning round on the audience and seeing he was black, that has stayed with me. It was the most electric moment of the whole show.

'We always used to see the dress rehearsals but the comics never used to do their routine on the dress. They used to come on and say their opening words, so they would be fresh to us, whereas all the singers and dancers and xylophone players, we would see.

'With Lenny, he just walked on and walked off again, so that was all that we were aware of, just a big young guy ambling on and ambling off again. Then on the actual show it opened with him with his back to us wearing a long raincoat and a black beret doing 'Oooh Betty' – Frank Spencer from *Some Mothers Do 'Ave 'Em* – which every bloody kid did at the time. There was a sort of silent moan down the panel, an absolute groan of, "Oh, shit not another Mike Crawford," because every schoolkid did Mike Crawford, the playgrounds were full of it; you couldn't get away from Mike Crawford on the buses, on the tubes, everyone was doing Mike Crawford.

'But then this guy turned round and, it doesn't sound very politically correct now, but the spectacle of a black Mike Crawford was quite sensational. At the time, we had never seen a young black lad do an act like that, and he was absolutely superb. His voices were tremendous. I think he did Crawford and Top Cat, and he was very, very funny. It was obvious that he had a gift and the whole studio rocked, the studio audience exploded. We used to give marks for content, presentation and star quality, and he got full marks for all of that from all of us. Whatever discussion there was on air, there was never any group discussion as a panel. It was obvious he was going to be a star. There was no question of it. It was one of the few times when the panel got it right. I'm the guy, remember, who told Victoria Wood she might have a future as a songwriter so long as she never appeared in public.'

(Curiously, when Lenny was recounting the Michael Crawford story in Los Angeles nearly twenty years later during the publicity for his Hollywood movie, *True Identity*, he put a very different spin on events, claiming that the studio audience could barely cope with his outrageous racial boundary hopping; 'It freaked them out,' he recalled, laughing. 'They couldn't believe it. Blue rinses were standing on end. Then I did some other stuff and I won.')

It is often forgotten that when Lenny went on the grand final of *New Faces*, it was Marti Caine and not him who actually won the competition and the first prize, a booking in Las Vegas. The panellists still puzzle over how Caine won; it is generally thought that special influence was granted to the jury member from Las Vegas, who had, after all, to go home with an act that would not be an embarrassment to him or the New Face in question. The curious result did no disservice to either Caine, who was more suitable to an American audience, or Lenny, whose morale might at his age have crashed without survivors in the face of an uncomprehending Las Vegas audience.

'I'm glad actually,' Lenny told Sue Lawley on *Desert Island Discs* fourteen years later, 'because Marti had to go to Las Vegas, and she sent me this postcard which basically said everything's plastic, I want to come home. I'm glad because being sixteen or seventeen with all these show girls and in the middle of a lounge with all these people walking by saying, "Martha, can I play the machines?", well, I don't think I would have liked that very much.'

'Lenny Henry was always going to be something special,' Jackson avers. 'The amazing thing was that he turned into such an all-round performer. In a way any kid can get up and make funny noises and take off Top Cat and Mike Crawford, but to become what he has done proves that there was tremendous ability there. But he really was a very, very, very simple lad. I wrote the first piece about him between the Tuesday the show was recorded and the Saturday it went out. It was obvious when I interviewed him in the green room that he was something really, really exceptional. He was obviously keen to get on, but was very unassuming. I don't think he recognised the talent that he had – he was just the kid who everybody at school thought was the clown of the class. He was terribly in awe of his mother, and very worried about what her reaction was going to be. He kept on saying, "I don't know what my mum is going to say", talking about his mum, worrying about her and that she wanted him to have a proper job working in a factory.'

Back in Dudley, it has to be said, the amazement was of a different nature, since Lenny was already so well known. 'When I saw Lenny on the box that time it wasn't exactly a surprise,' says one fan of his pub appearances. 'I was looking and hearing this bloke and saying I recognise that voice, who the hell is that? I think at the time all I could see was the back of him, because he hadn't turned round or something, and then, as he turned, I thought, Good God that's Lenny. We didn't even know him as Lenny Henry, but just as Lenny.'

Jackson's interview with Lenny appeared in the *Mail* on the Monday, 13 January, following Lenny's first appearance on TV. It was being read at breakfast tables all over the country as Lenny was clocking on at British Federal. 'It has taken him since then [when he passed his audition] to persuade Equity, the performers' union, to accept him into membership and allow him on the show,' Jackson wrote. 'In the meantime he has been touring Midland dance halls with a local disc jockey and record-shop owner Mike Hollis, from Stourbridge. Lenny had won a Hollis talent show by singing Presley's 'Jailhouse Rock'. A week later he won again, this time impersonating Tommy Cooper. Since then the two have been inseparable.

'Says twenty-four-year-old Hollis,' the piece continued, ' "Lenny has a natural instinct. He has no nerves in front of an audience, on the contrary he just devours them. He has this incredible gift for mimicry, it takes only moments for him to capture a character. His Brian Clough and Eddie Waring are quite unbelievable.

' "They say there is a great opening for ethnic comedians. But in truth he is more Black Country than black. His parents came over here from the West Indies two years before he was born. But the audience want black jokes, so he tells them. My only worry is that he is so young he may be destroyed. This business is full of sharks. I don't want to see him hurt and exploited." '

CHAPTER 4

CONIC RELIEF

'I was sufficiently different to win.'

Lenny Henry on his New Faces *triumph*

The rustle on the Birmingham show-business grapevine in early 1975 was all about Lenny Henry, and who could best help this naive but brilliant young Dudley apprentice while at the same time, as agents will, best helping himself. Immediately after the programme, Dickie Leeman, producer of ITV's *Golden Shot*, who was in the audience, booked Lenny for his show. Other stars asked for Lenny to join them in cabaret, and offers arrived to star in summer season at various seaside resorts around the country.

Mike Hollis had a good claim on Lenny, and a terrific personal relationship, but was still very young and inexperienced. Robert Luff, meanwhile, a big-time entrepreneur and impresario based in Earls Court, down in London, retained a local PR and show-business agent, George Bartram, to keep a weather eye on the talent coming up through Birmingham. Bartram shared this watching brief with Robert Holmes, who, after Bartram died, took over the agency and still operates in the West Midlands.

Bartram was present at ATV the day Lenny's first *New Faces* appearance was recorded, but had his mind set on signing up a girl singer. A little disappointed, he told Holmes the next morning that the singer had not won, but that some black guy had instead. After the edition was broadcast, Luff, a former military man with a notably pugnacious manner, watching the show in London, phoned Holmes to demand why he had not been told about this chap Lenny Henry. Holmes could not say a great deal without incriminating his partner; but by the end of the week, with offers of up to half a million pounds rumoured to be winging around Birmingham to tie Lenny into a lengthy contract, Luff saw to it that Mike Hollis had technically been bought out of his interest in Lenny (although Hollis remained deeply involved with him) and placed decisively on the management books of Robert Luff Enterprises. Lenny was about to become a professional show-business personality, with all the pluses and minuses that status carries. 'At the time I think Robert Luff did the right thing,' Lenny has said. 'He came in and took me away and said, "You need to get experience."'

Luff was in many important respects not quite Lenny Henry's type. In his sixties when he first picked Lenny up, an ex-major in the Gordon Highlanders, but with the appearance of an archetypal Tin Pan Alley agent, he was the impresario who started the *Black and White Minstrel Show*, and steered Beryl Reid's career towards greatness. Luff, who was still Lenny's manager and father figure as late as 1990, sent his new star out into the world with a one-way ticket to variety-land. It seemed an unlikely relationship but, as the *Observer* wrote towards the end of their professional involvement, 'They have both learnt from one another. Luff cites Henry's involvement in last year's Free Mandela concert with the same pride as his own Burma Campaign.' Luff has been based for the past forty years in the same private house in Earls Court, with traffic rushing by outside and a giant Japanese Samurai sword hanging on his wall. A feisty old war dog, Luff once accosted a burglar with the sword and chased him up the road waving it at him.

Miraculously released almost before he had started from the world of welding machinery, conic sections and getting up at five in the morning, Lenny was instantly a teenage star, but without the kind of cultural or family backup such people often have. His mother was very worried, but said if he wanted to have a go, he should do it. But when he decided to give up the apprenticeship two days after the first show, his workmates and family friends told him he would never make it, and gave him three weeks. British Federal said he could have his job back at any time.

Winston Henry was also disappointed that his son was not going to pursue his apprenticeship. 'I thought of the glamour, girls, fast cars and fabulous food in swish night spots that show business was bound to offer,' Lenny said in an unusually confident 1983 interview, 'then weighed it up against the prospects of three years' day release leading to an O.N.C. in engineering. It took me exactly ten seconds to make up my mind which I wanted to do.'

It was not merely the wholehearted backing of his family and acquaintances that Lenny was lacking. He had, albeit unwittingly, defined his own, unique form of comedy, but at the same time was professionally without any kind of role model. Muhammad Ali was fine as a personal development icon for a black lad, but not much of a stand-up comedian. For black, British, working-class provincial comics, the only example Lenny had to follow was that of Charlie Williams, a Yorkshireman and the only black British comic with a national reputation. Williams specialised in gags about work-shy 'darkies', and made a good living out of the white audiences in working men's clubs. Lenny was not yet the politicised idealist he was to become, and he worked a few racial jokes into his material, but he was aware there was more honourable comedy to be found. Williams had kindly offered Lenny the chance to join him, but it did not appeal, young and impressionable though he was.

'I began upside down,' Lenny willingly confesses. 'I went out immediately as a "star", but I had no experience to fall back on and certainly not enough material to sustain top-billing. When I started out, I honestly didn't know what I was doing. I pinched jokes from all over the place and nothing in my act was original. I did impressions of about 100 people – even Kojak!' His age caused problems that might not have been foreseen. 'I'd heard all these jokes about mothers-in-law and not having a mother-in-law, put me mum in instead, and couldn't understand why the jokes died. It's hard when you're sixteen.'

In the haze of it all, Henry received some advice from Tony Hatch, who had been the most infamously critical of the *New Faces* judges. It was guidance which he would later put to good use: 'Tony Hatch told me to listen to Bill Cosby albums. I was sixteen, I had top marks, but he said: "You're not going to be an impressionist for ever. You are funnier than what you're doing now."' Although Lenny did not like everything Cosby did, he recognised the sense of what Hatch was saying. 'There's a way of structuring material so it doesn't rely on an impression of Frank Spencer. I also learnt not to take it too hard, because if you're any good, you will bounce back,' he says now.

In the meanwhile, however, bookings he was ill-prepared for were rolling in. Shortly after the first *New Faces* appearance, he did a couple of turns at a country club: 'I had appeared on Monday, done quite well, and repeated the act on Wednesday. After a few minutes I heard shouts of: "Rubbish! Get him off." It was virtually the same audience again. I had not realised and did not have enough material to develop a new act.' He had another bad experience at a night club in the north east. 'I hadn't been told it was a stag night and there were going to be six naked girls on stage with me. I'm not a blue comedian and I was really upset. But I was determined not to be put off and I went out and did one of the best shows I've ever done.' In Sunderland, he had the character-building experience of playing to three people, two of whom, he suspected, were staff. In a club in Hull, the manager said to him, 'Well you didn't go down very well. You should do material like Charlie Williams.' Before a gruelling date in Morecambe, Henry called a friend from Birmingham, fellow comedian Don Maclean (of Crackerjack fame, and now a religious programme presenter on Radio 2) to cry on his shoulder. Maclean talked to Lenny for several hours about comedy. Lenny would watch Maclean's act night after night to learn the more refined tricks of his new trade.

After having been initially mortified by Lenny's hasty decision to leave the security of British Federal, just a few weeks later, Winnie was frequently there with him on the road, clapping the loudest from the front row of the audience (to the point where he sometimes had to ask her to 'cool out') and supporting him ferociously when he died. 'He was only sixteen when he started to travel around,' she recalls. 'He was so fragile and green I had to follow him everywhere. I couldn't leave him on his own, he was so young. People took advantage of him but you've got to pay to learn anything.' Sometimes, Lenny's elder brother Hylton and sister Beverley would come to these gigs with her. 'I used to come home crying after doing badly, but the family were always there,' he says now. 'One of the first dates I played after winning the show, I was introduced and given a sixty-minute standing ovation,' he jokily recounted once. 'I stood there, basking in the applause. Then when I started my act, the audience began talking among themselves and ignored me. I did about twenty minutes and ran off. I phoned my mum and said: "I'm packing it in," and she said: "Well, you know you can always go back to working in a factory and cutting your hands on a lathe." '

Material was a constant problem when Lenny went on the road, and even ruthlessly plagiarising bits of other people's routines frequently left him several jokes short of a round of applause. He was often aware that he was trying to make a six-minute act last for the best part of an hour. Once, in a club in Wales, he did what he thought was a forty-minute set, and came off, only to find the manager hissing at him in the wings, 'Get back out there, boy, you've only done ten!' As it happened, Lenny had just bought the LP of *The Comedians*, an ITV comedy show of the time that showed club comics at work, and was able to remember enough material from it, racist, sexist and mother-in-law jokes included, to make it to the finishing tape. The anomaly of a seventeen-year-old unmarried youth cracking jokes about his mother-in-law did not seem to trouble anyone other than himself.

His mother's ironically delivered words about Lenny giving it all up and returning to his lathe made perfect sense to him nonetheless, even when he was psychologically down. In June, the day before the *New Faces* winners' show, the *Daily Mail* reported that Lenny had turned down a two-year contract worth £300 a week, fifteen times his wages at British Federal, and the equivalent today of close to £60,000 a year. 'He reckons he can reach stardom without any entanglement,' the *Mail* explained. He was probably right, but the next five years were to be a ferociously busy and frequently miserable time, as he simultaneously did summer season, pantomime, continual club cabaret, the occasional TV appearance – plus one very strange departure; in the summer of 1975, Robert Luff prevailed upon his new star to do something which, if it seems bizarre now, seemed, at the very least, downright eccentric then.

On 20 October, in Stoke on Trent, Lenny Henry was to become the first real black man ever to appear on the *Black and White Minstrel Show*. The BBC TV version of an early radio show called *The Minstrels*, the *Black and White Minstrels* was by then already fifteen years old and on its last legs. In a fatal miscalculation of the sensitivity race relations would assume in the 1960s, the show's name had been prefixed with 'Black and White' only because it was on TV – i.e. in black and white, rather than on the wireless; there were, of course, no black members at all – until Lenny Henry. The blacking up tradition had been borrowed from an obscure branch of Deep South vaudeville. It was as late as 1978 before the show was stopped by the BBC, the intellectual tide having turned to the point where it was no longer considered quite nice for white men to black up and pretend to be black men of the 'Lordy, Lordy, massa' kind. Incredibly, rechristened *The Minstrels*, the show went back on tour in 1992, and played to packed theatres in Scarborough and Torquay. It was now, however, in a slightly emasculated form. The Minstrels blacked up for only half the show; they still did *Black and White Minstrels* classic numbers like 'Camptown Races' and 'John Brown's Body', but without the hand waggling of old. And they also asked the audience halfway through if they objected at all to the Minstrels putting on make-up for the second half of the show. Having paid to see the *Black and White Minstrels* as they remembered them, not surprisingly, nobody objected.

'I wanted to bring him forward slowly,' Luff explained several years later in defence of putting Lenny in the *Black and White Minstrels*. 'People don't become overnight successes in show business, you've got to do a lot of hard work. Mainly people go in direct. Well, Lenny had no background of that sort. He won the *New Faces* heat, I think he won two heats – and there he was, and I think he had to be handled from the point of view that he was starting from scratch ... I don't think he enjoyed it but it was very good for him. He learnt stagecraft. He was raw and he took advice.'

Luff's rationale for putting Lenny in a six-week *Minstrels* tour was more than just a hunch. He reasoned that, as the show's format did not allow any one performer on stage for very long, the pressure on Lenny would be less than in straight cabaret. Any comedy act in the *Minstrels* show would follow a big, spectacular scene, so the audience came pre-warmed – in perfect fettle, so the theory ran, for Lenny to wow them with a good, strong ten minutes.

Put this way, it was not such a bad idea, but the fact remained that, if the *Black and White Minstrels* was in abominable taste, putting a black man in the thing compounded the offence. Lenny, no friend today of the 'darkie joke', as he calls it, very nearly became one himself in late 1975; this was taking the Henry family maxim of fitting in with white people too far, and Lenny knew it. The Charlie Williams-style gags were unavoidable, and the derogatory phrase 'Uncle Tom' was bandied about. 'At least I shan't need any extra make-up,' he said at the time. 'Seriously, though, I don't think they expect me to wear white Pan-Stik make-up and croon Maa ... aammy. I'll just be doing my act – about fifteen minutes of it ... Doing the show will be great experience. for me and I'm very grateful to them for signing me up.'

On his opening night at Jollees club in Stoke, he told the audience: 'They picked on me because they thought they could save money on make-up – there was no way they were going to get me to white-up for the show.' One scene opened with the back of Father Christmas flanked by two white dancing girls singing 'We're dreaming of a white Christmas', whereupon Santa Claus turned round to reveal Lenny, who said: 'You got no chance.' Lenny's gags included wiping sweat off his face and saying it was chocolate, and threatening hecklers that he'd move next door to them – the latter joke a clever one because it brings a warm glow to racists and liberals alike.

Lenny has not rejected the whole of the concept Luff presented him with. In 1988, he delivered the first and probably the last defence of the *Black and White Minstrels* to be heard on *The South Bank Show.* 'The *Minstrels* is good because people come to see the Minstrels – they don't really care about who is on in between,' he explained. 'It's nice and they feel very glad that there's a comedian there. But really the comedian is there fill in the gap between the Minstrels getting changed and coming on. So I was very protected for about five years, and in that respect I'm very grateful to the *Minstrels* because it gave me stagecraft. It taught me how to use a microphone and all that stuff . . . There are some things which just blow your mind, like going out on stage at the Blackpool Opera House and seeing 3,000 people lusting after blood. But I managed to cope, and just about pulled through.

'But the big thing,' he added, 'was people blacking up and I couldn't reconcile myself to that.' The role he was cast in on the *Minstrels*, as the funny darkie, the guy whom the jokes were on, the young Charlie Williams clone doing gags about black people, jokes about blacking up ('Does it come off?, When I cry, I get white lines down my face, I'm leaking. It's chocolate,') was ultimately soul-destroying for Lenny. At times over the five years he was involved with the *Black and White Minstrels*, he became depressed, and ate for comfort, his weight hitting seventeen stone when he was still seventeen. It was a disturbing time, although one he did not elaborate on, or even refer to, in his autobiographical comic strip book, in which otherwise he exposed many layers of his personal trauma.

He did several other things for comfort, apart from overeating. 'I had various relationships with different girls. When you perform each night you are on a high and you don't want to come down, so you go clubbing . . . I used to go out with dancers and girls I met in clubs, where the conversation went: "What is your name?" "Would you like a drink?" and then (with a leery look) "Do you want a lift home?"'

Stories got about on the show-business gossip mill of Lenny being an enormous stud and exceptionally free with copious quantities of money. This might have been all right for most young showbiz personalities, but Lenny had a morally upright and religious past behind him, and a future ahead as almost the prototypical politically correct new man. The image of a free-spending Lothario was not, therefore, something he wanted either then or now. 'It was largely because girls thought I was in the money that I got labelled a womaniser,' he explained in the *Sunday Mirror* when he was twenty-five, his original words seemingly massaged a tad to resemble authentic tabloid-speak. 'All the stories of me making love to a flood of women are baloney. It was never more than a trickle. But I must admit I was taken in by some of the beautiful, sexily-clad girls who turn up at trendy nightspots just to get off with the rich and famous. I know better now.'

He attributed his ability eventually to handle money to his working-class background, and the continued support of family and old friends. 'It's that sort of thing that has stopped me buying huge limos and living in the South of France. When you come from a working-class background there are quite a lot of people around who will tell it to you straight. But only those who know you really well can do it. In show business there are plenty who'll tell you that you were brilliant when you weren't. You have to take what they say with a pinch of salt because they will try to schmooze you ... It's nice to have money, but I am not obsessed by it. I have a lot of possessions, but I wouldn't cheat my best friend for an object.'

Alongside his early profligacy, Lenny also admitted to several torrid on-the-road affairs with dancers in summer shows – 'You know what those chorus girls are like' – and to having had great difficulty communicating with such lovelies. 'Most of the girls that I've been out with I had to work incredibly hard to keep them entertained,' he said. 'At one time I would stay in bed nearly all day, a bit of a slob, really. Then I'd get up at 4 p.m. and say to myself, "OK, go out there and be funny!" ... Life had become just one long round of partying and sleeping in.

'I just used old jokes and wasted time. I'd go to Hull, for instance, arrive in the snow with my suitcase, find the digs, find the theatre, go to the band call and discover the band couldn't read music. I'd go home and cry, come back at 10 p.m. to go on. There'd be four people there and nobody'd laugh. So I'd go to the bar, get legless, crash out, wake up next day, get all the papers, spend all day doing absolutely nothing.'

Unsurprisingly, Lenny's early determination not to drink even when he was old enough had not quite held up. A seminal experience in his drinking career, or non-career as it really was, had been getting drunk to the point of having hallucinations on home-brewed beer at his friend Greg Stokes' house, after his sister's wedding. Lenny had got quietly sozzled while entertaining Greg's family 'for hours' with his impressions. Lenny was fourteen, and did not enjoy the experience of drunkenness, only starting to drink again in moderation when he was on the road as a cabaret star and sometimes had nothing else to do. He never smoked, however, after having tried and hated it back in Buffery Park. He also never showed any interest in drugs. In 1976, Lenny was voted number one non-smoker on a list issued by the National Society of Non-Smokers; Margaret Thatcher and Angela Rippon were also in the top ten.

Lenny declared on being bestowed with this honour that smoking was now unfashionable for young people. His dislike of cigarettes (which is shared by several night club performers, subjected as they are to continual second-hand tobacco smoke from the audience) put him off the idea of marijuana, to which he had been introduced in Buffery Park, and seemed to have a natural aversion. The only addictive behaviour he has ever displayed is nail biting, which he has always been prone to. As far as drugs are concerned, although he discusses the subject knowingly in his act, he is virulently anti. Once, he used to say in his act (and, embroidery apart, the story has the ring of truth about it), he was in Jamaica on holiday with a white friend, when the friend asked if he could get him some ganja; Lenny was embarrassed to confess that he had no idea how to do so, as well as being mildly offended that he should be expected as a black man to know about such matters.

The one thing he did admit to going crazy with was money although, in true Lenny Henry style, he had matured and settled down in his spending habits by the time most ordinary people have just begun to go through their youthful extravagance phase. 'I just grabbed the opportunity when it came. I could make a lot of money, but it's rubbish to say that I'm becoming rich,' he said aged seventeen. 'I'd like to buy a big car – but first I'll have to learn to drive. My family still live in the same house at Dudley, and we've no plans to move.' By the grand age of eighteen, he was talking like a thirty-year-old might in the same position. 'Like any kid with a few bob in his pocket, I went a little mad. Money was burning a hole in my pocket and it began to flow like honey,' he admitted. His bank manager, he says, had to step in. 'He began to talk like a Dutch uncle about things like overdrafts. I took note, stopped acting like a dummy and now I have an accountant who tells me what to do with my money – like saving.'

By twenty-six, he had moved fully into 'when I was a young man' mode. 'In those days [before *New Faces*] I used to give half my money to my mum and maybe I'd have enough left over to go out for a drink and buy a pair of trousers occasionally. *New Faces* changed all that. Someone said we'll give you all this money to mess about on stage for half-an-hour and I said "Oh yes, please." When you come from a family that's not used to having money and someone offers you large amounts – well, I had a good time. I was going to parties all the time, going to the bank, saying, "I'd like some more money please," and buying all the clothes and records I wanted. I thought I was being really trendy. My accountant never had much grey hair to start with but he rapidly went bald. I nearly went off the rails several times. Luckily, my father was always very helpful to me. He gave me the advice that helped me keep my feet on the ground. He used to say, "Remember who you are. Stay yourself."'

Sometimes, when he reflects on his five years with the *Minstrels*, all those nights, some of them passably steamy, in Bournemouth, Yarmouth, Blackpool and the like, Lenny is simply philosophical about it. 'It was just all these white people coming in and blacking up and going on and singing these songs, and then me going on afterwards. It was just such a weird place to be. I had to put up with a lot of jokes.'

At other times, he is quite angry about it, feeling he was compelled to do it. 'I was sort of being forced into doing stuff that I didn't want to do, and in the Seventies there are these terrible pictures of me wearing those flares and platforms and frilly bow ties because that's what the other comedians did at that time,' Lenny says.

'They [his fellow minstrels] were actually nice people,' Lenny confessed to Sue Lawley, 'but as I got on I really did take offence to blacking up and those stupid Stephen Foster songs and all the doodah-day – Jesus – and,' he added, as a slightly bitter joke, 'having to give black consciousness awareness to all the minstrels. "You know, Lenny, we're trying to cope with being black but it's so difficult for us because really it is a facade." So I'd raise their consciousness about blackness, teach them to dance and stuff and how to have rhythm, so it was pretty cool.'

In an interview in the *Sun* just after he left the *Minstrels*, Lenny said of show-business people in general, 'They resented all the money I was getting, but there was never any resentment against me because of my colour. I'm lucky, show business is a wonderful business to be in because there isn't any prejudice at all. Twelve years later, in a *Daily Telegraph* interview, he was not so sure: 'There was very little racism where I grew up,' he said. 'It was when I went into the business and saw how the cards were stacked that I realised there was racism. In this country it's more guarded, in America you get called nigger to your face.'

In a contemplative interview with Alan Franks in *The Times*, Lenny dealt with the question of the kind of material circumstances forced him to do. 'I'm not ashamed of what I used to be. I was just growing up, and trying to get a handle on who I was. In the working men's clubs there had been Charlie Williams, Sammy Thomas, Joss White and a couple of others. They were fine; they did jokes that were against themselves. But in those days, in the days of *The Comedians*, that's what you did. There were Paki jokes and darkie jokes and jokes about being sent home, and moving in next door ... Charlie Williams, who was born in Yorkshire, doing jokes about how all the blacks were talking about going back to Africa. He'd say: "Send the booggers home, that's what I say." And I did them because Charlie was doing them. He was the only successful black comedian in this country I could look to.'

Very quietly indeed, the politicisation of Lenny Henry was underway. It was not the raw, shocking experience of being called a black bastard by a fellow apprentice at British Federal, and Lenny punching him in the face. This was more the growing awareness in Lenny that there was, after all, a subtext to him, an intellectual side. It was by no means overt, and for the public and show-business colleagues, the old, accommodating, sunny-side-up, over-easy Lenny had not changed. But, even before he met Dawn French, which he says was the beginning of the process by which he realised darkie jokes were wrong, he was realigning himself.

First, it took the form of seeing himself as a kind of secret black man. While he kowtowed to white audiences on stage, as he puts it, 'I had this parallel life. On stage I'd be singing "You Need Hands". Off stage I'd be going to clubs and staying out all night checking out the new James Brown record.' Then there would come the question of trying to include gags in his act that had some deeper meaning. 'When I was a kid and first started, people used to say to me, "Now you don't want to talk about bloody politics on stage, the stage is for entertainment. If you want to talk politics, go out and be a bloody politician." That's what the comics used to say to me. When I told comics I wanted to be like Richard Pryor, they said, "This is Batley Social Club, we don't have that around here." As I grew up I realised that everything you do is politics...'

Lenny was, and continues to be, immensely proud of his one anti-racist joke at the time, which, he claims, he told from the beginning; it is the joke he always mentions in interviews to show, and quite convincingly, that he was not completely of the world which had apparently sucked him into itself and digested him.

'I remember one of the first jokes I told when I was sixteen. It was just after the Enoch Powell Rivers of Blood speech, and he was still making the odd foray into the news with the same stuff, and I said: "Enoch Powell has offered us a thousand pounds to go home, which suits me fine because it's only 10p on the 54 from here to Dudley." It went down really well, and it was true, because Powell hadn't thought of the British-born population, the British-born Asian/West Indian population that were there, that were English, walking round ... "What's he mean he's going to send us home? I live in Tipton." To tell that joke, even as naive and as young as I was, there was something there that said, "Yeah, this is a good thing to say." '

For the most part, however, the culture in which he was surviving demanded that he fit in, however uncomfortable this made the real, deep-down Lenny. 'I was this monster: Len who went around telling horrible jokes. But they weren't malicious, and I'd nicked them all from white comedians anyway. I don't regret that because I was a child in showbiz terms. I'd do gigs where there were no blacks in the audience, so after a while I had to examine why I was getting laughs, and it was for all the wrong reasons. They were laughing at me instead of with me . . .

'I was using sexism and racism – jokes that were very laddish and very fwoaargggh!! which, being seventeen and eighteen I shouldn't have been doing at all. I was doing jokes about being black. It wasn't like, "Hey I'm a black guy," and being rational and reasonable about it. It was telling jokes that everybody was telling about black people. And nobody ever said don't do those jokes – until 1981, when I met Dawn.'

CHAPTER 5

... AND LENNY HENRY

'For the first four years of my career I survived and could eat because I was a black person. It was after then that I realised I could rely upon my talent. Far from being a hindrance, being black was a help.'

Lenny Henry

As the wave of interest in Lenny Henry gathered momentum in 1975, Michael Grade, then at London Weekend Television, and some producers at the station had a brainwave. Lenny's story – working class Midlands family, secondary modern school, engineering apprenticeship – was all over the newspapers. A tape had come over from America of a series called *Good Times*, broadly about a loveable working-class black family.

Was it possible, the well-meaning liberal establishment types at LWT wondered, to do their own bit for race relations in Britain by inventing a feelgood ethnic family over here? And was Lenny Henry the key to such a series, a real-life friendly, sassy, hip black kid from such a family? Was the time ripe – or could it be ripened – for a British all-black sitcom?

Black actors in the mid-Seventies were in some demand. Rudolf Walker and Nina Baden-Semper were doing well in *Love Thy Neighbour* (despite its racist theme), the distinguished actor Norman Beaton (who died in 1994) cropped up from time to time in *Rising Damp* alongside the black star Don Warrington, and the TV hospital series *Angels* provided work for black actresses as token black nurses. Beaton, who was greatly admired by Bill Cosby, and once appeared on an episode of *The Cosby Show*, said at the time, 'There's no discrimination in show business – talent tells.' Walker and Baden-Semper were more sceptical about the black acting boom. 'Let me put it this way – when *The Avengers* was relaunched, there was a poll in which viewers could suggest who played the new girl. I got the most votes – but no one offered me the part,' Baden-Semper said.

Grade invited Lenny to go to his office at LWT to watch an episode of *Good Times*. Grade and Humphrey Barclay, a great campaigner for blacks on television, then offered him the part of Sonny, the eldest son in a British version of the American product, to be called *The Fosters*. Also at the meeting was Stuart Allen, who would be the series producer, and had been a major influence in bringing Lenny down from Dudley.

To do the first series (over two years, he did twenty-seven episodes in two series) Lenny had, of course, to live in London for thirteen weeks, the first time he had been properly away from Douglass Road and the family. 'Every day I'd have to walk from my hotel to the rehearsal rooms,' he recalls. 'It was one of the most awful experiences I'd ever had. On that walk, nobody spoke to you. Nobody even looked at you. I felt like the Invisible Man. I was so depressed, so low, that I couldn't wait to get back home.'

He spent too much money, drank and ate too much. He would call his mother from the hotel, saying again that he felt like jacking it all in. Winnie was encouraging again, not having to raise the spectre of the lathe – that was no longer a realistic alternative – but talking him up with what might be the family motto – 'Keep going, keep your feet on the ground and work hard.' In London, as a TV star (although not one that was stopped in the street a lot) he became arrogant, he admits, towards the lesser mortals of show business. 'I went through a time of having the wrong attitude, particularly with a lot of agents in the north,' he said in 1984. 'I think that even today some of them still say: "Lenny Henry. Phew – very bad news."'

He became a little vain, buying good (albeit large) clothes in expensive shops. He spent a lot of money on collecting classic comics, especially 1960s editions of *Marvel*, *Daredevil*, *Spiderman* and *X-Men*, which could be a great comforter and reminder of childhood when you are living for three months at a stretch alone in a hotel room. He also bought large numbers of records and, as a by-product of trips to music shops, made some new discoveries about his own line of work. 'My influences early on were people like the Marx Brothers and Tommy Cooper. I didn't really know these black comedians existed. But then I went into a shop on London's Edgware Road, and this black guy behind the counter had earphones on and was roaring with laughter. He held up an LP and on the cover was Richard Pryor tied to a stake, with fire shooting up round his feet, and he had all these Ku Klux Klan men dancing round him, and it was called "Is It Something I Said?" That made me start collecting comedy albums from then on.'

As ever, Lenny was saved by his rather precocious, mature sense of self-awareness and desire to do the right thing. 'I suddenly realised that I was doing too much partying around,' he says of this time in London. 'I thought, "I cannot afford to do this. I'm going to burn myself out." I had to come to terms with the fact that what I do is a job – a very serious job. Comedy is perhaps the most difficult thing in show business.'

He would redouble his efforts to follow his father's advice and be true to himself. There are always two sides to giving, and he derived great pleasure from being nice, good Len alongside his other life as loud, swaggering, showbiz Len. As Meg Newton, one of the Henrys' neighbours in Douglass Road, recalls: 'A lovely memory I have of him was when I had a baby, my son, who's now eighteen. Lenny was beginning to be quite a big star by then, and one day he knocked on my door. He had his hands behind his back, and said he was sorry because all the florists were closed, but he'd like to give me this. And it was the most beautiful red velvet rose. I kept it for years and years, until I just lost it. It didn't seem as if any level of success could change him.'

The Fosters was about a West Indian family living in a council tower block in south London. The first episode was made in London on 23 September 1975 and shown on 9 April, a Friday evening, the following

year. The credits at the beginning gave some impression of Lenny's role
in the scheme of things, as a television star on approval; the star of *The
Fosters* was Norman Beaton (as the father, Samuel Foster); Isabelle Lucas
was Pearl, the mother, Sharon Rosita, the daughter Shirley, Lawrie
Mark, brother Benjamin – 'and Lenny Henry'.

The opening sequence pinpointed both the precise geographical
location of the Fosters' flat (in Theed Street, less than 100 yards from
LWT's offices on the South Bank) and the black community's location
in the social hierarchy. We saw a black traffic warden (female), a
cricketer, a cricket fan, a black motorbike traffic cop and happy black
children in London settings. (In the programme's closing sequence, a
black policeman – accompanied by a white officer, of course – was also
glimpsed.) The scene was clearly being set for a jaunty portrayal of
black Britain; social realism could wait for the moment.

The ironic parallels with Lenny's real life were obvious; here he was,
a black working-class youth, portraying a similar character to himself.
Yet by doing so on the television, he was in reality taking the first step
away from his background. For the record, he did point out at the
outset, lest any viewers might have thought Sonny Foster was a bit of
a waster, that, 'I wouldn't get away with half the things I do in the
series. My mother wouldn't allow it. She brought us up very strict –
there's no messing around at home.'

Lenny, who was sixteen when shooting began, appeared as a seventeen-year-old in the series. In the opening sequence of episode one,
he was seen shouting at his sister Shirley, who was in the bathroom.
'Shirley! You still in there. I've got a date, don't you know.' Lenny's
accent, a slightly West Indian-ised London, with Dudley still poking
through curiously for a Londoner (the West Indies twang was a less
than entirely successful attempt to cover up the Dudley) was not as
much of a surprise as his appearance. He wore a vivid yellow T-shirt,
extremely tight blue jeans, a baggy blue cap and, after a few moments,
a scarlet PVC short anorak.

The Fosters, the senior ones at least, we soon learnt, were from
Guyana – an attempt to get viewers away, perhaps, from the notion that
all black people came from Jamaica. The plot was not very complex:

the mother finds the typewritten script of a research document entitled 'Sexual Behaviour in the Black Community' in the flat. She wants to know why Sonny – it *had* to be the preening, girl-mad Sonny – has brought such 'filth' into her home. The Fosters clearly have no way of establishing this is a respectable educational paper.

The father then arrives home from an unspecified job – but we are not encouraged to think he is a brain surgeon – and far from being shocked by the discovery of the paper is thrilled that it proves his son is a sex maniac, just like he was back in Guyana. Sonny/Henry, now changed to go out (white trousers, a black-and-white striped jacket, yellow formal shirt and broad-brimmed hat) denies all knowledge of the document. Then it is discovered that the paper is the work of sixteen-year-old Shirley's terribly serious, soberly suited twenty-one-year-old boyfriend, a lecturer. Father is furious, for illogical reasons he refuses to explain, but insists on gating Shirley, who is expecting the boyfriend, Matthew, played by Joseph Charles, to come over at any moment.

When Matthew arrives, Samuel is exceedingly cold towards him. Then boyfriend explains that he only met Shirley while writing his thesis, a word that Samuel, naturally, can't understand. Things get worse, until boyfriend points out that Shirley's role was to illustrate how the rate of unexpected pregnancy in black teenage girls was almost nil – in stable black families with a strong father figure. This flatteringly explained, of course, Samuel gives his blessing to the relationship.

The show, although clearly a vehicle for Lenny as a cameo, did not exactly dwell on his character. Episode one concluded with Sonny returning from a date some minutes after having gone out on it; his girlfriend for the night's father, we learn, smelled his mouthwash, checked out his carefully preened appearance – and slammed the door in his face; another triumph, it seemed, for a strong West Indian father figure. The End.

Very rapidly, more of Lenny's talents were allowed to appear. In a later edition, 'Who Needs Friends?', Lenny (in tight blue trousers and a black shirt with an enormous collar) is going for his fourteenth job interview in two weeks. After it, he saunters into the pub (with a black hat and purple patch silk jacket added to his ensemble) and announces that he has got the job – as a dustman. 'Well I'll be working outside, I get free gloves and overalls and all I can salvage from the bins,' he says. The facial mobility which was to become his trademark in later years was in evidence by now, but quite toned down. We later see him on his dustcart in a brightly coloured rasta hat. As he tries to hide the truth of his new profession from his father, he adopts one of his many accents.

By the second series, recorded in March 1977, Lenny's role had developed further, with the chance to use a full range of mimicry and accents. He also sang a little, and seemed to have a spontaneity that the other characters lack. Any viewer, by this time, would have been able to pick him out as the actor who was also a comedian.

He was by this stage of his career filming six days a week, and doing cabaret nights around London at the same time, during which he stopped doing his impersonation of the Ugandan dictator, Idi Amin: 'He's not a figure of fun any more. I wasn't getting laughs. So I've dropped him,' Lenny said.

The question of Lenny's workaholism was beginning to concern both him and his friends by now. 'I think that if I stop work for a second, something terrible will happen,' he has confessed. 'I never worked hard at anything before I became a comic, because I didn't know what I wanted to do. But I love my work now and I work very hard at it. Too hard, sometimes. There's another little Lenny who often sits on my shoulder in Bermuda shorts and sunglasses with a cocktail in his hand, saying "Take a nap, Len!" But I can't let up.'

The suggestion that he was some kind of idler before he became a comic at sixteen is again something of a giveaway if the search is on for evidence of workaholism – yet that word thoroughly irritates Lenny. 'Someone said I was a workaholic. I don't know why that's bad,' he complained on a different occasion. 'People in our business are driven. They must be. Why else would you do such stupid things? . . . I was really cheesed off because I thought, "I'm not a workaholic. I'm a comedian and I like what I do." A part of me is driven, but I don't think there's anything wrong with that. I'm very ambitious. If you've no goals what are you? . . . I was in the right place at the right time but

I've also worked incredibly hard. You have to be lucky, but you've got to work until you almost collapse to get any result at all.'

Lenny reads, cooks and uses relaxation tapes to stop his mind speeding, but admits these diversionary tactics do not always work. He has also increasingly developed the classic workaholic symptom, a chronic, nagging dissatisfaction with his own work. 'I don't think I've ever been entirely happy with any performance I've ever done,' he has said. 'There have been things where I've said to myself, "Yeah, that's fine, that's OK," but I'm always slightly disappointed. I'm not just talking about my stand-up routine but the TV stuff, films – the lot. I'm not completely despairing, but there's usually some niggling thing … It drives me on: if I were to finish something and say, "Oh, that was great. I'll never give a better performance than that," then I'd give up.'

Even in his mid-thirties, the balance between work and sustaining a normal home life was troubling to Lenny, especially after having married a similarly driven comedienne. By this time, Lenny had settled into his current pattern of waiting until his wife and daughter are asleep to get out his Apple Mac Powerbook laptop computer and work on the next project. 'Dawn has a thing,' he commented, 'that there's got to be something else apart from work to live for – and she's right. 'Cos if you're not wanted on television there's got to be something else to support you, someone who cares enough to say "Don't worry."'

'I was always confident,' he said at this time. 'It's only as I get older that I get a bit nervous about things. When I was a kid, I was like a brick wall. I'd come bouncing back. I could fall in a vat of horse manure and come up smelling of Eau Sauvage! But now I feel vulnerable and I feel I've got to be funnier than anything I've ever been at any time.'

Like virtually all comics, Lenny had a deeply unconfident, insecure side. While fans expected him to leap about in fits of laughter, or to be the sex god he (jokingly) says he was on stage, he saw himself as a thoughtful, introspective person. To be funny for a living, he maintained, it was essential to be meticulous and disciplined. People who are flippant and superficial in everyday life – the archetypal life-and-soul-of-the-party types – could never be professional comedians. He admits to being 'a bit grumpy sometimes,' intolerant, egotistical, tenacious and very disorganised. But he also says he is gregarious, self-deprecating and, interestingly, 'I'm a very good audience. I love to hear a joke.' (This was very true; years later, on a trip to Africa for Comic Relief, he would spend half the night telling jokes to the aid workers and journalists – and laughing enthusiastically at theirs.)

Despite having such a confident aura, Lenny felt he had to learn, or relearn, assertiveness the more experienced he became. At one time, he has explained, he was the kind of man who would bite his own arm off rather than confront an adversary, or even hurt somebody's feelings. He was beginning, he claimed as late as 1994, to be consciously more assertive. 'Now I'm not afraid of anyone – except my mum,' he said.

Being a public figure from the age of seventeen was also a mixed blessing. 'I love it,' he said in 1985 of being recognised by the public. 'I love working to people, but sometimes it's a drag. You're always the public's property, they talk about you really loudly, as if you're on the telly and you can't hear them. I get angry sometimes when you go out for a meal, just the two of you, and they draw up a chair and say, "Ullo Len, you all right?"'

Lenny became used to being approached in the street, frequently to be offered a joke. Some were good, he says, and he would use them. Others were disgusting. Once, he used a joke somebody told him in a bar in Liverpool and made the mistake of telling it in the same city the next night; the entire audience seemed to have heard it before. Being asked, as he sometimes was, to tell a joke in the street irritated him from early on; 'If I was walking along with a couple of pipes and met a passing welder I wouldn't ask him to weld them,' he says. 'I still get annoyed when, say, I'm having a candlelit dinner with a girl and a bloke thrusts a bit of paper in my soup and demands an autograph for his mate 'cos I can't stand you. People can often be quite unintentionally rude.'

(In 1989, Lenny attracted some rare bad publicity when he was accused of saying 'Fuck off' to Gregory James, aged twenty-five, who organised a whip-round for Comic Relief in a Soho bar, having spotted Lenny at another table. Gregory collected over £20 in a hat and approached Lenny. 'I didn't hassle him,' James insisted. 'I just said, "I'm sorry to disturb you." That was as far as I got. He left the cash on the table and watched Henry count it without a word of thanks. Lenny's spokesman denied he swore but apologised if he appeared 'short'. 'He told the man he wasn't supposed to accept money and that it should be sent direct to the charity.' Lenny denied saying fuck, and added: 'We were just having a few private drinks when this bloke suddenly plonked this money down in front of us. I told him it wasn't the way to do things. But before I could explain properly he stormed off in a huff. Now everything has got out of proportion.')

In 1977, just after recording the second series of *The Fosters*, Lenny was called urgently back to Dudley from Stockport, where he was due to do a series of shows. There was a family crisis. His father was in hospital with kidney failure, and it had been made clear that he was unlikely to survive. It was now that Lenny spent longer talking with his father than he had ever done before, finding out as much as he could as quickly as possible about the family history. His father's death was the most traumatic event of his life, yet he found it difficult to cry until the night after the funeral.

The points when he most expected to cry – seeing his father's body at the undertaker's and standing by the graveside – he felt, as he put it, 'like someone had superglued my tear ducts closed.' The funeral service, in a Church of England church, made him laugh in retrospect, as the large crowd of black mourners responded to the vicar's kindly platitudes with whoops of 'Yes, Lord!' and 'Praise the Lord'. Winston Henry's friends and relatives would also break into melodies in the middle of the lustily sung hymns in the church. There were then more hymns by the grave, as Lenny and the other male mourners followed the Jamaican tradition of each shovelling some earth on to the coffin. Lenny found it all uplifting. ('People from other funerals were defecting to us,' he joked in *The Quest for the Big Woof*.)

Back at Douglass Road, it was open house, with friends arriving constantly with food and cakes, and Winston's mates dropping by to pay their respects and play dominoes. Winifred was busy cooking, and Lenny, according to his own account, became increasingly disturbed. Eventually, as the generally social atmosphere warmed up, he says, he 'went loopy,' and asked everyone to leave. It was only his mother explaining that the tradition of having an open house for nine nights went back to the West Indies, and previously to Africa. Lenny toed the line from then on, and obediently helped wait on and amuse the mourners for the next eight nights. On the last, he recalls, when he went to bed, he cried for the first time.

'It's only recently that I have been able to write these things down,' Lenny said in a moving *Sun* interview when the book *The Quest for the Big Woof* was published in 1991. 'If you are scared or upset about anything, talking about it gets it out of your system. Making a comedy out of something that upsets you so much diminishes the pain. Writing it all down has been so beneficial. I can look back at the funeral now and see how funny it was.

'The idea,' he said of the wake at which he temporarily lost his cool, 'was to help my mother through her grief as my father's spirit went to heaven. I still feel that my dad is looking over me, guiding me in some way.'

CHAPTER 6

FALLING OVER BLACKWARDS

'Oooookaaaay.'

Algernon Winston Spencer Churchill Gladstone Disraeli Palmerston Pitt The Younger Pitt The Elder Razzmatazz

Even though he decided at sixteen that he didn't want to be like Charlie Williams, and felt deeply discomfited in the late 1970s at having to play in the *Black and White Minstrel Show*, the black side of Lenny Henry at this time was almost kept under wraps as far as the public was concerned. He may have had his 'secret life' as a black man, marvelling at Richard Pryor and buying the latest and coolest in black music, but to all outward appearances Lenny had developed into a regular English entertainer, as familiar a sight at British seasides as deck chairs and seagulls.

It was not simply a case of Lenny turning a blind eye to black consciousness as part of his comedy deal; he was, according to his public statements, expressly opposed to it, a bit like those traditional working-class Tories who take moral exception to trade unions. Any thought that the sassy Sonny of *The Fosters* might have had some basis in the real Henry was dispelled; it seemed that Lenny was happiest when his blackness was ignored, except, of course, when he was using it as a way of getting laughs. At times it actually seemed to embarrass him. 'I don't want to be thought of as a black comedian. I'm a British comedian who happens to be black,' he was quoted as saying. 'I don't go on about the hardships of being black and all that rubbish. I'm proud to be black – but I'm also proud to be British.' In another interview, he said the same, adding, 'I've never been uptight about being black and British ... and I was like that long before I started to make it in show business.'

This was strong stuff, and there was more of it in a series of interviews in 1981. The *Daily Mail* began an article: 'If there's one word that can wipe the smile from Lenny Henry's rubbery features it's "black".'

'I really can't be bothered with colour,' he told the paper. 'People ask me what I think about the colour question, and I say "What's the question?" A friend of mine is the lead in *Jesus Christ Superstar* at the moment, and a reporter asked him "What's it like to be a black actor playing Jesus?" He said "I'm an actor, that's all. Does anyone ask a white guy what it's like to be a white actor playing Jesus?"

'I joke about colour as part of my stage act to break the ice with the audience, but the gags are not anti-black; they're anti-me,' he went on, repeating his favourite joke. 'I say I'm all in favour of being paid thousands of pounds to be repatriated – it's only a 10p bus fare back to Dudley. But really, I've got nothing to say about race. Being black didn't make it any harder for me to break into show business. It's hard for anyone. You have to be good, you have to be funny. Colour doesn't come into it.

'I get people asking me if I'd like to go back to the West Indies. But I say, "Why? I'm not from there, I'm from Dudley." I'm not into palm trees. I'm into Black Country bitter and the Baggies – that's West Bromwich Albion. Jamaica is somewhere far, far away where it's hot. I'd go for a holiday, but I'd want to come back to the cold where there are people I've got things in common with. A lot of reggae records chant "Back to Ethiopia, come to Africa, Haile Selassie." But black youths over here don't know who Haile Selassie is – yet they wear the clothes, put on woolly hats and say Rasta. They don't even know what it means. Those kids really worry me. They think it's hip to get into trouble with the police and be anti-white, anti-work, anti-everything.'

These seemed odd thoughts for someone who, a few years earlier, would probably *not* have won *New Faces*, or even made it through the audition, had he been just another white guy impersonating Frank

Spencer *et al.* Talented as he clearly was to the original producer at the Birmingham audition, and later to the panellists, his gimmick – and a very clever gimmick it was too – remained the fact that he was black. It was what set him aside from all the other aspiring impressionists – it certainly couldn't have been the quality of his material. He later, after meeting Dawn, admitted that this was the case: 'For the first four years of my career I survived and could eat because I was a black person. It was after then that I realised I could rely upon my talent,' he said. 'Far from being a hindrance, being black was a help.' He did not dwell on the obvious irony that it took a white woman to point out that his blackness was important.

Lenny's disavowal of any form of black solidarity extended to a stinging critique of unemployed young black people, which was the more surprising because Paul, his younger brother, was in the middle of an eighteen-month period of unemployment as he spoke. 'A lot of black youths have a negative approach to unemployment. It's no use sitting there saying, "It's not fair – everyone is picking on me." They hang out on street corners or at discos and get into fights because they've nothing to do. I say: "Try to make something of yourself. Don't sit back and moan about it." I might have ended up just doing something in a factory. But at least I'd have been better off than them because I'd have had a go.' (Later, Lenny modified his argument subtly by saying, 'I think all kids are having a rough time at the moment, black and white. I went with my young brother to the local job centre the other day. I'm not surprised they don't like going there – the kids are treated like morons.')

He seemed cheerfully to take any amount of racism and being patronised. A writer on the *Daily Express*, for example, observed: 'Lenny Henry is as black as the Ace of Spades and as British as roast beef and Yorkshire pudding . . . Incidentally, he's not going to complain to the Race Relations Commission about being called a "spade". He roars with laughter and says: "It's right, isn't it . . . after all, I am something of a card . . ." And he pulls that great big Lenny Henry grin. That's typical of his whole attitude,' the writer affirmed. 'He is probably the number one person in Britain most unhung-up about race.'

Lenny was still very young, and there had to be a change in his outlook. And there was, possibly, a simple and rational explanation for the things Lenny was saying in his early twenties. The essential difference between him and American comedians like Bill Cosby, Richard Pryor and Eddie Murphy was that his audience was a hundred per cent white; indeed, black people here had no experience or desire to go to see comedians – probably because they did not want to be subjected to racist jokes. If black people had comedic leanings, they would become disc jockeys. On the few occasions he performed at West Indian venues, such as a social club in Southampton, Lenny found he had to explain first what he actually did, and how the audience should respond. Even after he had diplomatically set out the ground rules, there were still people who thought the evening's entertainment was a kind of conversation, and interjected with stories about their own lives.

It was not as if the seeds of Lenny Henry's growing up had not already been planted. The 'fitting in' ethic so deeply implanted in him allowed him to go so far, but he finally, and with some embarrassment, had to confront Robert Luff over his continuing involvement with the *Black and White Minstrels*. 'I realised that I was going the traditional route, this black bloke in a bow tie and a frilly shirt, and I was wanting more and more to be myself and not this happy-go-lucky token, which I had been for the beginning of my working life.' He explained to Luff that he no longer felt right with people who blacked up, and that he would henceforth do anything else rather than appear with the *Minstrels*. He was delighted when, rather than be forced into confrontation with his mentor, Luff said: 'Yes, you're right.'

'After about five or six years, I realised I was going down a road that wasn't the right sort of comedy for me. I realised I wanted to be on the right side of the line. There were a string of comedians doing racist and sexist humour and still doing it today very successfully, and good luck to them, but I didn't want to be a part of that. I knew there had to be a better way of trying to put your messages over, putting your jokes over without having to pick on people because of their colour or because of their race or gender,' Lenny said many years later.

Chris Tarrant's half-improvised children's TV show *Tiswas* is often acknowledged as the first stage in the turning of Lenny Henry from the all-purpose, utilitarian British showman he was in the late 1970s into what he is now. There was, however, a slightly odd interregnum between Lenny the Minstrel and Lenny the born again, radical black performer. This was his period, once again at Luff's suggestion, supporting Cannon and Ball during their first summer season on Blackpool pier(where Roger de Courcy and Nookie Bear were also in attendance), and later during two seasons in Great Yarmouth, while at the same time breaking new ground in *Tiswas*.

In the case of Cannon and Ball, Lenny's enthusiasm for the new and slightly unsuitable, as ever, all but ran away with him. 'Cannon and Ball are hilariously funny people,' he told a visiting reporter from the Dudley *Herald*. 'At first, they yelled at me and shouted abuse, and I thought they were being serious. Then they just folded with laughter and looked at me in amazement. They are very friendly, really.' Yet at the same time, a new, more discerning viewpoint can be detected in Henry in some of his comments on Cannon and Ball. 'The audience had come to see comedy as opposed to music, and for the first time I found an audience willing to laugh at me – and I got good reviews for what must have been the first time in my life. It was fantastic. What Bobby Ball did was really dangerous, confronting the audience, pointing at them. I was very influenced by him and Tommy ... Basically, what you had was these two guys arguing on stage, going through pathos, body comedy, different voices, repetition, everything. The tenor of their material was reactionary, but its execution masterful. There's no getting away from the fact that Bobby Ball is a genius.' (Henry, in his stage shows, still uses the device of pointing at members of the audience and embarrassing them.)

It was with Cannon and Ball in Great Yarmouth that Henry, his sense of black identity growing, took his first real, political risk. 'When I started, people liked me because I was Len, had been on *New Faces* and said hello to my mum. I spent five years in the *Black And White Minstrel Show*,' he said later in his career. 'It was a job and I didn't really question it at the time, but I got loads of stick and racist remarks. In the end I couldn't deal with it, so I changed tack.'

Lenny's great gamble was to use the Brixton riots as a source of comedy material. Under pressure from *Tiswas* to come up with more and newer impersonations, Lenny had hit on the idea of inventing non-existent people, caricatures, as a vehicle for not just his imitative talent, but his inventiveness and observation too. It was a step not dissimilar to a journalist, fed up with seeking out facts, taking up fiction writing, where they can be made up.

With the riots spreading around Britain in the summer of 1981, the first Lenny Henry character, Algernon Winston Spencer Churchill Gladstone Disraeli Palmerston Pitt The Younger Pitt The Elder Razzmatazz (a Rastafarian, whose catchphrase was a vast, croaked, 'Oooookaaaay') emerged at Yarmouth, prior to a national airing on *Tiswas*. The demystifying, viewer-friendly Algernon was an instant hit on TV. It was a daring and commendable idea (although not unlike Eddie Murphy's Buckwheat on *Saturday Night Live* in the US) to introduce such a gentle and likeable character to children's ITV at a time when racist feelings were running high in both directions between whites and blacks.

Although Henry, true to form, denied at first that Algernon had a political agenda ('Algernon is just a funny lad who wears a big woolly hat. That's all there is to him. I had enough of all that racial bit at school'), he did concede that there might be something more tendentious about his creation – that it might even do something to alleviate the inflamed situation. 'I suppose white kids see ole Razzmatazz on *Tiswas* and suddenly they are not so frightened. Next time they see a Rasta, they think, "Ah, that's OK. That's only Algernon." ... I've only had four letters of complaint, and two were from Rastamen. I got a potted history of how black people had been put upon during the last 400 years. "Haven't we blacks suffered enough without you ridiculing us?" one guy said. I wrote back that one of the best qualities in a person is a sense of humour. If you can't laugh at yourself, then you're not able to laugh at all. I told him to watch the character of Algernon carefully. He's not actually ridiculing black people, he's doing something positive for them.'

Lenny did, nevertheless, eventually come round to seeing that

Algernon might be construed as a racist stereotype and dropped him after Dawn French convinced him that Algernon was too similar to white people's negative idea of a Jamaican. 'I wanted to do something big and bold and cartoon-like. In the end it was too much of a caricature. I was only eighteen when I did it,' Lenny confessed to the Chicago *Tribune*.

Algernon certainly did strike a chord with white children, so much so that Lenny's character was used that November in a firework safety campaign. 'During one performance at Great Yarmouth, a kid suddenly stood up in the audience and bawled "Oooookaaaay" at me. It was an incredible sound.' Teachers and parents reportedly wrote letters to Lenny saying that their children were damaging their vocal chords trying to get the authentic Caribbean twang into the catchphrase. Lenny claimed to hold the world record for making an Oooookaaaay last for two minutes in the bar at ATV. Algernon also began to turn black youngsters, who had only the vaguest idea of Lenny Henry's existence, over to his side. Black people began at last to become fans.

Before Lenny came to *Tiswas*, Chris Tarrant had come to see him compering a stage show. Lenny had tripped on the stage steps, fallen flat on his face and split his trousers. It was just the thing for the anarchic Saturday morning show; 'Marvellous stuff' said Tarrant. Lenny was a fan of Tarrant, too. 'Whenever I meet him, he makes me laugh so much ... not many people can make me curl up. Tarrant is one.'

Lenny was extremely unsure of the idea of becoming pigeon-holed as a children's entertainer, but, with a national showcase for the unexpectedly successful Algernon, endless Saturday morning buckets of water emptied over his head and countless condensed milk sandwiches consumed, *Tiswas* (and its sister programme for grown-ups, *OTT*) turned out to be the great turning point in Lenny's career.

'It's what Saturday mornings were made for!' was one of the show's promotional slogans. 'The children's programme which breaks every rule in the book' was another. Madcap was the description most critics assigned *Tiswas* – the word anarchic had yet to be imported from politics into the light entertainment field. Buckets of water were thrown if the gags weren't any good, and the air was thick with custard pies, which would now be intellectually analysed by journalists as stylistically retro or possibly ironic custard pies. Show-business stars lined up to take part in The Cage, and Compost Corner and be ambushed by the 'Phantom Flan Flinger'. All guests would be assaulted by flying food-stuffs, as would the children in the studio. By reverting in this way, to be dry about it, to traditional circus tactics, *Tiswas* broke the ground for the 1990s irony boom, of which Channel 4's *The Big Breakfast* was the prime example. It was Britain's irreverent answer to *Sesame Street*, and ITV's sophisticated answer to the earnestness of BBC children's programming, especially *Blue Peter*. Six years before the phrase 'pol-itically correct' had been uttered, *Tiswas* was soaring ahead into the reaction against it; where else in 1981 could Bernard Manning and Frank Carson have appeared on a show with Lenny Henry? Or Michael Palin broadcast a spoof appeal for the rights of plankton endangered by whales?

Any weaknesses in the show's structure or content were bulldozed by the strength of personality of people like Tarrant, the sheer energy of Lenny and the freshness and audacity of what it was doing – soaking guests and being impertinent. More than anything, *Tiswas*'s brilliance was in its masterful way of appealing on two levels to a dual audience of parents and children. For example, Tarrant did a sketch about a campaign to reduce the alphabet to twenty-five letters, and managed the entire routine avoiding the letter P; viewers were asked to write in to the Ost Office in Lymouth and so on, which was entertaining to an adult because it was very clever, whilst a child could simply enjoy the sound of the gobbledygook. Even Algernon had a kind of dual standard; parents could savour the political daringness, while children could be amused by the ridiculousness of the length of the name.

'You couldn't help but like Lenny,' Tarrant said. 'When we used him on *Tiswas*, kids immediately warmed to him, they just thought he was wonderful, this big, cuddly Lenny figure.'

What cuddly Lenny might not have realised when he first joined *Tiswas* is that it would bridge the gap between his being a working-class icon, another bow-tied seaside entertainer and inhabitant of telly-media-Jaffa Cake land, to someone taken seriously (for what it was worth, and to Lenny by this time, it was worth a lot) by the *Guardian*-reading classes.

There is a special mixture of gimmickry, brains and talent that will occasionally turn middle-class heads; it happened increasingly in the Eighties, as educated people and serious journalists began to reassess and re-evaluate some of the ITV and popular entertainment favourites. Intelligent interviews would appear with people like Bob Monkhouse or Max Bygraves, and such performers would rise to the occasion, turning out to have depth – and far more interesting lives to talk about than the usual run of arts pages interviewees, the authors, earnest actors and opera singers. Lenny Henry, whom middle-class parents would not have watched on *New Faces* or *The Fosters*, but could not avoid seeing as their children watched *Tiswas*, virtually started this 'low culture for highbrows' process.

Yet on the programme, there were, behind the uproarious scenes, serious problems for Lenny. He was nearly twenty-three, a wealthy young man who had moved up in the world, but even now, it was a variation on old stand-by from Buffery Park, Dudley – impersonating a TV favourite – that was to save his career. 'I was very, very tough on him,' Tarrant says. 'Although socially I was a mate, when we're talking about a television show upon which my career and everyone else's depended, I was actually very hard on him. We very nearly dumped him off after about six weeks, which would have been very sad. But he really wasn't very together. He had all the ideas in the world, tremendous enthusiasm – which he still has ten years later – but he hadn't disciplined it at all.

'It was at that time – I don't know if he'd heard any mutterings – but he said: "I've been working on this bloke David Bellamy." Now to me at that time the idea of this big, gangling black kid doing David Bellamy was so ludicrous, with the stuck-on ginger beard and silly shorts and his big, long black legs, but he had the voice and the idea was so bizarre . . . and that took off instantly and massively and I think in some way that it kept him very much on at *Tiswas*. On the strength of that, he did about three hundred live shows. He did television for ever on the strength of that. But that was very much a turning point for him, I think, and his confidence grew from that.'

With the help of a new technological development, the home video recorder, Lenny was able to fine tune his impersonations more precisely than when he was twelve. With the VCR handy, he could morph himself all the more effectively into the Trinidad-born ITN newsreader Trevor MacDonald, reading the news in black preacher style with a gospel choir behind him, or into 'Dr David of Compost Corner' – Henry's version of Bellamy, whose beard kept falling off – as a *Tiswas* character, as did Worzel Gummidge. The real 'Trevor MacDoughnut' even joined Lenny on a live show, which quite genuinely thrilled him. ('I had no idea he was coming in. Suddenly there he was in the studio, it was brilliant, and he said he enjoys my impersonations of him,' burbled Lenny.)

Increasingly conscious of his image, Lenny knew *Tiswas* was making him a great deal more fashionable, but was deeply wary of making another career error. 'For years I tried to get on by rolling eyes and making weird noises and doing frantic impressions,' he said in 1987. 'It couldn't last. When the novelty of a young black impersonating whites like Tommy Cooper wore off, I went through a very lean time.' He went to America for the first time in 1981 and his eyes opened a little more. 'For the first time, I realised there was much more I could do that was much more real; I could use my blackness in a much more positive way.'

Where *Tiswas* was really an open road, and one well worth following, it appeared at times to him like a cul-de-sac. The London publicist Mark Borkowski was at the time working for the Wyvern Theatre in Swindon, which had booked Lenny for the night. 'It was completely sold out,' Borkowski recalls. 'Here was a theatre which did things like the Swindon Amateur Light Operatic Society and the Thamesdown Singers, and along comes a name that really hadn't quite made it yet, and the public went completely bananas. We had to get a photocall together for the local paper, and I had to try to persuade Lenny to do the picture. He was asking exactly what he was supposed to do, and he said, "Look I don't want to be a bloody kids' entertainer. That's not what I want to be seen as. You're not going to put this in the kids'

press, are you? Because I'm desperate to get out of that." Then a load
of schoolkids turned up wanting autographs. He didn't mind meeting
them but he was absolutely determined not to be photographed with
them on the basis that, yes, *Tiswas* was a cult and he was a huge part of
it, but he had a very keen sense that he had a career in front of him and
he didn't want it to be always doing that. He was quite paranoid about
the media even then.'

Lenny was ranging widely in his search for new direction. One of
his less celebrated initiatives was a brief stab at reviving a career he had
dabbled with at seventeen – as a recording artist. In 1975, during the
fuss over *New Faces* and under the guidance of a songwriter and producer
called Jack Fishman, Lenny had recorded an inexplicable though ven-
erable song called 'Boiled Beef and Carrots'. Even by 1975 popular
entertainment standards, this was a venture to make his later joining
the *Black and White Minstrels* seem like becoming a member of the
Metropolitan Opera in comparison. In the song, Lenny's voice wavered
from pure (if slightly querulous) Dudley to cockney to American; thus
were cockney 'potatoes' rhymed with 'tomaytoes'. The refrain was:
'When you're hungry/It rings the bell/Keeps you fit and it keeps you
well/Don't live like vegetarians on food they give to parrots/From
morn to night/Keep living right/On boiled beef and carrots.'

Pye, which released 'Boiled Beef and Carrots', had been guided to
some extent by Lenny's ideas on suitable songs for a young lad to sing.
Those who had thought that Lenny's schooldays renditions of Max
Bygraves' 'You Need Hands' had just a tinge of cynical teenage irony
about them had a surprise coming. 'I won't sing love songs, I'm too
young,' he said at the time his first record came out. 'It would look
ridiculous. Imagine me singing "I'll Do It My Way". I can't sing about
broken hearts and sad songs about autumn love and "We haven't got
much time." ' He liked, he insisted, to sing songs like 'You Need
Hands', or 'How Much is That Doggy In The Window?' – and
especially 'Boiled Beef and Carrots'.

'Properly handled, Lenny will become a great recording, television,
film and stage star,' Mr Fishman said, not totally without perception.
Undeterred and apparently unembarrassed by 'Boiled Beef', Lenny

rode the back of the Algernon craze by recording in 1981 a single of his 'OK Song'. With a Caribbean beat, and a vastly more assured-sounding Lenny, it was possibly a thousand times better than 'Boiled Beef', but still flopped. 'Most promising hits come in at 100 with a bullet beside them,' he said as the 'OK Song', or correctly 'The (Algernon Wants You To Say) OK Song' slid from nowhere to pop oblivion. 'Mine came in at 99 with an air gun pellet next to it. Lord-eh, did Stevie Wonder ever suffer such cruelty?' The flip side of the single, for old time's sake, was a version of 'Mole In The Hole', with Lenny as David Bellamy introducing Lenny as Algernon doing a Jamaican 'I am a mole and I live in a hole'.

Far more the ticket was *OTT* (the acronym for Over The Top, a World War One phrase that became fashionable among early yuppies), the Saturday evening show which took to its logical conclusion the nearly accepted fact that *Tiswas* was really an adult show disguised as a children's programme. *OTT*'s provisional title was *Big Tis*. Made by Central, the successors to Lenny's nursery, ATV, *OTT* was first shown on 2 January 1982, starring and produced by Tarrant whose mission statement was, 'How outrageous can you be without getting arrested? How far can you go without being dragged off the air? With *OTT*,' he expanded, 'all we really want to do is to send people to bed early on a Sunday morning with a smile on their faces and perhaps a few mucky little thoughts in their heads.'

'Some of the stuff that went on *OTT* was very, very good,' Tarrant said after the show ran its course. 'It was live, it was late night, but some of it was awful. It was not that well-written, it was certainly not that well-presented. But the one shining jewel in it was Lenny Henry. Lenny took off in that series far more than years of rattling about in custard and beans on *Tiswas*. I think *OTT*, in amongst a lot of quite weak material around him, actually set him up for life.'

Lenny had seen *OTT* when it was first conceived in the autumn of 1981 as a chance to expand: 'People associated me exclusively with my *Tiswas* characters,' he said. 'I've got to come up with some new ones in a hurry. I'm too young and lovely to get stuck in a rut with Algernon, Trevor MacDoughnut, Doctor David and that lot ... I now realise I've got to develop if I'm going to survive. Like Sellers, Dick Emery and Benny Hill, I've got to move on from doing impressions. This will lead on to acting. I'd love to be a movie star.'

Unfettered by the constraints of children's television, Lenny's *OTT* characters started springing up even more prolifically. The menagerie of his creations was becoming crowded, and it was sometimes hard to be sure whether he was dangerously reinforcing stereotypes or popularising warm caricatures – an issue which has yet to go away for Henry. *OTT* saw the birth of a mouthy African TV host, Josh Yarlog, who, by shouting it out at unpredictable intervals, invested the word Katanga (a rich mining province of the former Belgian Congo, which tried to secede in a bloody 1960 civil war) with something that millions found funny. ('When I started using it in *OTT* people wrote in saying, "Did you know Katanga was the scene of a massacre in Zaire?" Others wrote saying, "Did you know Katanga is Swahili for sheik and can also mean a vegetable or fruit?" I mean, you can't win, can you?' Lenny said in an interview at the time. Some cynics would say you could easily win, by not constantly yelling Katanga.) Yarlog was originally called Robert Mugabe Nkomo Amin Zimbabwe Yarwood and would typically appear in a suit with leopard skin trim to do parodies of gameshows ('The Price Is Correct') and Ken Dodd impressions in a Robert Mugabe accent.

Yarlog did not amuse some black people. Lenny was once accosted in the street by an African who disapproved of the character's witch-doctor drag as racial stereotyping; Lenny patiently told his critic that he had leant over backwards to avoid 'going into a "jungle-bunny" thing'. Later, he reportedly seemed disturbed by the incident. 'He's supposed to be a hip African character, very Zimbabwe, very jet-set comedian,' he said. 'People will take offence at anything, but I just feel that I'm black and will do black things.' (Ben Elton has defended Henry stoutly against those who accuse him of creating black stereotypes. 'It would be a terrible thing to exclude a group from the cultural experience by being too terrified of insulting them: that would be contra-racism,' Elton says.)

Delbert Wilkins was also new for *OTT*. While the front line of racial conflict in London was, in 1981, Railton Road, Brixton, Delbert lived a safe distance away, in Ladbroke Grove. Delbert was a street-wise pirate disc jockey with vastly exaggerated views on police harassment, Mrs Thatcher, apartheid, clothes and clubs. 'He's a young black cockney revolutionary, a very flash dresser,' Lenny explained. 'He's from the Clothes Line of racial ferment, rather than the Front Line. He's an incessant rabbiter. His motto is "Bring Cardboard Windows Back to the High Street." ' Like Algernon Razzmatazz, Lenny hoped Delbert would be a diffuser of racial tensions.

(Delbert Wilkins first saw the light on *OTT* as a Brixton milkman who dealt on the side in shares, televisions, dodgy airline tickets, wicked suits and the like. 'I was working with this guy called Kelvin,' Lenny explained, 'and I had this one car journey with Kelvin and he said, "You know" and "You know what I mean" about 4000 times all the way.)

Theophilus P. Wildebeeste, a sexy, black and slightly overweight soul singer in the tradition of Marvin Gaye and Barry White, was another new character. In an open shirt, medallion and leather waistcoat, Theophilus would say things like, 'Hello Ladies. I've got a mirror on my kitchen ceiling – that's how cool I am. I am a love machine.' How and why he had a cod Afrikaans name was not entirely clear.

Then there was Deakus, the most close-to-reality of these characters, and the one that black people find the funniest of all Lenny's characters. Deakus was an old Jamaican man with a slow, deliberate way of talking and a love of all things British, however cruel Britain had been to him. ('When I first come to Henglan', everybody used to keep lookin' at me, starin' at me, starin' at me. I used to get annoyed. Hey what's the matter with you? You never seen a black man before? They said no. You can't argue with that.') Deakus, who Lenny still uses, was recognised by Americans when Lenny first started performing in the US as the spitting image of Richard Pryor's Mudbone character.

Deakus wears a hat, checked shirt and cardigan and came over to England on a boat in the early 1950s. He gives his thoughts on life amidst much lip sucking and musing. One of his early routines concerned how he tried to get a job in England when he first arrived. He had heard of 'the old school tie network', and only worked out after three years of wearing his Jamaican school tie and getting nowhere that he might have got the idea a little wrong. 'Deakus's function,' as Lenny once explained, 'is to let you know about the changes the West Indian has seen in England since he arrived. He shows you life through the eyes of an old Jamaican guy who remembers how the Fifties landlords ripped him off. He'd come home from work to find another man in his bed, and realise his bed was doing shift work too – they were letting it out, day and night, without changing the sheets ... There are wonderful old boys like Deakus sitting in every corner of every pub in this country – all waiting to tell you to slow down, man, and listen while they tell you these terrific stories.'

One character Lenny dreamt up during this prolific, though awkward and shifting time (yet did not finally do on TV until his 1994 BBC show) was a drag creation: 'She'll be a glamorous jet-setter with sequined gowns and all that. A real wow, man!' Lenny promised the *Sunday People* in 1982. Deeva (it stands for Daring, Explosive, Electric, Voluptuous and Animal) appeared finally as a black Lily Savage-inspired character wearing Vivienne Westwood-style clothes and singing a song 'for all big girls'.

(Critical response to Deeva did not quite justify the fourteen-year gestation period; 'I'm very, very jammy,' Lenny has admitted. 'A certain amount of people are locked into my sense of humour.' One of them on this occasion was not the London *Evening Standard*'s TV critic, Matthew Norman, who wrote, 'We moved seamfully to Mr Henry's new character Deeva, a dominatrix in red PVC who sang of humiliating members of the Cabinet [as though that's something they can't do on their own]. The delusion here was that kinky sex is so innately hilarious, it negates the need for a decent script.')

It was during the 1981 to 1982 period that a little difficulty arose – inevitably, but disturbingly – between Lenny and his mother, back in Dudley. As he started to edge his way back to black culture, she was busy finding God. Winifred had been a widow for five years, and Sharon, her youngest was now nearly fourteen and needing her less. Always a keen and observant Pentecostalist, she now became a mission-ary worker for the Church of God of Prophecy, pointing out to friends that going to church and being saved were quite different issues. Winifred's decision to up the religious ante meant an end to her one small vice, bingo; it also meant that she could no longer attend Lenny's shows. He received the news with a mixture of amusement and disappointment; he had been expecting such a conversion for some time. With great kindness, he told her that he understood her decision. She astutely pointed out to Henry that he now had Dawn to back him so he didn't need her any more. 'Lenny has now accepted my feelings. He's very nice, very humble and every time he phones me now he asks how Church is. He knows that it's my life,' Winnie said some years later, in an extraordinary interview she gave to the *News of the World* (or perhaps had had teased out of her).

'Since I found God I've only been to see Lenny twice while he's been performing,' she confirmed. 'Each time I only sat in his dressing room and watched him on a video monitor. I didn't think it was a place for a child of God to be. If I go to places like that and enjoy it, I just don't feel right. I'm pleased to read about Lenny's progress in newspapers, and I know what he's doing. But it doesn't come as a crown of glory to me. The show-business world is not of Christ's world. TV can be very good. It can spread the gospel but I don't mix with what is going on out there. When the Variety Club of Great Britain named Lenny as Personality of the Year earlier this month, I was asked if I wanted to say anything about it. I declined because it is not my line any more.

'If people don't know I'm Lenny's mother, I wouldn't really want to tell them,' Winnie continued. 'I don't feel I should put him in front of the Lord. I'm glad for him, but I won't boast about it. I never thought of him getting so far, but I believe in him. It's what he wanted.'

She went on to give intimate details of her state of health, and how she had been the lucky recipient of a miracle from The Lord after her foot gave up the ghost when she was carrying a banner at a religious rally in Birmingham. Two years later, the problem recurred and Winifred spent nearly seven months in hospital, and asked the doctors at one stage to cut the leg off below the knee because it hurt so much. She also suffers from diabetes and, in 1989, had a heart attack. Whenever she went into hospital, she revealed, Lenny would send her huge baskets of flowers. 'Other patients keep asking me who they are from and I worry they'll find out they are from Lenny. Lenny normally comes to see me when visiting hours are over. Otherwise everyone wants to come and talk to my famous son!'

His mother's religious developments aside, Lenny's own rebirth, in the form of a comic renaissance, was continuing apace. In London, he encountered for the first time the burgeoning non-sexist non-racist alternative scene based on The Comic Strip, a comedy club that set up camp in Raymonds' Revue Bar, and later became the Comedy Store in Meard Street, Soho.

The records of Richard Pryor had opened Lenny's eyes originally to the possibility of comedy that did not rely for its laughs on pandering to the proclivities of drunken, prejudiced white audiences in seaside towns. Now, ironically perhaps, it was white British comics, specifically Alexei Sayle, a Jewish Liverpudlian, who made Lenny realise that he himself was in a perfect position to do the same kind of material as Sayle.

CHAPTER 7

DAWN OF THE NEW ERA

'I will look back on 1982 as the year I really grew up.'

Lenny Henry, January 1983

The received wisdom that Dawn French introduced Lenny to alternative comedy is not recognised by all those on the scene at the time. Stan Hey, one of his script collaborators, doesn't put Henry's change in direction entirely down to Dawn. 'Lenny heard the new comedy and worked things out for himself. He was part of the climate of awareness. He'd started his career within a conventional showbiz framework – but by the time he did *Tiswas* and *OTT*, he was already an anarchic comic in his own right. He was perfectly capable of doing his own changing.'

'I decided to change,' an adamant Lenny said in 1985. 'I wanted to go out to a different audience, wider and with more black people, and do more adult material. It coincided with going to see the Comedy Store and the Comic Strip and listening to Richard Pryor and all that ... So now the act I do is very me, it's the sort of stuff that I laugh at.' He realised from devouring Pryor and Bill Cosby on video (and Steve Martin too) 'that you need to write your own material, get away from just telling gags, but develop your own personality and let the humour grow.'

Another point never quite appreciated is that Lenny only once worked at the Comedy Store in Meard Street, Soho, and never at the

Comic Strip. It was not quite the case that the showbizzy, working-class graduate of ATV's gag factory and punishing years of traditional summer season variety suddenly mutated into an upmarket product. He did not instantly drop punch lines and jokes in favour of the new comedy, with its reliance on recognition, 'you-know-what-it's-like' humour and Sayle-style vituperation. Lenny had, after all, signed up for a second season with Cannon and Ball when he began to mix with his new crowd. Just as finding common cause with the grammar school boys in Dudley had taken time and happened unconsciously, becoming socially accepted by the intellectuals of the Comic Strip did not happen automatically. Lenny Henry first knew alternative comedy as a member of the audience, the only one at times who was neither drunk nor a liberal arts graduate.

'Lenny was really very impressed,' recalls Chris Tarrant, of his talented protégé's new enthusiasm for 'alternative' comedy. Tarrant had taken the cast of *OTT* to the club as part of a search for new writers in April 1981. 'He saw the likes of Rik Mayall and Alexei Sayle, who had a tremendous cult following. But I think it's been a very positive influence. You actually can still see in his work certain areas of sexist humour, racist humour – they were very standard parts of club patter that he'd learnt as a kid – suddenly he started to question them and they quietly went away.'

It was a new television series, *Three of a Kind* – his first for the BBC – that sent Lenny to the Comic Strip again. Paul Jackson, a young BBC producer then, who would later become a major comedy innovator and conduit for young talent, had been given the job of coming up with a fast, pacey prime-time sketch show based on the tenets of the new comedy. His brief was to find new faces, while using experienced script writers with a BBC track record. In keeping with the new breeze in comedy, producerly autocracy was to take a bow to democracy – the performers would have a choice in the material they did. The consumer therefore had an implicit guarantee that the people on screen found their gags funny. To acclimatise writers and performers to what was new, he sent them to the Comic Strip to watch the likes of Sayle, Rik Mayall and Nigel Planer.

There needed to be something daring about the choice of per-formers, a sense of novelty within novelty. The first gimmick was that the comedy was modern; the second was that the people performing it, instead of being university types, would be more along the lines of old style entertainers. The original title of the show was to have been *Six of a Kind*, but finding that many presenters of the right calibre was too taxing; three would do. The first two of the new on-screen faces would be Lenny, a children's TV star currently supporting Cannon and Ball, and David Copperfield, a northern night-club singer. The third, Tracey Ullman, an unknown actress with virtually no TV experience, had yet to be chosen. Jackson sent Henry and Copperfield to see Ullman in a play at the Royal Court. 'We just fell about laughing,' said Copperfield.

The pair, both something of a curiosity to Ullman, met her afterwards in the bar. 'She was being very much the actress,' says Lenny, 'talking all posh – "Oh hello, boys! How are you?" – and there we were saying, "Come on, luv, 'ave a pint! Get it down yer neck!"' Ullman was deemed highly suitable to complete the three, who, as the title suggests in a lateral way, were not of a kind at all. 'It must be the only show on television where you've got a woman, a black guy and a northerner and it really doesn't matter,' Lenny said before the show's second series in 1982. 'We play everything and anything. For instance, in one show we're doing a send-up of *Brideshead* – 'Brideshead Regurgitated'. I'm playing Charles Ryder and Tracey's not only playing Julia and Cordelia, but Anthony Blanche as well.'

'Right at the beginning Paul Jackson called a meeting of writers and there were about seventy of them sitting in this room,' Ullman remembers. 'We all had to get up and say something, which I hated because I'm very shy when I'm being me. So I got up nervously and said, "I'm not a blonde, I don't have a big bust, and I don't want any sexist jokes. Thank you very much!" and sat down again. We haven't had any, either. If there is a line in a sketch which is even a bit sexist, I don't even have to speak – the boys will say "Oh no. We're not doing that!" and out it goes!'

The democratic ground rules worked out surprisingly well for something so idealistic. 'There's a key to it all which in the end you learn is hard work, collaborating with writers, bouncing ideas around, coming up with original thought as opposed to jokes,' says Lenny. 'It was a slow process, it was a growing process, and it was the *Three of a Kind* experience where we were doing eighty characters a week and leaving impressions behind.'

One of the notable new features of *Three of a Kind* was its extensive use of computer graphics and references well ahead of its time. A typical show, the first of the second series in November 1982, included some Monty Python-type material, although a little more accessible than Python, which was on its last legs by then. Much of the writing for *Three of a Kind* was by Grant and Naylor (who later took comedy into space in *Red Dwarf*). In his first full sketch, Lenny played a formerly submissive person who decides at a cocktail party to become aggressive. Later, he was a bus conductor ('Anybody want this stop? OK,' he says and gives it to the passenger). In a pub sketch, he asks if anybody would mind if he played the piano; he then gets a handful of darts and offers the instrument a game.

Sketches would be interspersed with computer-style 'Gagfax' coming up on the screen: Britain's prisons crumbling to bits – says the governor of Wood Worm Scrubs. In a musical number, all three stars dressed as The Supremes ('The Ruinettes') did a cod version of 'Then He Kissed Me', based on a disco fight. Lenny, who a year earlier had said he 'couldn't be bothered with colour', was now working the racial theme into his work. In a ten second sketch, he is a black man stopped by the police; 'What's the charge?' 'None. I do this for nothing.'

Lenny was given yet more scope in the new show to develop his characters. In the first series he introduced Fred Dread, Minister for Reggae, a Deep South black preacher, Nathaniel Westminster (Nat West) and a black community policeman, P.C. Ganja, with dreadlocks, a Rasta hat on top of his helmet, a Walkman in place of a radio and a dog called Selassie. In the second series, he dropped Algernon and Josh Yarlog. He prided himself on having rounded his characters so that they had their own life inside his head. 'I could even tell you what Fred Dread would eat if he came into a restaurant.'

Three of a Kind was greeted by critics as an enormous success from its first edition in the summer of 1981. The *Daily Mail* called it 'a rampaging roller-coaster of a show, utilising a quick-fire, hit and run style of comedy not seen on TV since Rowan and Martin's *Laugh-In.*' The stars 'flit on and off the screen in a bewildering welter of two-line gags and mini-sketches. There is no time to get bored. By the time you realise a joke has not worked you are laughing at the next.'

Although *Three of a Kind* gave Tracey Ullman her first national exposure, it was Lenny who gained most from the show. He saw it as his rehabilitation from the world of darkie jokes; after all, even on *Tiswas*, there could sometimes be racial undercurrents, however innocently they were meant. Bernard Manning, who was on record as saying Lenny should put up with racist digs in the same way he had to put up with people being rude about his fatness, once came on as a guest. And on another occasion, a *Tiswas* technician, filming Lenny continually being soaked with water was heard on air to comment, 'You're right. It doesn't wash off.'

'This was the first time that he was able to do grown-up comedy and work on characters that he believed in and ideas that were long trousers time rather than pies in the face,' Kim Fuller, his principal writer explained on *The South Bank Show.* 'It was a stage on from that, and he was keen to develop an of awareness of what he is – black, British, living in the Eighties.'

Fuller, then thirty, was a lecturer in the English department of Lewes Technical College in Sussex, and was in a theatre group which performed in the Brighton area, doing anything from shows for foreign students to children's parties. He had started out in comedy by sending on spec sketches to Radio 4's *Week Ending* show, but had nothing used. He then began sending material to *Not The Nine O'Clock News*, which finally used one of his scripts in 1980; he then bombarded them with about ninety items, ten of which made it on to the programme. Paul Jackson wrote to him when *Three of a Kind* was being planned, and invited him to a meeting. Naturally chuffed, Fuller was disconcerted to discover it was actually a *mass* meeting, attended by seventy other writers – the conference at which Ullman (whom he particularly clicked with, and today writes for in America) made her manifesto speech.

Henry said of *Three of a Kind*, 'I think both Dave and I set out with the attitude, "Great! Let's get it done!" But then I saw how much work Tracey put in on her characters, and it really worried me, so I went away and started trying to do the same! Now I think it's great. After that first series I found I really wanted to do things better, and work harder.' (Lenny so admired Ullman, that he successfully suggested her to French and Saunders for *Girls On Top*, the TV comedy about four women flat-sharing, which also starred Ruby Wax, whom French and Saunders had met at a party.)

'In the end we managed to have a prime-time show that was non-sexist, non-racist going out with the *Two Ronnies* on Saturday night, which I'm very proud of,' Lenny was later to say of *Three of a Kind*. He then sat down with Kim Fuller and Paul Jackson and put together a completely new act, again expunged of all racist and sexist jokes. 'This was the prototype of what my act is now. I went to this club up in Northampton and I did this show and it was great. It was stuffed with *Three of a Kind* characters, my own characters, still doing a couple of impressions. I found I was getting laughs but with material that didn't have any kind of offensive tinge to it. I was so chuffed.'

The ultimate beauty of this liberation for Lenny was that the glittery side of his profession, which he did not feel under any compulsion to drop along with the dodgier material, did not cease. Aged twenty-three, he was a regular on an extraordinarily naff TV game show called *Celebrity Squares*, and had performed at the Royal Variety Show, where he was introduced, his nails bitten to the quick for the occasion, to The Queen. Winifred was by Lenny's side at the London Palladium for this event, her 1950s notion that she would be bound to bump into Her Majesty in her new country fulfilled for all practical purposes. 'The Queen was very nice when I met her,' Lenny said. 'She told me she thought my act was very funny and had laughed a lot. She wished me the best of luck.' On Christmas Eve, before rushing home to Dudley for turkey with the family, Lenny even appeared as a guest on *Blankety Blank*.

None of this was the kind of thing that was bound greatly to impress Dawn French, the twenty-four-year-old Plymouth-born daughter of an RAF officer and a poodle parlour proprietress. French, who within three years of Lenny's first wandering into the Comic Strip would marry him, did not even like him very much the first time they met. At five feet tall, she was a foot shorter than some of the leggy but vacuous dancers Lenny was used to dating, and nearly a head and a half shorter than Lenny himself.

On the surface, there was not much to attract one to the other. Dawn was privately educated at a weekly boarding school in Plymouth, where her grandparents lived; because her father was in the forces, the family moved round a lot and the RAF paid two-thirds of her fees. She trained in teaching at the Central School of Speech and Drama, where she met Jennifer Saunders, then taught drama at a north London comprehensive. Dawn shared a flat with Saunders, and the two started performing at Comic Strip in 1980, when the club began.

There were in fact several points of contact for Lenny and Dawn. Both their fathers had died when they were nineteen; Dawn's mother, Roma French, had dropped out of the poodle business to become a counsellor in a Plymouth drug and alcohol rehabilitation unit, and addiction, be it to drugs, tobacco or alcohol, was a subject Lenny was deeply interested in. Despite the death of their fathers, both Dawn and Lenny had enjoyed very happy childhoods. Dawn was also quite a plump woman, as Lenny's mother was. Dawn's mother had been a big woman too, but had lost a lot of weight when Dawn's father died. 'I made a choice at a very young age to either be big and worried and nervous or to say, "Look, this is how I am," and be confident about it,' Dawn was later to say. 'We are actually quite a big family – Devonshire dumplings – we are short and wide.'

Not surprisingly, both Dawn and Lenny had been funny as youngsters, but another similarity between them was that neither had quite fitted in to the teenage dating game in their respective home towns. While Lenny went frantically through prototype comedy routines only to watch the girls he hoped to make an impression on go off with other people, Dawn was suffering her own adolescent misery. 'It was slightly sad,' she says, 'when I used to be the funny girl at the weekends in the cars with the lads but never the girl they wanted to take home. Everyone would have a good laugh but you weren't the one getting snogged at the end of the evening.'

Like Lenny again, Dawn gave the outward impression of great confidence. 'Obviously I haven't got confidence at all times, but I couldn't believe that other people weren't as confident as me,' she confessed to Mavis Nicholson on one TV programme. 'I've always been surprised by that. I thought it was something that everybody had. And then I realised that it's something not very many people have ... I can only put it down to that healthy childhood ... always being encouraged.' Lastly, although it was probably not necessary, Dawn had had some happy contact with young black people (who are not numerous in Devon) while teaching in London, while Lenny had been out with dozens of white girls – as he used to say cleverly in his act – 'I used to out with white girls. I didn't mind.'

The first meeting between the two was not a success, all the same. Lenny liked French and Saunders as well as Alexei Sayle, and met them all. 'I asked Dawn if she would write for me. I said, "Hello, my name's Lenny Henry. I'm from *OTT*. We're doing a new series and we'd like to have you to write some material because I think it's important to have women writers on the show and there aren't any." But she was really cool and off-hand and said, "No." She didn't have the time. She said, "Well, you know, it takes a long time to come up with our material – at least six months a sketch – and I just don't think it's possible." That was it. And apparently she went into her dressing room with Jennifer, and said, "God, he's a famous person," and screamed. I don't think she liked me at first. She said, "Oooh, you're the one who used to eat those dreadful condensed milk sandwiches on *Tiswas*. Yuukkk!" I really did want her to write for me, it wasn't just a chat-up line. I saw her as an artist before I started meeting her socially.'

Dawn's version of the encounter is similar. 'I remember him waiting in the bar, and I remember thinking, "God, there's a famous person, a famous person," and trying to stay very cool about the whole thing,' she has said. 'I thought he was loud and revolting. He was starring in the telly show *Tiswas* and specialised in eating condensed milk sand-wiches and wearing a four-foot high Rasta hat ... He was quite successful and I thought he was a real showbizzy person. You know, on an ego trip and doing the celebrity bit.' One side of Henry that Dawn, as a former teacher, was less than keen on was his snobbish belief at the time that the only interesting people in the world were in show business. She has said she had to wean him away from this view early in the relationship.

They met again a few months later in the foyer at a recording of an Alexei Sayle show at a BBC studio in Shepherd's Bush. 'We ended up sitting next to each other and talked throughout the recording,' he says. 'Afterwards she suggested we went for a drink and we carried on talking. Then we went to a disco and carried on talking. It was the most I'd ever talked to one person in one night. It was clear there was something going on ... I talked about things with Dawn that I'd never talked about with any other person, male or female. It was just so easy being with her.'

'We met again at a jazz club with some other friends,' continues Dawn. 'Suddenly everyone started snogging and we were left like a couple of gooseberries, and we just began to click. I found out he's absolutely not a showbiz person at all. I just realised how funny and gentle and shy he was. He rang me later. And that was it.'

It was the first time Lenny had been serious about someone; 'I felt it was worth giving up whatever it is that goes with bachelorhood,' he said. 'I was very big-headed when I met Dawn, very loud-mouthed, a bit cocky. I was just full of myself. I was doing *Tiswas* and I was a bit, "Hey Saturday morning live, that's me." When I met Dawn it was time to be doing something different, both personally and professionally. When I started going out with Dawn my life went off into another direction.'

Going out with someone if you are young and a popular public personality is difficult enough, but doubly so when the someone is famous too, as Dawn was rapidly becoming. What was later to become regarded by some as a paranoia about personal publicity started for Lenny around this time. Well into the relationship with Dawn, about which no newspaper seemed to have any idea, Lenny talked about girls in an interview with the *News of the World*.

'Girls certainly seem more interested in me now,' he said. 'But I'm suspicious of them. You can tell the ones who just want to be seen with you. That's the way they get their kicks. They always hope there's going to be a photographer around and that they'll end up getting the glamour. But they miss out – all the photographers are somewhere else taking pictures of Pamela Stephenson . . . It's boring if all they want is to hear you shouting "Katanga" or "It's weeird", but I'm always approachable. I prefer them to come over and say hello, and not sit in the corner of a bar staring at me for half an hour . . . I was hopeless with girls when I was a kid, really useless. They didn't take any notice of me. But now I'm much more confident with them.'

By the autumn of 1982, the press had wind of Henry's romance with somebody, but the *Sun* only knew his girlfriend was called 'Frenchie'. Henry told them: 'The last time I revealed something about a girlfriend we split up two weeks later. Now I have a new lady in my life I'm not taking any chances. He went on to say that the divorce rate in showbiz circles put him off marriage. 'I think once you're married you should be faithful or there's no point.' Two months later, nobody even among the tabloid show-business reporters had worked out who Frenchie might be. As part of a private joke with Dawn, in December 1982, Lenny told a persistently probing *Sunday People* reporter: 'She's a dancer from Blackpool. But I like to keep my personal life quiet.'

In doing so, Lenny and Dawn unwittingly turned the revelation of their affair into a sort of public Dance of the Seven Veils. The interest generated, which was rather modest at the start, grew in proportion to the discretion they invested in it, to the point where some Fleet Street gossip veered towards the faulty but inevitable conclusion that Lenny did not have a girlfriend at all, nor would want one, and some publicist had thought up the wheeze of inventing a non-existent relationship.

Even when minced through the tabloid processor, Lenny's words hardly suggested any deceit. Asked by the *Sunday Mirror* about 'his mystery blonde', he reportedly said, 'We met last April and it has been great ever since. She's white and a very funny lady – and those are all the clues you are going to get to her identity.' Lenny then added, to muddy the waters a little, 'I'm much too young [to marry] and my career takes up so much of my time it would be hard to make a marriage work. The way things are right now suits me.' It was October 1983 before the *Daily Mail* was able to reveal that 'Frenchie' had been Dawn French all the time.

Privately, the relationship was going tremendously well, although there was a huge amount of adjustment required for Dawn to understand the downmarket show-business world Lenny just about still inhabited. To her, seeing his cabaret audiences was almost like descending into a live, grotesque Hogarth engraving. She later said she had been 'utterly shocked,' both by his continuing darkie jokes and the Neanderthal audiences who lapped them up.

Soon after Lenny and Dawn met, she went to see him at an RAF club in Wiltshire, where he did his customary run of self-deprecatory gags. He thought the show had gone particularly well, but she could not stomach much of his material. 'She said, "What are you *doing?*" I was very defensive at first. I thought: I've been doing this for years, I'm a professional, I'm a veteran. But when I realised that she was right I had to take a step back and think what I wanted to do.'

'The audiences were raw meat-eating people who drank bones for blood,' Dawn said, of gigs even after they were married. 'They would be shouting out, "Where's the sambo?", and Lenny would go on and gradually bring them round. It was like the Christians and the lions. No one from the alternative circuit could have survived until the end of the month, and that includes me.'

Although he denied that Dawn went through his material with a blue pencil, he acknowledges that it was she who convinced him of what he already knew – that the racial jokes were no longer necessary. Even with the many new influences he had come under, he still had a hankering for being what people said he could be if he wanted – the new Max Bygraves, the most popular entertainer of the time. Dropping material that made him a fat living was not easy for him; 'The problem with being a comedian,' as he put it, 'is that if something gets a laugh you will cut your leg off before you will kick it out of the act. So I had to be very brave and lose a lot of material which actually got huge whoofers – as they are known in the trade . . . My ambition was to have an act that lasted half an hour, made people laugh and allowed me to get off stage without being bottled. Dawn made me realise it would be great to make people laugh without having to sell out.'

Instead of contrived gags, or stealing jokes from other people, he started actively seeking out material that was about himself. 'That's the real stuff, because people immediately recognise it,' he enthused. 'They go, "Yeah, that's happened to me," and only you can do it, only you have your voice. In the beginning I think black audiences didn't come out and see me because they thought they were going to get offended. Now there's a lot of people saying they respect me, which is nice.'

Henry's politicisation took some time, all the same. He was horrified when, at an awards ceremony, a radio reporter asked him to comment on the Toxteth riots: 'I've had people coming on to me and being very heavy, saying "You should be doing this and that for your brothers." But no way, I'm a comedian not a politician,' he said in response. 'I mean, what does it matter what I think? We're entertainers, not politicians,' he said sharply on another occasion. 'When a white football hooligan carves up another white on a bus, do they blame Jimmy Tarbuck for doing nothing about it?'

In late 1982, Lenny bought his mother her new house in Kingswinford, where she lived with Paul and Sharon, who was now fourteen. The move to the bungalow coincided with her finding God and officially ending her active interest in Lenny's career, and Lenny deciding to settle down with Dawn. The process of getting to know each other's families was in train. Dawn rang Roma before she took Henry home for the first time saying: 'You remember the big black boogie man you said would come and get me if I didn't get to sleep? Well, he's come, he's got me, and I'm bringing him home this weekend.'

'She was very sweet,' Dawn told Mavis Nicholson. 'She rang and said, "Just checking. Does he eat chicken?" She hadn't met any black people ever.' Dawn explained that Winnie always put the best china out when Lenny took girls home. 'His mother tested me by piling a lot of Jamaican food high on my plate, and if I could get through that food I was in the family, and the funny thing was my mother did the same thing to him of making massive great pasties . . . she tested him to see if he could eat them. She's a very open person and she loved Lenny straight away.'

Having passed his pastie exam with honours, in June, Lenny tried something else new, a Radio 1 show called *The Lenny Henry Sunday Hoot!* that was described in the *Radio Times* billing as 'two hours of music and the freewheeling, frenetic style of comedy that has become his trademark'. Delbert Wilkins was in evidence, plus still more new characters, Big Winston, Freaky Deaky and Gronk Zillman, space-age detective, whose adventures give you 'excitement, danger, suspense and a funny wobbly feeling in the black holes of your socks'. There was also a 'totally laid back' LA record producer called Con Dominium, and Dr Rydim, a Rasta DJ.

For all but the press, the pair had become an established item, spending a large slice of the summer of 1982 together in the US, checking out American comedians. 'When I first went there, New York scared the life out of me,' Lenny said. 'When we walked down 42nd Street, people kept offering us drugs. We stayed the first night in a very dodgy hotel. There were women running from room to room wearing only towels. And the guy at the reception desk was protected by a metal grill and a sheet of glass eighteen inches thick. You had to speak through a microphone to talk to him – and there was blood on the grill. I only stayed there one night, and then I phoned a friend in Staten Island and begged for help.'

He came back from the trip with forty-five minutes of new material derived from listening to people and jotting things down, and with a new resolution to keep up the habit of cataloguing thoughts about his past and current life to assist him in his mission of exploiting it for ideas.

There followed several months of testing the new, more highbrow waters Henry was paddling in. He bought a flat in Central London. 'Yes, I'm going to play Wendy Houses,' he confirmed to the *Sun*, as the precious crates of records and vintage comics were being transported down from Kingswinford. He added: 'And the most important room will be my little work room where I do my writing.' Lenny's old friends and teachers might well have done a double take on reading this – the last time his writing had been discussed, after all, was when his infant teacher marvelled at how neat and rounded it was. But one of the many spin-offs of Henry's finding Dawn was to give him the confidence to write, even if penning his own material would also provide him with a great deal of frustration over the years; the subject of his book, *The Quest for the Big Woof* was, after all, his struggle to come up with original, funny writing without the benefit of a team of writers.

In January 1983, Lenny set off on a tour of nineteen universities and polytechnics, starting in Manchester. His first big expedition into student land (he had done a couple of earlier gigs at universities), it was his way of saying he had changed, by appearing at non-flashy, £2.50-a-ticket gigs. 'Students aren't easy to please and are good judges of an act. I'll do two half-hour comedy spots, play records and sing,' he said, modestly describing his voice as 'a cross between Stevie Wonder and Lassie'.

When the tour ended, he started work on what would be the last series of *Three of a Kind*: 'Basically we didn't want to become The Three Ronnies,' he said bluntly. 'I don't want to go on just doing impressions,' he told a doubtless disappointed interviewer from the *Daily Star*. 'David Bellamy, Trevor MacDonald and all those other characters are all right to fall back on, but I want to do better than that. Look what happened to Mike Yarwood. He's ended up doing Benny from *Crossroads*. Now what's he gone and done *that* for? Dick Emery, poor feller, had the right idea. He worked very, very hard at his characters. He would introduce them very gradually and build them up. But Dick then put his characters into fresh situations week after week, making them thoroughly believable ... Tony Hancock was another perfectionist. He created a character so real you knew exactly what he would say in a given situation before he said it.'

The extent to which the broadness of Lenny's constituency had developed was increasingly in evidence. Black, but somehow white too, working-class but middle-class too, populist but simultaneously elitist, he had taken on a role as a kind of British mascot, a position in the culture not unlike that of Frank Bruno or Daley Thompson, in some respects. In March, Henry promoted a special set of Post Office stamps celebrating the Commonwealth. 'Personally I come from British West Dudley, in the protectorate of Birmingham,' he commented. 'But my folks come from Jamaica so I am very pleased to see special stamps celebrating this huge international family.'

Lenny's full-blooded celebrity status was recognised at home in Dudley all the more now he had formally moved to London. He was going to the Midlands at least twice a month, and the local press in his home town dutifully recorded every turning point in his life, be it his purchase of a video recorder to help with impressions or signing up for another summer season at Blackpool. He loved any chance to perform in Dudley or, more often, in Birmingham: 'Doing a live, one-man show in your home town has got to be the best thing ever,' he has said. 'It's the ultimate show-off's paradise, with everyone looking at you. You want to do a lap of honour afterwards.' In the summer of 1983, he caused great local merriment when he mistakenly opened the wrong hospital fête in Dudley. He arrived at Burton Road Hospital, did the honours to the amazement of the crowd, who thought it was tremendously cool of the organisers to have secured the services of such a star and kept quiet about it, and then had to be told that it was the Corbett Hospital in Stourbridge where he should have been. He then went off and repeated the whole ceremony.

It was September 1983 before Lenny and Dawn became officially engaged in Plymouth. The announcement came less than two weeks after the *Sun* published an interview with him in which they still had no inkling who 'Frenchie' was, and in which Henry said he didn't rate marriage very highly because of the high divorce rate in show business.

Looking back at the interview now, the clues (apart from any as to the identity of 'the girlfriend') were there that a famously single young man of twenty-five very shortly would no longer be a bachelor. 'I am a much more serious person than I was when I started in the business,' Lenny said. 'Then I used to go night-clubbing all the time, trying to impress the girls. I still pop my head round the door of Stringfellow's or Gulliver's occasionally. But I'm more likely to go to the theatre now, or the pictures, or just stay in and watch the telly. I still like parties, but parties full of people I know, not parties where you go to pull. Discos are really full of airheads. There'll be a line of people sitting at the bar and if you did a brain scan of the lot of them it would just be one straight line, no activity at all. They're really pathetic. I'm much happier in the company of my close chums. I like people who are honest with me. My mum does it and my girlfriend does it and my friends do it. They say, "Be cool, calm down, stay the way you are." I've had fun and I've learnt a lot along the way. But I've wasted an awful lot of time.'

'He hummed and haa-ed a lot before he proposed,' Dawn told a world intrigued by this rather unexpected coupling – black to white, working-class to middle-class, tall to small. 'Then one day he gave me this ring all wrapped up inside three shopping bags. Lenny thought the way to show somebody you really loved them was to buy them the biggest diamond he could possibly find. But he couldn't decide what it was for. So I had to say "I don't know which finger to wear it on," then he pointed and that appeared to be the general direction we were going in.'

Although neither was inclined to go public on the intimate details of their relationship, the odd revealing glimpse slipped out in their delight at having found one another. 'Before Lenny, I know a lot of people misunderstood me,' Dawn confided in the *Daily Mail*. 'I think once you've been established as the kind of joker in your gang, it's very hard to lose that. Guys were a bit frightened of me because they couldn't see further than that shell. I didn't want anything too gooey. I just wanted proper people who didn't take me for my image. Lenny and I laugh a lot together. But I was glad that he was someone who could tell me when I'd had enough of a good laugh.'

'We have talked about the problems of having children in a mixed marriage at some length,' Dawn told another interviewer, 'and we have decided we can deal with it. We don't worry about the difference in colour. Our families don't, it doesn't come into our relationship at all and I don't see why the public should care.'

'I have somebody I care for and who cares for me. There is no

▶ Young love: Dawn and Lenny soon after they first met.

◀ Dawn and Lenny's wedding day, 20 October 1984.

▲ Out on the town
with husband Lenny,
co-star Jennifer
Saunders and her
husband Adrian
Edmondson.

◀ 'Now look here,
I'm the funny one!'

▶ Dawn and Jennifer with actress friend Miranda Richardson.

▼ Dawn French and her friend Ruby Wax, whom she has worked with many times over the years since their sitcom *Girls on Top*.

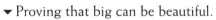
▲ ▶ Promoting her clothing
company, 1647.

▼ Proving that big can be beautiful.

▲ Dawn French *au naturel...*

▲ ...And dolled up to the nines for a *French and Saunders* sketch.

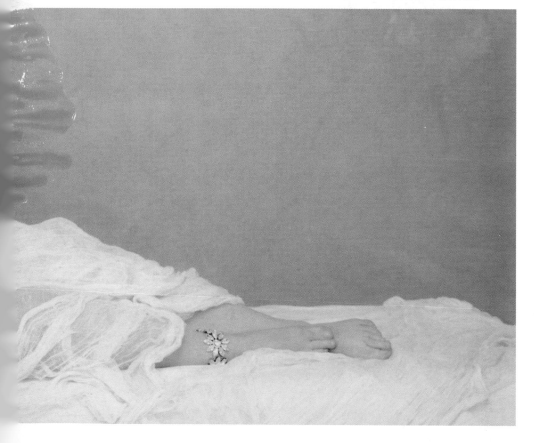

▲ Making a point.

substitute for having a woman you can go to and talk over problems, get advice, laugh and cry with,' Lenny said. 'That's what counts.'

The Lenny Henry of the autumn of 1984 was a mellow man, more mature than he needed to be at twenty-five, but clearly settling comfortably into his changing lifestyle. He drove a sober two-year-old Renault 20, and, when he wasn't at his London flat, stayed in modest rented accommodation in Blackpool, where he topped the bill for the first time (with David Copperfield) in the summer and autumn of 1984. In the middle of that season, he gave an interview to Peter Dacre of the *Daily Express*, in which his scepticism about the flashiness of show business – and even a trace of despondency – were evident.

Part of his melancholy throughout that summer was the result of missing Dawn desperately. In his old life, long stints at the seaside were livened up by flings with leggy dancers, but he obviously had no taste for that any more. He spent a great deal of time on the phone to Dawn from Lancashire. Some of this was arranging the details of their wedding, which they planned for the autumn, but, if the bond was not already deep enough, it was cemented by this separation. A romantic joke grew up between Lenny and Dawn during these phone calls; he would ring and when she answered the phone, sing Stevie Wonder's 'I Just Called To Say I Love You'. Soppy as both realised the routine was, it became their favourite song; when Stevie Wonder sang it live years later at the Mandela Day concert, which Lenny compered, it was a particularly poignant moment for the now very married couple.

'I don't know what being a star is. It seems a redundant word to me,' Lenny told Dacre. 'I'm not very flash. I live a fairly quiet existence. The only time I like to be flash is when I'm performing ... People who see me in the street sometimes say "Doesn't he look miserable?" But what's your face like when you walk down the street? That false face, that hypocritical show-business grin is not for me. I can't do it and I won't. I smile when something's funny. I don't go around saying: "Hey, look, I'm funny. Here's a joke." When I started in show business I tended to be always on stage. A lot of comics want to be on stage all the time. But I think it shows a basic insecurity if you're trying to be funny all the time.'

One of the other ways Lenny whiled away the twenty-week summer season of 1984 was, a little unpredictably, by taking two O-Levels, in English language and literature, at a college of further education a few miles away in Preston. His motivation for doing such an apparently self-flagelatory thing (instead of just reading a few books) was simple and unashamed; he felt inferior to most of the people he was close to in his profession – even his fiancée. The feeling had been developing for several years; Don Maclean, who had taught Lenny so much back in the Midlands, for instance, had been a teacher, as had Chris Tarrant, Alexei Sayle – and Dawn.

One day, between the matinée and the evening performance at the North Pier, Lenny started phoning around colleges in the area, explaining in the vaguest possible terms that he was an actor and was looking for private tuition in English. The teacher he clicked with was David Emery, a tutor at the W.R. Tuson college in Preston – which Lenny was not to know was considered rather the inferior of the two Preston colleges at the time, although this turned out not to matter.

Emery said he would have no problem putting Lenny through O-Levels in twelve weeks. It was obviously too late for that summer, but the November exams were a reasonable target; Lenny was a prolific reader already, and for the whole summer he would come in from the theatre, write an essay and hand it in the next morning. In literature, he studied *Cry the Beloved Country*, *Henry IV Part Two*, Tennyson, Yeats and Burns – his favourite. When Henry sat the exams at the Preston college, he'd had to be separated in a different room from the other examinees in case he distracted them.

Lenny was in America when the results came out, and Emery phoned him there to say that he had got two grade-B passes. Dawn immediately coined the joke that he was now to be known as BB Henry, the new English literate blues singer. 'A lot of people I know have got degrees and are supremely intellectual,' Lenny reflected a couple of years later. 'Like my wife Dawn French. They talk about the morality of art and things like that, and I'd be going: "Whaaat?" I can go toe to toe with anybody, but I got my O-Level just to prove I could. I didn't actually feel any different, after I passed them, so I haven't done any more. But at least I proved the point to myself. It wasn't that I was stupid at school. But I wasn't taught to educate myself. I learnt that later. Now if there's anything I want to know I've learnt how to look it up. As you get older, you see more of life, and you learn more and you observe more. And your material changes.'

CHAPTER 8

LOVE IN BLACK AND WHITE

'People have this idea that she's a Nazi in knickers telling me what to do all the time, but she's very sensitive, loving and caring and would never ever presume to say I had to change things.'

Lenny Henry on Dawn French

Lenny and Dawn married at St Paul's Church, Covent Garden on 20 October 1984, the day after his comedy album 'Stand Up, Get Down', came out. Lenny was twenty-six, and came to the ceremony fresh from the North Pier, Blackpool, where he had been performing the previous evening. Dawn was twenty-seven. Some 350 friends and relatives came to the wedding. Winnie looked magnificent in a raw silk dress, all Lenny's old Dudley friends came down, plus the likes of Rik Mayall, Nigel Planer, Chris Tarrant, Robbie Coltrane and Tracey Ullman, who made herself inconspicuous in a brown bowler hat and dog-tooth check suit. Henry had already postponed the wedding once because someone leaked the time and place to press; the delay made little difference, and a scrum of reporters and photographers got under the feet of Saturday afternoon Covent Garden shoppers anyway.

Martyn Thomas – Tommy, who dropped out of officer training in the Navy and later went back in as a rating – was Lenny's best man, while Dawn's brother Garry gave her away. Tommy was on hand to tell the reporters how he and Lenny 'grew up together in Buffery Park', leaving a group of them in a huddle conferring over the spelling of

Buffery. Greg Stokes, who had been due back from a lengthy trip to the Middle East the day of the wedding, came home a week early, and managed to be in London on the big day. As Lenny and Dawn got to the 'I do' part of the marriage ceremony, a pigeon with a sense of humour got tired of flapping about in the rafters, swooped down over the sixty-strong gospel choir and settled down beside Lenny. There was one of those minuscule wedding sensations when the vicar read out Lenny's full name, Lenworth George Henry, which none of his show-business friends had ever heard. Henry's press agent Robert Holmes explained, 'I used to call him Lenworth for a gag, but I don't think anyone else knew it. Holmes imaginatively described the feathered interloper at the ceremony as a dove, and acted as the reporters' eyes and ears inside the church. 'You couldn't hear Lenny at all,' he revealed. 'It was the first time he's ever been lost for words. But he seemed to say all the right things.'

After the ceremony, as the shutters clicked like firecrackers, Lenny looked sheepish and slightly bashful, smiling awkwardly and saying little. He seemed emotional; asked if he was nervous he mumbled, 'Yes, I suppose I am, but it wasn't too bad.' Dawn looked extremely pretty and slimmer than the public normally saw her, the result of a two-month crash diet; she had told the lady making her wedding dress that she was a size 14, only to discover she was at this stage a size 20. Ullman said it had been a beautiful, happy wedding, and 200 of the guests went off to a champagne reception at the River Restaurant of the nearby Savoy Hotel.

Although, under Dawn's influence, both Henry and French liked to regard themselves as trailblazers for the modern show-business affectation of refusing to say anything about their private lives except to the compliant reporters of fan magazines like *Hello!* (or on stage to paying customers), they actually indulged in something of an orgy of self-revelation for the vulgarians of the tabloids. 'My marriage is a very, very wonderful thing. She makes me laugh a lot, intentionally. She's a very funny woman, on and off stage. She's good at listening too, and tells me off when I make corny jokes,' Lenny informed the *Daily Express*. 'It's wonderful, and the greatest thing in my life,' he burbled in another tabloid, 'but I'm such a chatterer I might say too much, and that's not fair on our private lives. I'll just say Dawn's terrific and funny, and I agree with her strong feminist views – feminism is a way of looking at life, not rushing round the kitchen reading bits out of *Spare Rib.*'

Lenny's new-found feminism made it OK, it seemed, for him to reveal intimate information about Dawn in his stage act. 'The stairs have disappeared. She's chopped them up with her bare hands,' he said ruefully in reference to Dawn's apparently severe PMT. Feminism also made him a devout anti-fatist. Just three years before his marriage, Lenny said that his dream Sunday would be spent basking on an Antiguan beach with a beautiful girl at his side. Asked whom he had in mind, he said, 'Oh, Miss America, Miss Jamaica, Miss England, Miss Japan. I'm not choosy. After all, this is the age of opportunity. All the girls should have the chance of the treat.'

The summer before the marriage, however, he refused to judge the Miss Blackpool beauty contest (in the illustrious company of Les Dawson, Ruth Madoc, Su Pollard and Paul Shane) because such contests were pointless and 'they're degrading to women'.

'I'm not that fussed about beauty contests. My fiancée is a feminist and once you talk to somebody like her about it you see it's all a bit pointless,' he said. 'I don't do sexist jokes because I don't find things like women's bottoms very funny,' he added, a little stuffily for some. 'Women's bosoms are just not very funny,' he said elsewhere.

This youthful sobriety, which the alternative comics made fashionable for the whole of the 1980s, seemed to have mellowed by 1994. In that year, Dawn French, joint owner of 1647, a London clothes shop for big women, stripped off as part of a Big is Beautiful campaign. 'I'm her greatest fan when she's got no clothes on,' Lenny enthused. 'For me, it's natural to be surrounded by big women. Most of my female relatives are over a size 16. Like most people, I'm tired of catwalk stick insects. I can't understand what any man sees in skinny women. In fact, Dawn is the most beautiful girl in the world.' Lenny's feelings on thinness in women are to be respected, but one wonders if there were not slim ex-dancers all over the country reading his well-publicised comments at this time, and wondering if it was their minds, after all, that the young Lenny had been attracted by on those torrid evenings years before in the likes of Yarmouth and Bridlington.

At the time they married, in the blue heat of the Margaret Thatcher yuppie years, both Lenny and Dawn were keen to mix business with pleasure at every opportunity. Children of their time, Lenny a remorseless workaholic and Dawn every bit as motivated, they happily enthused about the delights of work taking precedence over normal life, and especially the advantage of marrying someone in the same profession. This attitude, too, was to mellow in time.

'I think marriage could only work for me with someone in the same job,' Lenny said in 1986. 'I would hate to have all these things going on in my head and not have someone at home to talk to about them. Imagine going home every night and you just turn on the telly and go to bed. Horrible.

'People have a funny idea of comedians being married to one another,' he went on, explaining that such a marriage was no laughing matter. 'They seem to think we wake up in the morning with Tommy Cooper hats on and tell each other jokes and behave like comedians all day long. It's not like that. Jennifer is her partner. I'm just her personal partner. But I ask her to work with me occasionally because I think she's good. Believe me, if I didn't think so, I wouldn't work with her. She's very funny and she makes me laugh a lot. But mostly we work separately. She does her writing in the office she shares with Jennifer and I do most of mine on the road, and then we show each other cassettes of our shows and pick holes and criticise or advise.' Dawn, whom Lenny said proudly was very strong-minded, challenged his intelligence and didn't suffer fools, would come to his shows and make notes for discussion afterwards.

'Our careers take up so much of our time, it's hard to make a marriage work. But we are very happy. I had to be very sure it would last because I have never had any intention of joining the divorce statistics,' he said a year later.

Sexual jealousy did not seem to be a problem within Lenny and Dawn's social circle. At one time, in *The Comic Strip Presents* (a kind of alternative best-of variety show) Lenny played, 'the funniest comedian in the world', with Dawn as his long-suffering wife, and Jennifer Saunders as a slutty student who had a nude scene with Henry. 'Talk about jumping in at the deep end,' Lenny commented on this pioneering venture for him. 'Not only was there a lot of snogging, we also had to perform wild, abandoned sex. I was so nervous I didn't know what to do with myself. Jennifer ended up having to take charge. She got really carried away and kept banging my head against the headboard. We had to rehearse it over and over again and I ended up with a whopping big bruise on my head.

'It was awful having her writhe about on top of me,' he continued, a trifle ungallantly. 'I found it so embarrassing because I'm a friend of her husband, Adrian Edmondson. Even though it's only acting you feel guilty, like you're having an affair or something ... Dawn thought it was hilarious that I felt so uncomfortable. She never stopped telling me how she didn't care. "Oh well, we're all friends. It doesn't matter, it's just what you have to do for the job," she kept saying. I'd seen Dawn kiss lots of people on TV. In fact, every time I showed up on the set of the Comic Strip she was snogging either Adrian or Nigel Planer. I didn't mind seeing Dawn snogging – she treated it like a laugh. I don't know why, but I think it's different for guys. It's like carrying on with someone who's not your missus.' (Dawn, incidentally, later evened the score by snogging Saunders herself in *Me and Mamie O'Rourke*.)

By the end of the Eighties, there was a subtle change in Lenny's attitude to the supremacy of work within the marriage. The couple had developed a system under which, if one was in the spotlight, the other would take a back seat and provide support from the wings. 'We manage to be supportive of each other,' he said, 'And we try to be home together every night. We cook or watch the telly. We don't have to be out on the town.'

'We enjoy each other's success,' Lenny said at around the same time, 'even when I know her series got nine million viewers and mine got only four million. But most of all we try to leave our business at the door and get on with our lives.'

Because Dawn was big and had an image (largely based on her acting roles, but with some back-up from Lenny) of being bossy, the idea took root that she was orchestrating Lenny's career and censoring his act. This was not just a public perception, but one prevalent within the industry. 'Dawn is essentially Lenny's biggest script editor,' says Andy Harries, controller of entertainment and comedy at Granada Television, and one of the major influences on Lenny's career. As a young current affairs director who was gradually moving into the arts, Harries had the idea of making a *South Bank Show* film on Lenny, and went on to conceive and produce Lenny's groundbreaking 1987 on-the-road film, *Live and Unleashed*. Harries got to know Lenny well, Dawn less so.

'When we were on tour making *Live and Unleashed*, it happened at least twice that we didn't go to the show for a couple of nights, and found that Dawn was going on those nights. It made more sense for her to go then, but often the show was quite different after she'd been. Material that we were quite keen on would have disappeared, scenes that we were developing were out. He really listened to her. She would go back stage and give Lenny all the notes she had made, and say, "Cut this, cut that." They work as a comedy team.'

Lenny was as proud as ever to admit that Dawn remained his biggest influence, but continued to insist that she was not censoring his comedy, denying that she is 'a Nazi in knickers', or even, 'a dictator in a dress'. Why he felt the need to think of alliterations to hammer this point home, is interesting. The explanation may have something to do with the couple's sensitivity towards tabloid simplification of issues; while there is no evidence of any journalist being as rude in print to Dawn as to call her a Nazi in knickers, it is probably fair to say that Lenny is more popular with the mass-market newspapers than his wife.

The two have never denied that there were and are tensions in the marriage, as there were in the long relationship before it. Both Lenny and Dawn admit to monster egos, and joke about these crashing into one another 'like asteroids'. Once, Lenny said in an interview, 'Dawn and I have been through a great deal together and we know what the cycles are. In most marriages it is the predictability that kills it off. As Richard Pryor says, "Every day the same bloody person." We try and make it different. If it is predictable, we make fun of it.' Another time, he said, 'Dawn and I have had a bumpy ride, like any relationship, but we went in with our eyes open.'

The dynamic of the marriage, in the sense that every couple has its underlying theme, is that it was generally Lenny whose behaviour was up for restructuring, rather than Dawn's. This agenda for change did not cover just his stage act, from which he promised that all sexism, racism and even unnecessary swearing would be excised, but his social being too. And as men so frequently are, he was quite open about how he was prepared to be radically reformed. 'I used to bulldoze through situations,' he has said. 'I was very much the loudest person in the room and had this thing about being the life and soul of wherever I was, but Dawn's helped me realise that being the loudest person doesn't mean you are saying anything.'

She tore away at his tendency towards a snobbish disregard for anyone not in show business, demonstrating that even normal people could be quite interesting. She increased his regard for privacy and middle-class reserve. When the couple eventually adopted a daughter, Dawn had strong views on protecting her from prying interest. Lenny, on the other hand, has always been a little vague about any changes he wrought on Dawn in the marriage. 'She's tough and doesn't shirk away from situations, but I think I have made her tougher,' he said once. He made no other claim.

The race difference between the two has never been even remotely an issue; the class difference has. Close friends have a telling anecdote that illustrates this minor but wearing clash. A friend of Lenny and Dawn, the pop musician Thomas Dolby, once offered them the use of his cottage in East Anglia for a fortnight. Instead of handing over the key, Dolby stayed on to welcome his guests and show them the rather sparse facilities. If one thing characterises the English middle-class, it is the delight they take in a simple way of life. People like Lenny Henry, on the other hand, who were brought up in simple conditions, have no shame in enjoying relatively more luxurious surroundings once they can afford them. Dolby has related to friends how, simultaneously, as they walked in, Dawn looked utterly enchanted by the cottage, while

Lenny's face fell. It was obvious, says Dolby, that he would have been much happier in a five-star hotel, but was far too polite to say so.

Lenny and Dawn's racially-mixed marriage, and their obvious success in it, may have been a source of delight to each other and to intelligent people, but it greatly upset the dimmer and nastier end of the market. Lenny could joke about the racial divide ('It's never been a problem. I've been out with all sorts'), but within a short time of their marriage, they were victims of a National Front hate letter campaign.

They made the decision to go public on what was happening out of public spiritedness. They were keen to show they were not immune to intimidation simply because they were famous and relatively rich, and aware that they could raise public consciousness of such outrages. When the same things happened to people who were not well known, they recognised, it would not even merit a mention in a local newspaper.

Dawn said of one of the racist letters, 'I was terribly upset for about a minute. Then I was angry. I just ripped it up and threw it in the bin. It was horrible hate mail. Lenny was angry too, but he's had to cope with racist nastiness all his life and deals with it a lot better than I ever could. I think it's a shame that he has to go through that. But as long as we have bigots in this country then it'll happen ... Some people have a go when they see us in the street,' Dawn went on, 'but usually it's under their breath, nothing I can actually confront them about. Others do it openly thinking it's funny – look at all the racist comedians there are. People make jokes about his blackness more than anything else when they meet him. I find that so juvenile and ignorant.'

Henry told a live audience at the Alexandra Theatre in Birmingham about the racism he and Dawn had encountered after they moved to a tall Victorian house in tree-lined Agate Road, Hammersmith, in west London. 'I know what these people are like,' he said. 'I came home with Dawn one night and noticed that the letters NF had been smeared in excrement above the door.' Henry also described a poison-pen letter he had received, in which even the word 'coon' was misspelt (the mind boggles at the idea of a National Front member so lacking in the basics of his trade). The letter accused him of 'inter-breeding'. He laughed as he told the story, and the audience, too, chuckled, if a little uncomfortably. It was indeed, quite funny to imagine, as he did, how precisely the morons had come by the shit, and how they had gone about smearing it. But there was no hiding Lenny's fury at the outrage.

The five-bedroom end-of-terrace house, which Lenny and Dawn bought for £150,000, was a splendid place for a couple so young, with its garden, roof terrace, thirty-foot L-shaped sitting room, marble bathroom, thirty-two-foot kitchen-dining room with stripped wood floor and exposed brick fireplace, but came to be a magnet for criminals. Burglars in search of Lenny's computer, video and hi-fi equipment caused the couple to install a number of alarms and security systems, but that was less of a problem than the weirdos. 'We had a strange thing put through our door which was like a tile you hang on your kitchen wall, with a picture of St George on the front,' Dawn related. 'On the back it said: "You have been visited by the Ku Klux Klan." I couldn't believe something like that would still happen. Those people are cowards ... complete cowards. I suppose we are a fairly public mixed-race couple, so if anybody's got a hang-up about that, we get it. I got a letter at the theatre yesterday from somebody who writes to me regularly as a "Nigger Lover".' She had also received newspaper clippings of herself and Henry covered in racist scrawls. 'It's disgraceful, but what can you do?' she asked. 'These are tiny-minded people who have nothing better to do than be vitriolic.'

It was often said to be racism that eventually forced Lenny and Dawn to move from their London home out to the country, but they stuck the problems out for several years. 'I won't say anything because I don't want to encourage them,' Lenny said after the move, but went on, 'I wrote a sketch about it which I did on stage to help get it out of my system, but contrary to what some people think, it didn't make us move to Berkshire. That would have been very weak. We still get the odd letter, but generally people leave us alone now.'

Despite the slightly incongruous fact that at the time of the wedding, Lenny was still performing on the North Pier, his act was, by late 1984, almost completely restructured. The month before the wedding, the first edition of a landmark BBC 1 venture, *The Lenny Henry Show*, started at 7.30 p.m. on a Tuesday; he was unable to watch it go out, of course, as he was on stage at the time, but video-ed it for himself and, he said, his mother, who was now happy to watch his safer early evening TV material. *The Lenny Henry Show* fulfilled the first of two promises Henry had made to himself when he first won on *New Faces* – that he would have his own show. The following week, the second promise he made came true, when he sent Winifred on holiday to Jamaica, the first time she had been back, or even flown. 'She's going on to America from Jamaica,' he said proudly. 'I'm really thrilled to be able to give her the trip she's been talking about since I was a child.'

The new TV show featured established Henry characters like Theophilus P. Wildebeeste and PC Ganga and Deakus, plus Billy Bradford, a Brixton wideboy (Delbert Wilkins being based north of the river, in Ladbroke Grove) and a new member of the cast aimed cleverly at the young audience, Derek the Teacher. Derek was a merciless lampoon of the eternal student teacher. 'We always had one a term,' Lenny explained. 'He always walked in, dressed very casually, and said, "Hello, call me Derek", or Dick or Sidney or something. Of course, we ripped him to shreds, poor soul.'

Including a school sketch based on personal experience rather than a generalised stereotype exemplified the enormous change that had overtaken Lenny's comedy. Gone was the happy-go-lucky nodding to racism; the very personal comedy of the new age was now marching all over his work. The first five minutes of *The Lenny Henry Show* included observations of being in a relationship and dealing with periods. 'It was quite truthful and there was pain in there and it was good,' he expounded in the *Guardian* late in the 1980s. 'I experimented a lot with those two series, and I don't apologise for it. I felt that I needed to exorcise all of that other stuff.' Whether Henry's motivation for the show, which was, after all, in an early evening light entertainment slot, was quite as militant as this in 1984 is doubtful; it certainly has an air of wise-after-the-event about it, but it may simply have been that he did not quite dare to describe in quite such dour terms at the time.

He had not turned his back on impersonations, but they were somehow now even better and more pointed. The show included brilliant parodies of Tina Turner, Stevie Wonder and Michael Jackson, which appeared on the first show in a pastiche of Jackson's contemporary fifteen-minute video, *Thriller*, which was the hottest thing around, having sold 35 million copies. 'It was just such a big idea, the public's imagination had been captured, and it was just ripe to have the mickey taken out of it,' Lenny said. He did not seem to have an enormous amount of respect for Jackson, despite the two having been born on the same day; in 1987, he would impersonate Jackson's song 'Bad' with slightly adapted words, 'I'm sad, I'm sad ...' Jackson's apparent rejection of his own blackness did not appeal to the new Lenny Henry.

With the construction of his new, more *Guardian*-esque persona almost (but as ever, not quite) complete, Henry occasionally adopted an ever-so-slightly jarring intellectual snobbery, the minor failing of many converts. He was, for example, unhappy about the music for the first series of *The Lenny Henry Show*. 'When I wanted to do Fred Dread, the reggae politician, I tried to explain that it should sound like Linton Kwesi Johnson,' he complained in the *Guardian*. 'The bloke in there had a Keep Music Live sticker on his forehead – he'd probably just come back from arranging on the *Black and White Minstrel Show*. He didn't know what I was on about.' (Linton Kwesi Johnson was a late 1970s reggae poet half-remembered from Rock Against Racism fundraising events where, in a trilby, goatee beard and glasses, he would recite such works as 'Di Anfinished Revalueshan'.)

Lenny's earnestness control also went on the blink from time to time. 'I'll never use dancing girls on my show. They don't add anything to the programme,' he said sniffily to the *Daily Express*. 'It's old-fashioned and boring to go in for that kind of thing. Nobody would have dared to say to me, "Let's have Lenny's Angels." They'd soon find themselves flying out of the window.' Although it is perfectly reasonable for a young man to grow up and his attitudes to change, these comments still seem a bit rich, bearing in mind Lenny had only a few years earlier been living on a staple diet of dancing girls. Swearing on stage seemed a new way to express his radicalism, and he started doing it with verve, only to say a couple of years later, 'I've tried swearing and it's not good. I went through a very sweary stage a couple of years ago but I'm not really comfortable with it. I can't do the offensive stuff – me mum watches everything I do.'

In November, keeping up the unique personal double act of being a mass and an elitist entertainer, Lenny embarked on an eleven-week tour of universities and polytechnics. 'I'm on the same wave length as students,' he boasted. 'I can say, "Do you remember Top Cat?" and they'll all shout back at me.' His university act was bluer than TV shows, but Lenny promised, 'I'll probably be doing more jokes about sex and puberty on TV next year.' Theophilus P. Wildebeeste was a star of the student show; at the Great Hall of the University of Wales, in Cardiff (the night after Lenny Henry's last O-Level paper, as it happened), Theophilus tore his shirt open in front of a blushing female student volunteer, leering, 'Let's roll around, baby, on my deep pile carpet.' Instead of the performer's traditional little glass of water, Lenny drank from a mug of Coke and ice to cool himself down while working to student audiences. He had yet to be invited to Oxford or Cambridge: 'I've been asked for after-dinner speeches, but I'd much rather go with a band and rock the house,' he said.

As young and hip as Lenny liked to regard himself in the mid-1980s, the students in his audience were almost to a person former *Tiswas* viewers, for whom he was very nearly a cuddly uncle figure. He had first experience of this phenomenon in Blackpool, when parents would take their young children to see him because they too thought of him as a *Tiswas* person. When he got into some perfectly clean, but by parents' standards risqué material about teenage snogging, they would be shocked. Now, in student venues, the man the audience could not yet dissociate from David Bellamy impressions, custard pies and buckets of water, seemed halfway to being a radical feminist, who, at one moment would be semi-ironically evoking cartoon favourites, the next be in full menstrual flow on some right-on aspect of gynaecology.

'I suppose a lot of the stuff I do is designed to break down – I don't know about this – it sort of breaks down barriers ... It's going for the better laugh as opposed to the cheap laugh. It's easy to get a laugh doing jokes about darkies and women's bosoms and things: it's a lot harder to make jokes about ... something else,' he said in an *Observer* interview. Lenny, the all-purpose, all-things-to-all-men, universal showman was by now a master of tailoring his statements to a given audience. For the heavyweight, broadsheet journalists, he could shift into the requisite verbal gear – a touch of academic self-deprecation here, a hint of scholarly avoidance of vulgar oversimplification there. For the *Mail* and the *Express* he was skilful in appearing serious and thoughtful, not too ITV, but fun all the same, and would always be careful never to patronise lower-middle-class readers, In the tabloids, meanwhile, he was still good old Len from Dudley.

Cordell Marks, a writer for *You* magazine, described Henry's jumble of thoughts while testing a new part of his act: 'Henry felt, he said, that after fifty or fifty-five minutes on stage that the audience had become his pals and when you have a pal you can share secrets. He'd been caged inside, he wanted to feel free as a bird and – pause – he knew that was a cliché but, er, you know, that was how it was. The gist of this confession was that a lot of people had trouble with this kind of thing. Had been forced to enter secret clubs, wear weird clothes, even funny suits, but, er, to be real about it – he had made a discovery. He was black. Gloria Gaynor would be writing a song about him.

'The majority of the audience saw the joke,' Marks noted. 'There was laughter and cheers, but entwined also was a thin strand of confusion. "Now," said Henry, "for some biting racist satire. Why do white people have normal noses? So they can breathe." The material was purposely pathetic. "We had some white people move in next door to us. That means the rent is going to be the same." ' Lenny said he preferred to work on stage: 'You can be more aggressive. I don't want to be the warm guy. If you do that all the time you get labelled Mr Family Entertainment and you're a wimp.'

CHAPTER 9

Sweet Charity

'I don't like to see human frailty, deformity and illness.'

Lenny Henry, November 1984

The show-business personality performing great and well-publicised deeds 'for charity' (preferably while dodging income tax, the less flashy method of giving to lesser mortals) has become such a figure of fun and derision that it is surprising Lenny Henry never did a comedy caricature of the type.

Instead, along with a few other inspirational people like Bob Geldof and the scriptwriter Richard Curtis (who later wrote *Blackadder* and *Four Weddings and a Funeral*), Henry reinvented the whole tradition of charitable work by performers. If only because of its appearance year after year, the plastic red nose may have become a slightly tiresome symbol, but Comic Relief must qualify as the best-known example of the quality of having one's heart in the right place. Henry's tireless efforts over more than a decade for the charity make it a sure bet that, by the time he gets a few grey hairs, he will be Sir Lenworth Henry.

Lenny's charitable instinct was awakened in that dynamic year for him, 1984, at the same time as his life and career were settling into their new, sober, responsible – and above all, middle-class – pattern. He had middle-class friends, was married to a middle-class woman, told middle-class jokes, and was now getting into the ultimate British middle-class activity – fund-raising. In November 1984, Lenny did charity shows for multiple sclerosis and miners' children. On 2 December, he appeared at Stringfellow's in aid of the Ethiopian Famine Appeal.

It was another year, however, before Lenny was part of the team of comedians that launched Comic Relief on the *Late Late Breakfast Show* on Christmas Day 1985. (Charity Projects, the group out of which Comic Relief was formed, was founded by Richard Curtis in a New Oxford Street office simultaneously with Geldof's Band Aid. Charity Projects' aim was to help disadvantaged people in Britain and Africa.)

But Lenny's philanthropic activity was mushrooming before that. A fervent opponent of drugs since he was a teenager, in March 1985 he made an anti-drugs film for the YMCA, *Chasing the Bandwagon*, in which he starred with Helen Atkinson Wood. With an original script he had been sent rewritten by himself and Kim Fuller, he played six characters, from a TV news reporter to Delbert Wilkins to a teenager whose life has been ruined by addiction. To highlight the stupidity of drugs, mustard was given the status of heroin, and Henry's various characters ended up hooked on it.

'I have watched people I like taking drugs,' Lenny said in the publicity for the film, which was shown in schools in September 1985. 'A lot of them are people you watch on your TV screens most nights, and they put stuff up their noses and into their veins. If they carry on doing it for much longer, they won't be allowed on your screens again. Drugs have never had the slightest attraction for me. I've been offered them but never touched them.

'Of course, show business has people who take drugs,' he continued. 'But I always think they're so miserable – six blokes huddled together in one toilet cubicle. Cocaine is so unsociable. By the time they've got themselves organised, they've usually missed the party. And heroin seems to turn people into pathological liars. It's dreadful. Many youngsters idolise pop groups and show-business stars who take drugs, and it's easy for them to follow suit. The excuse you get from those stars is that they need to do it to help them carry on working. That's a cop-out answer. The crazy thing is that there are often forces that get a lot of bands and showbiz folk into drugs. There are some people who get money for cocaine written into their contracts. It's written down as "running around money". Managers take the view that if they put up a lot of money to launch a group they want them awake for recording sessions, concerts and everything else, and so drugs are brought in to see they get what they want.'

Lenny had more than jokes and interviews to give in his crusade against drugs. He took particular interest in Broadreach House, a rehabilitation unit in Plymouth, Dawn's home town. After learning about Broadreach being in financial trouble from Dawn's mother, Roma, who worked as a drugs counsellor, Lenny started pouring money into it – nearly £200,000 to date, by means of fund-raising and personal donation. Ian Wilson, Broadreach's manager, said bluntly in 1991, 'Lenny saved our bacon – we wouldn't be in existence without him.'

One spectacular fund-raising effort for Broadreach House was a live charity concert at Plymouth's Theatre Royal in April 1986. Such was Lenny's pulling power among his professional colleagues that, alongside French and Saunders and Jennifer Saunders' husband Ade Edmondson, he also managed to get Elvis Costello, Jools Holland, Nigel Planer, Ruby Wax and Alexei Sayle down to the west country. The show raised £15,000.

'Broadreach is a brilliant place. They give an eight-week course to addicts followed by some aftercare, and they have a seventy-five per cent success rate,' said Lenny. 'But Dawn and I found it a very frightening experience going round there. Drugs are evil, but not until you see how they affect people do you realise just how evil they are. I think they are really scary ... But after looking round Broadreach, the more I learnt, the more I wanted to help. I met a girl who'd seen her best friend become addicted to heroin and die. And these days it is so easy to get heroin ... We've got to help. The kids can't do it on their own.'

Another field Henry involved himself with in the mid-1980s was sickle cell anaemia, the blood disease that mostly affects black people. His eighteen-year-old niece Angie was suffering from sickle cell, and Henry was thinking of taking a test for it himself: 'Angie is coping with the disease at the moment because it is not affecting her mobility,' he said in 1987. 'But I find it scary because when Angie was diagnosed, I started thinking, "What if I have it?" People should be screened. It would be nice if the Government interceded and decided to give some money for research.' In 1989 he opened the Lenny Henry Sickle Cell Clinic at King's College Hospital, London, where a doctor already bore the title 'The Lenny Henry Senior Lecturer'. By 1990, he had given £18,000 of his own money for research into the condition.

Lenny claimed that Dawn had influenced him into becoming a charitable crusader. 'She made me be brave. Before, I'd support the odd fête, but I'd never commit myself to a big issue,' he said around this time. 'Dawn helped me to take a stance. She helped me to shape my opinions. I wish I was more articulate about this ... There is a danger of people perceiving you as Mr Cause, and getting cheesed off with you turning up again. That's why I try to do the things that make the most impact.'

All this charity work did not mean that Lenny's career was slackening off. If anything, he was busier than ever. At the beginning of 1985, he hosted the ninety-minute pilot for Channel 4's *Saturday Live* at the LWT studios on the South Bank. A successful kind of youthful, studenty variety show, the pilot included a filmed parody of *On The Waterfront*, with Henry as Marlon Brando, along with music and live acts by the familiar faces in such circumstances – French and Saunders and Rik Mayall and Ade Edmondson as The Dangerous Brothers.

In the August of the same year, Lenny took his one-man show to the Edinburgh Festival, performing at the Assembly Rooms with most of his material fairly or brand new. This included a sketch about having his wisdom teeth pulled out (based on his own recent experience) and a new character, Davey Boy, a Liverpudlian who thinks he is everybody's mate in the pub but nobody wants to talk to him.

September saw the second series of *The Lenny Henry Show*, on BBC 1. 'This marks the end of my career in sketch shows,' he announced. 'I don't want to just pootle along. I'm twenty-seven now, lookin' over my shoulder now. I go round saying that there should be more black comedians on television. I think, "Hey, wait a second ... I'm not different any more." ... I've been doing sketches now for four or five years, and I really want to do something more ambitious, something

Lenny (he's the white man to the right of Frank Langella) ODs on make-up in *True Identity*. (Rex)

Lenny as *Theophilus P. Wildebeeste*. (Rex)

(*above*) The centre of Dudley in the mid 1950s, when Lenny's parents arrived from Jamaica. (Dudley Public Libraries)

(*below*) Douglass Road, Dudley, in 1995. Lenny's was the corner house.

(*above*) Lenny with his fellow *New Faces* performers, 1975. (Rex)
(*below*) New-Face: Lenny as a baby.

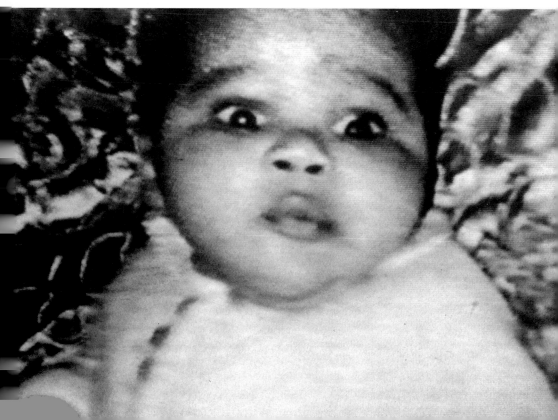

Lenny, aged 12, with his little sister, Sharon. (Meg Newton)

(*right*) Lenny grimly surveys a rudimentary hospital in Burkina Faso, on a fact finding trip for *Comic Relief*. (Ken Lennox)

Lenny in Burkina Faso. He had just been asked for the fifth time by a film crew to try a salt sugar rehydrant solution for the cameras. (Ken Lennox)

(*right*) Lenny and Griff Rhys Jones spell out the message. (Rex)

The best wedding picture. (Mail Newspapers)

Couple about town: Lenny and
Dawn. (Nikos Pictures)

Lenny with Ade
Edmondson, apparently
impersonating bouncers at
a dinner. (Alan Davidson)

Lenny as cheeky chappy Sonny Foster in *The Fosters*, 1975. (LWT)

Lenny and mother, Winifred, in 1981. (Express and Star, Wolverhampton)

(*above*) Lenny practises cooking at London's *Le Gavroche* for his series *Chef!* (Mail on Sunday)
(*below*) Lenny's first day as a Black and White Minstrel, Stoke on Trent, 1975 (Mail Newspapers)

Cause celebs – Lenny and Dawn do their bit for trees. (Sport & General)

with a bit more class.' Slapstick humour, Trevor MacDoughnut and Dr David were consequently abandoned as Algernon Razzmatazz had been previously. The first show included a send up of the recent craze for Raj drama, called 'A Jewel in India's Passage'.

In November, Lenny made an appearance back in the Midlands on *Pebble Mill at One*, in the foyer of the BBC complex in Birmingham, with the afternoon traffic behind him. It may have been the fact of being back in the Midlands, or that he was on a relatively downmarket show, but Lenny's chameleon tendency to adapt precisely to any given public was again in operation. In a snowflake grey jumper, he nervously fingered his right sock with his left hand and mouthed 'Hello Mum' at the camera.

When he was asked to describe the formula of *The Lenny Henry Show*, he stopped in the midst of his analysis and scolded himself: 'What am I talking about, utter rubbish.' It was a stylish way of preventing himself from boring the home audience. Did he model himself on any one talent, he was asked? 'I think my main model is He Man in *Masters of the Universe* because he does have the biggest nipples in the world.' He then started doing his David Bellamy impression with the foyer flowers as props.

As he had promised it would when the second series of *The Lenny Henry Show* was aired, his professional repertoire had progressed by the time a new BBC Thursday evening show, *Lenny Henry Tonite*, was shown in September 1986 to an audience of over 10 million. It was, yet again, a new departure in his career; if Lenny Henry knew one thing that only the cleverest people in show business do, it was not to let any period of his career go on for too long. The reason he, now best known as an alternative comedian, attracted such an enormous audience was that it was never quite certain what Lenny Henry would do next – he was brilliantly unpredictable.

Lenny Henry Tonite featured him in several mini-films. One moment, he was a twenty-first-century private eye, Grank, the next a London motorbike messenger, then the god Jupiter in a musical. Another episode was set in Dudley Zoo, where Henry used to perform. Called 'What A Country!' the story drew on Winnie's experiences as an early immigrant; for a rare glimpse of Lenny at work, she paid a state visit to the film set. Dawn starred with Lenny in another episode, in which he was a politically active driving instructor, she his bossy and pregnant wife. Then there was a story set in a barber's shop, based upon a West Indian hairdresser Henry visited just off the Edgware Road. ('I used to come here and just sit and listen, especially on a Saturday afternoon. You got all the young dudes packing this place out, smoking, talking, telling really rude stories. Dud [the greying proprietor] would start talking about when he was young, and all the women he used to have ... [Deakus's voice] "You must save yourself for de right woman, because you young people like to give yourselves to too many women ..." ') In 'Neighbourhood Watch' Lenny and Dawn played two liberal, but priggish, protest-marching types, who are alarmed to find themselves on the side of the police when a drug dealer moves in next door.

The writer Byron Rogers had the chance of a revealing glimpse of Lenny and Dawn in rehearsal together in west London; 'It was a room the size of a gymnasium, fenced off by poles, so that, in turn, it was living room, police station, prenatal exercise class,' Rogers reported. 'But the fascination was in seeing two professionals at work, discussing emphasis, expressions, all the seams which on the night will not show ... 'In the police station, a desk in the middle of the floor. Lenny Henry, dressed in a red T-shirt with "Touch up de key" on it and baggy grey trousers with a bunch of keys dangling from the waistband, was trying to overawe the police. His wife, he was telling them, had a friend Sarah "who just happens to be a researcher on the Esther Rantzen programme." Dawn French, a small cube-like pretty woman, broke in: "Weigh every word," she advised him.'

The same year also saw Lenny make his first film, *Coast to Coast*. Film-making was an experience he loved, and has yet to be fully recognised for; even people who are not sold on his comedy have had to concede that he is a good actor. Lenny had first seen the script for *Coast to Coast* the previous year, and had been champing at the bit to be given the joint starring role, desperate for a change of tempo, and an opportunity not necessarily to be funny *all* the time. *Coast to Coast* was a full-length TV comedy thriller that opened the 1987 Screen Two season. In it, he played an itinerant Liverpudlian 'DJ Ritchie Lee, who had been fired from a job with British Telecom, is foul-mouthed and a dead loss with women.' Lee has a mobile disco in a converted ice cream van. His partner is an ex-US Air Force pilot (played by the American 'heart-throb' John Shea, who starred in the film *Missing*). In *Coast to Coast*, Henry and Shea are forced to go on the run after a gangland murder.

One of the great attractions for Lenny was the unusual script – he used to be given dozens – which specified the 1960s Tamla Motown music with which the film was to be liberally punctuated. 'This was the first script that really excited me,' he said. 'All the great names – The Four Tops, Otis Redding, Marvin Gaye – were there. I was bopping round the room as I read it. When it said things like, "Junior Walker comes on the car stereo and they both drive off into the sunset", I knew I just had to do it ... Ritchie is just like me when I was younger,' added, fractionally glorifying the waywardness of his past: 'I was clumsy with girls,' he went on, 'very loud and absolutely crazy about music.'

Lenny's acting was a revelation, especially to the producer, David Wilkinson, who admitted to having been dubious when Henry was put up for the Ritchie Lee part. 'I was very anxious when Lenny Henry's name was first floated as the star. But he really knocked us out. We could not have hired a better actor. And the amazing thing is that he is such a nice person to be with. He has no big star mentality,' Wilkinson said. Lenny reported being very relaxed making the film. 'There wasn't the pressure of having to be funny every time I walked on to the screen,' he said tellingly. 'All acting excites me now. It's just like dressing up in your mum's shoes when you were young.' A sequel to *Coast to Coast* was planned to be made in America, called *Brother to Brother*, and scripted by Stan Hey, but the BBC decided it could not afford it.

By the age of twenty-eight, Lenny Henry had already been in show business twelve years. His track record was astonishing; he had squeezed into that period entire careers sufficient to satisfy a lesser man – as a TV star, seaside variety entertainer, stand-up comedian (trad and alternative), as a sitcom star, a film actor, recording artist, writer, charity motivator, political spokesman, anti-racism advocate, anti-drugs campaigner and even as a mature student.

It was of no surprise to his wife and friends that he suddenly found himself feeling very old, even though he was the age of many people starting out in their careers. He slightly missed being a prodigy; 'You can't be complacent – there's always some young guy coming up,' he fretted. 'Twenty-eight is getting quite old really. And it's harder when you're older. When you're young you're willing to do anything. When you're older, you tend to stay within the guidelines of your philosophy. Between the ages of thirty and forty,' he concluded gravely, and with no hint of irony, 'I'll really have to step things up.'

'I'm doing OK,' he accepted in another interview, 'but I am very ambitious. I stumbled into all this, but now I intend to get better and better. I need a blitz on all forms – TV, stand-up, music, live shows and films.' Would Henry like to be a multi-millionaire black star like Eddie Murphy, he was asked? 'I'd love it – that or a pop star like Michael Jackson. But who could stand the pressures of being so well known – 35 million albums? No wonder Jackson's gone loopy. I don't want to play *Othello* – I leave that to Ben Kingsley. And I'm getting the film star bit out of my system in my new TV series [*Tonite*]. I'm happiest as a clown ... I respect what people like Bill Cosby and Richard Pryor have done, but I set my own standards, which are very high. I want to do good stuff, work with the best writers, the best directors and the best actors.'

With what was close to superstar status in the bag, in the spring of 1986 Lenny also found himself in a role he definitely would not have chosen, in a personal drama close to home. On the afternoon of 15 April, his close friend in Dudley, Greg Stokes, was fuming about the American punitive bombing raid on Libya, which Mrs Thatcher had that day permitted President Reagan to launch from USAF bases in Britain. A socialist like his father, Doug, who worked for the Co-op, Greg had also travelled extensively in the Middle East and was knowledgeable in Arab affairs.

Greg regarded the F-111 raid on Tripoli, in which thirty-nine Libyans were killed, including Gaddafi's eighteen-month-old adopted daughter, as an act of state terrorism. He was additionally worried because his father and mother were in Morocco on holiday, and he suspected that, with Radio Tripoli encouraging all Arabs 'to kill every American, civilian or military, without mercy and ruthlessly,' some locals might not differentiate between Americans and British tourists – and that anyway, British people might be in some danger because of Thatcher's collusion with Reagan.

That afternoon, Greg happened to be in Buffery Park and passing Lenny's old house in Douglass Road, on his way from having checked the mail at his parents' house to the Lamp Tavern, a pub in Dudley. He planned to go to J.B.'s, a club in Castle Hill that hosted rock bands on Tuesday nights. Around 11 p.m., while Greg was at J.B.'s, his sister, Jill, received a knock on the door from a policeman bearing bad news. Doug Stokes had been stabbed to death by a lunatic in the souk in Marrakesh seeking to avenge the raid on Tripoli by an act of Jihad – Holy War. It was ironic in the extreme that Mr Stokes, his victim, was a lifelong socialist who, had he known of the raid, would have been disgusted by it. Greg's mother, Avery, had survived the attack by Hasdi Ahmed Ben Abdelkrim, but a friend they were travelling with was badly injured.

Obviously, Jill wanted to contact Greg immediately, but thought he was in London, staying with Lenny and Dawn, as he had said he might for his birthday. The police went straight to Kingswinford and woke up Winnie, who for a few moments thought something terrible had happened to Lenny; when she heard it was Lenny's friend's father, she prayed for Greg. The police in Hammersmith were alerted, and phoned Lenny at around 11.30 p.m. He then took over the grim task of finding Greg and telling him his father, whom Lenny knew very well, had been killed. He phoned another of his Dudley friends, known as Mac, who lived in Burton-upon-Trent. Mac remembered a vital fact of Dudley life – if it was Tuesday, Greg would be at J.B.'s.

It was there that Lenny located him by phone. Greg was tapped on the shoulder by a doorman and told there was a call for him in the dressing room. To Greg's great surprise, it was Lenny on the phone.

'Listen, I've got some bad news,' he told him. 'Your father has been killed. He's on holiday in Morocco and he's been killed.' Lenny recalls the line going quiet, then Greg giving, 'a howl of pain and rage and sadness ... the most upsetting noise I'd ever heard'. Greg, who later wrote superbly about the tragedy in a locally published book, *A Witness For Peace*, remembers telling Lenny, 'No, they can't have killed Dougie,' and Lenny passing on the incorrect story that had gone from mouth to mouth during the day – that Doug had been heard speaking on the phone in English, 'So they blew him away.' Greg remembers then going quiet, and Lenny saying Greg had to go to Dudley Police Station and to phone his sister. Lenny asked if he was all right, admitting it was a stupid question, to which Greg answered, 'Yeah,' and thanked him for phoning. He asked Greg to phone him when he got home. Lenny, who wrote the foreword to Greg's book, says he didn't realise he himself was crying until he put the phone down.

Lenny needed no reminding by such a horrible experience that, while he was living the life of a big star, he was missing out on much of the warmth and comfort, and even, in better circumstances, the humour, of life in his home town. Just after Christmas, he announced that he was not going to do any comedy gigs in 1987. 'I'm going to ease off and have a rethink about my career,' he said. 'It's very difficult to do the observational comedy of life that I do if I'm not actually living it. Besides, I have been touring the clubs since I was sixteen. I decided I needed some time away from that.'

The year was to have two major landmarks for him – the making of a *South Bank Show* on him, perhaps the surest sign for an artist or performer that he has truly arrived – and his first visit to Ethiopia for Comic Relief. He and Dawn also bought a country cottage at Erlestoke, near Devizes in Wiltshire, a venture which was slightly spoiled by some locals expressing their racism in thinly veiled terms.

The episode developed into what would have made a good enough storyline for *The Archers* to sustain the radio show for a month. Lenny and Dawn's country retreat was a converted stone Victorian school-house, which they bought for £75,000 and spent £25,000 doing up, reportedly to include a balconied bedroom and gold-plated bathroom

taps. One close neighbour, the parish council chairman and an elec-
tricity board worker, fifty-nine-year-old George Phillips, was prodded
by the *Sun* into allegedly muttering something about the English
'getting their own country back from this crowd that's come in'; a
garage owner Dennis Turner, sixty-five, was quoted as saying: 'We're
pretty conservative around here. It's not just that he's a six-foot comedian that makes him different. We haven't got anyone else like him
about for miles.' Other villagers were said to have petitioned to stop
the conversion from going ahead, although a housewife, Margaret
Pocklington, was quoted as saying, 'Lenny's a lovely chap – just what
this village needs. It's dying on its feet. All the children here are bored
to tears.' The *Sun* later apologised to Lenny for having delved a little
too deep into the psyche of Erlestoke.

He did, as it turned out, do some comedy in 1987 – a charity gig in
Birmingham, and the Amnesty Secret Policeman's Ball, at which his
Delbert Wilkins ran into a minor barrage of right-on flak. Henry's
Delbert was attacked by a (white) critic for being patronising, racist
and playing to a white yuppie audience. Lenny was thoroughly irritated
by this; 'My material goes through me, then it goes to Dawn, then the
guys I write it with. I censor my own stuff. I don't need anybody to
tell me it's racist or stereotypical,' he snarled to a *Guardian* writer.

Lenny went on the attack himself in defence of Delbert, devoting a
whole TV show in October to what he said was his favourite character.
'There are dozens of real-life Delberts in south London. The slicked-
back hair, the baggy trousers and the pointed shoes. I love him because
he's so flash. He can say things that as myself I could never say . . . He's
just wall-to-wall jokes. He's twenty-two, very black, very cool. He
lives in Brixton and he's totally up-to-date with fashion, keeps all these
pictures from *Vogue* and then gets someone round the corner to make
them for £10. And he's got this customised street machine with flared
wheels. It's a Ford Escort really. The police are continually messin'
with him 'cos they feel he's up to no good.

'I want to do Delbert right,' he insisted. 'People have said it'll be
difficult to make him the main character in a series. But I know he can
do it. He's going to talk about everything – sex, nuclear arms, shoes.

Delbert will have a lot to say, but he's not going to preach. People will always listen when you make a serious point in a funny way. I go to see the writers every day with chocolates and champagne just to make sure that they keep producing funny lines for Delbert.'

While *Lenny Henry Tonite* was topping the ratings, Lenny was on his way to Ethiopia on behalf of Comic Relief. It was his first trip into the heart of Africa. He travelled with a TV producer, Helen Fielding, and a small group of journalists to see how Comic Relief's money was being spent and to make three short documentaries and lots of brief 'commercials' for the 1988 Comic Relief show. Griff Rhys Jones went to Sudan on a similar mission at the same time.

'The idea of sending comedians rather than news reporters was precisely because people will recognise that they didn't start out by being better informed than ordinary members of the public,' Fielding explained at the end of the trip. 'They're ordinary people with an ordinary amount of information, a sense of humour and a love for life. They represent the way an ordinary bloke would feel about it ... We very much wanted to talk to the people themselves rather than to aid-workers or people in the know. In Africa we made a rule that we weren't having any British spokesmen – only local people.'

A diary of Henry's Ethiopian experience published in part by *You* magazine proved a mixture of funny and sad stuff. He did a 'command performance' of President Reagan on the Tarmac at Addis Ababa airport. Of Day Three, he wrote: 'We start filming at a water pump crucial to the survival of one village. Comic Relief put a lot of money into water supplies, which prevent diseases and help agriculture. I have to carry a water pot and explain how heavy it is – and how women have to carry these for miles. The Ethiopian ladies looked on in sheer wonder as the great big clumsy wimp picked up the water pot, staggered under the immense weight towards the camera, delivered his lines in grunts, pants, wheezes and coughs and then, when Butch [the TV director] shouted "Cut!", almost dropped the bloody thing.

'The crew cracked up, and so did the Ethiopian lady who, when she realised the pot was no longer needed, just picked it up in one swift graceful movement and walked off without a hint of strain towards her home.'

On Day Seven: 'We went to an immunisation programme which we hope to support this year. That's when I met Mohammed – two years old and dying of TB (if he'd been immunised, he wouldn't have had it). He is a beautiful boy, very docile, and although in a little pain, he didn't cry once ... I couldn't think what to do. He didn't seem to be responding to anything. So I put my Comic Relief nose on and a grin just spread very slowly across his face. I thought to myself, well, if it can do that to a little kid who can't speak our language, maybe if we all wore one we could really raise a load of cash.'

A very different diary was published shortly after by *Weekend*, a tabloid supermarket magazine. 'Came across a group of children searching a field for food. They were real children, not in a film or something; just short, brown, grumpy and noisy kids. They could have been mine except they were starving to death. I watched them sieving earth through their bare hands, trying to find grains left from last year's harvest. There weren't any ... October 8th: Watched a little boy die today. They told me 50p would have saved his life. I don't know how old he was – six, seven maybe. There was nothing of him – just skin and bone. No one could do anything. He had TB. The doctor said a 50p inoculation would have saved him – trouble was, no one here has 50p. It sounds odd but this dying little boy gave me courage. OK, so I am only a comedian, but at least people know who I am. They *will* listen to me. If the only thing that comes of this is that I raise one 50p piece and save one little boy's life, won't that be worth it?'

The astonishing images were crowding in on Lenny so rapidly that some got pushed to the bottom of the memory pile, and he only recalled them later. 'I met one kid over in Ethiopia who was so frightened that he never slept at night because he saw that the crops had failed again,' he said in an interview several months later. 'It was so heartbreaking to see those kids dying of measles. Measles! When it costs 40p for an injection. I had to talk to children of five, whose parents had died. I didn't cry, but I had to keep stopping talking. That will stay with me for the rest of my life. I kept thinking that these could be my nephews and nieces ... What's happening to these people makes me very angry. It helps to know that even a weedy comedian can do something.'

Where he could, Lenny used his humour. In one village he entertained a group of children for over an hour by pulling faces, doing animal impressions and impersonations of the villagers' laughter. 'I am a comedian. I make people laugh,' he said. 'I found myself being incredibly buoyant and cheerful over there because it was the only way to get through it. I felt a constant need to make people smile. At least they'll remember the big black guy who turned up there one day and made noises.' A more poignant moment came when Henry, dressed in full Ethiopian costume, was mistaken for a local because of the deep black suntan he had gained. A man came up to him and started speaking in Amharic. When the situation was explained by an interpreter, the man simply said, 'For a moment I thought you were one of us.' 'It made me realise that nationality is only wardrobe deep,' Lenny said. 'But for the grace of God it could have been me standing in the middle of a field asking where all my crops had gone.'

The fact of being of black African descent, but having missed out on such a sparse life by a few quirks of history and geography, had never struck Lenny so forcefully; it is often brought home to black Americans for the first time by tame tourist trips to the Gambia. Lenny's privileged (in a sense) tour of Ethiopia was a far more intense experience than Roots tourism, and it set off thoughts of adoption in his mind. He saw one boy of eight in an orphanage, and could hardly avoid the comparison with himself in Buffery Park at the same age. 'I was so touched by him, I wanted to take him home. The kids in the orphanages and hospitals in Ethiopia really screwed me up. For just 50p they could have been inoculated against the diseases they were suffering from. It was so very emotional. But when I got back to Heathrow, I realised adopting him would be wrong. I know I could help more of them by encouraging people to give money to Comic Relief. We did. We got £9.8 million.'

It was not just the stick-thin children in Africa that disturbed him, but the frustration of seeing a beautiful country that wasn't working properly. The land would often be green and fertile but people would be growing the wrong crops on it, like coffee. Like Bob Geldof before him, and, more recently, Richard Curtis, Henry returned from Ethiopia, his everyday outlook changed: 'Suddenly I hated the way we threw things away – even empty coffee jars, tomato tins, old newspapers. I wouldn't go round the corner to the Indian shop to buy a packet of rice unless I knew we were going to eat it all.'

Still not aged thirty, Lenny had achieved all he needed to merit the professional tribute of a *South Bank Show* on him, yet the programme came about, as these things do, by a coincidence. Andy Harries was a freelance TV producer and director who lived in Hammersmith, close to Lenny. He was a couple of years older than Lenny, and had done two *South Bank Shows* already on two of his idols, Malcolm Maclaren and Truman Capote.

'I had quite a good relationship with Melvyn Bragg, and he had left the door open for anything I wanted,' explains Harries, who is now Granada TV's controller of entertainment and comedy. 'I was keen to continue the relationship with the *South Bank* because it was in a particularly prestigious phase at that time, although it was very unpopulist, and one of the things that I had tried to do was to bring Melvyn populist subjects. Maclaren was quite bold of them to go with, and I did a pretty thorough job on it. I think for the first time *The South Bank Show* did something with a little bit more edge, and it did very well.

'Then one day [it was a few weeks before Lenny's Ethiopian journey] I staggered off down to my corner shop in Hammersmith to get a bottle of milk, and there in the shop was Lenny Henry. I didn't know he lived so nearby – I had never seen him and I didn't know him from Adam, so I didn't say anything to him. But on the way back to the house I was thinking about how I've always been a huge fan of Lenny's. I loved *Tiswas*, and Lenny had been outstanding on it, and a key part of its success. It was then that I thought he would be a great subject. It was interesting, because he was terrifically funny and an old-fashioned guy, and he was also black; this was Britain's first black comedian who really said something about Britain.

'So I got a number for Lenny and I rang his answer machine – like all celebs, he left the answering machine on all the time – and explained who I was, and if he was interested in this would he give me a call back. I couldn't offer it on a plate, but I felt confident that Melvyn would be keen, as indeed he was. Lenny called back and asked me to come round, which I did, and called up Melvyn shortly afterwards.

'We got on very well,' Harries continues. 'I really liked Lenny immediately – I thought he was fabulous. There was the potted history to tell, from Dudley Zoo onwards, but I wanted an angle for the show, and the angle I thought of for Lenny was America. Lenny had never worked in America at this time. I thought, why don't we take him over to New York? I got the money for that, and rang up this club called Catch A Rising Star, and went off there for a week with Lenny and Kim Fuller. And that was how we embarked on the show.'

Keen as they were to foster new talent, Catch A Rising Star, which is on the Upper West side of Manhattan, was somewhat reluctant about Harries' plan to give a completely unheard-of black man from England a platform. It was one of only two comedy clubs in New York at the time, but it had its reputation to think about; normally, there would be five acts on the bill, and these would rotate, so each comedian would do two or three sets each. They agreed to allow Lenny, who was just back from Ethiopia, ten minutes on a freezing November Monday night.

For an indescribably minority taste, he did quite well in terms of pre-publicity. New York *Newsday* mentioned him as the last item in its 'New York Tonite' column: 'British Comedy: Lenny Henry, one of England's biggest TV comics (he co-starred with Tracey Ullman on a sitcom), performs this week at Catch a Rising Star, 1487 First Ave., at 77th Street. Henry is a skilled impressionist known for his roster of famous people as well as his own characters – Delbert Wilkins, a streetwise Cockney, soul singer Theophilus P. Wildebeeste and African comedian, Josh Yarlog.' A small photo of Lenny appeared next to the paragraph. As a result of this, the club was not packed, but surprisingly full of sceptical New Yorkers sitting with their arms crossed and amuse-me-if-you-dare expressions on their faces.

'On that Monday night, he totally died the death,' Harries recounts. 'It was horrific. I remember slumping at the back of the club thinking, "Oh, my God, this is a nightmare. This film is going to fall apart, my whole ending, the whole final twenty minutes is going to be a fucking disaster." *The South Bank Show*'s ethos is a sense of celebration, not a documentary fly on the wall approach. You are really saying, this guy is a great comedian, but it was obvious that he was unsuited to a New York audience. It just didn't work. I can't remember what the set was that night, but he was doing Jamaicans, and it just didn't hang together.

'He got off and was obviously was in a state of great concern, so a rapid rewriting of material started. And then Lenny came up with this idea which I thought was terribly clever and worked. He turned the whole thing round, by telling stories about being an English black guy in New York. You have got to remember that it was ten years ago now, and black British guys were kind of a novelty. Lenny speaks quite well anyway but when he wants to he can put on a very nice refined English accent, which just makes people crack up even more. We found that when we went round New York in the first couple of days, because he is big, they would go, "Hey, how are you man," in pure Bronx, and of course out would come this very refined English accent, and it would crack people up.

'So that's when he started to work up all these routines, and by the Friday night when we filmed, with the help of word of mouth in the English community that Lenny was in town doing this club, they were hanging off the rafters. He picked up a good review in the *Post* about the one he did on Thursday and all was well. That night he came out and said, "You don't know me. I'm Lenny Henry," and a crowd of British nurses in the front row shouted out "Katanga" and sang the theme from his TV series.

'The thing for me about New York was it was the first time I had really seen Lenny work. I had obviously seen him a couple of times in London and around, but even though I really loved him on telly, when I went to see his live act, I have to say I remember being disappointed. He didn't make me laugh as much as I thought he would do. I think that New York trip was the start of his material getting much better, being sharper.'

It was also, Harries admits, the start of his own successful career in the comedy world. 'Lenny was the one who got me into comedy, there is no doubt about that. I had always liked comedy very much and I really wanted to work in comedy. Up until the Lenny show I had never really done any comedy. It was in New York, when I was watching Lenny on that stage, that I came to understand and appreciate what a comedian does, that critical act of getting on stage in front of people you don't know and making them laugh – or not. It's not like a rock band who have got a couple of hits behind them and they just tootle up there and set up the speakers.'

The show was thus made, starting from the climax backwards. As Harries became more absorbed with the story, he became closer personally to Lenny, which was to have a rather unfortunate conse-quence two years later; but for the moment, they were unusually friendly for a film-maker and his subject. Harries went for lunch with Winnie and the rest of the family, and, although he did not feel he got to know Dawn well, he found her 'very warm and very funny and very keen to help and participate in the show. I think she is quite a difficult person to really get to know, as is Lenny, to an extent. You felt that she plays a very, very big part in his life – she was a very real guiding force in the relationship.'

A great deal of material Harries filmed was jettisoned because there was not space for it in a fifty-minute film. One sequence chopped was of Lenny as Joshua Yarlog running up and down the sedate street in Kingswinford where Winnie lived. Another showed Dawn and Jennifer Saunders knocking on a door in Hammersmith early in the morning (it was actually the door of Harries' house) and screaming through the letterbox. Saunders was yelling, 'Melvyn, we know you're in there. We've come to talk about Lenny Henry.' Dawn: 'I've got Melvyn's baby inside me.' 'Melvyn was not in a great mood when he came to the rough cut,' says Harries. 'At the time, I didn't think he would think this was terribly funny, so I cut it before he saw it.'

CHAPTER 10

UNLEASHED

'It's accurate, it's affectionate and it's extremely funny. But is it,
you know, OK?'

A Guardian *writer agonising over whether the newly politically correct Lenny*
Henry's pointed studies of black people are themselves politically correct

The South Bank Show was transmitted on 6 March 1988, with Melvyn
Bragg's introduction neatly summing up both Andy Harries' mission,
and Lenny Henry's life story: 'We attempt to show the transition of
someone who was prepared to be seen as a giggling victim of society
to the Lenny Henry of today who can take on the role of this Brixton
street hustler Delbert Wilkins and make a serious point about black
people in contemporary British society,' Bragg pronounced.

A few days after the well-received film went out, Lenny made,
arguably, another point about black people in contemporary British
society, by earning £75,000 for a day's work filming a TV commercial
for the Abbey National Building Society. His role was not too taxing;
he had to walk into a branch and say: 'There's more plastic here than
in Michael Jackson's face.' The fact that, at the height of the Thatcher
property boom, with banks and building societies at each others' throats
to get home owners to take out mortgages, or at least change lenders,
a black man from Dudley was seen as a purveying the right image for
the Abbey must, surely, have showed that things were improving slowly
for black people. Lenny had already stormed the bastion of the white

British breakfast table with advertisements for Alpen Muesli.

The most important thing Lenny did in 1988 was to go back on the road, with a series of gigs culminating in a run at the Hackney Empire, in east London. The purpose of the gigs, which he described as his comeback, was to limber up for a film of his stand-up comedy, called *Lenny Henry Live And Unleashed*. This film was to be yet another landmark in his career, suggesting as it does in the title that what was now being seen was the real, raw Henry, all previous appearances having been of a Lenny caged by convention. *Live and Unleashed* has been widely acknowledged as the peak of Lenny's stand-up comedy career.

He still did plenty of other things in 1988. One was hosting the Nelson Mandela Birthday Concert at Wembley, where he impersonated Michael Jackson so convincingly that someone in the wings, seeing the unexpectedly chunky figure on stage, was heard to say, 'Jacko's been on the doughnuts.' A few weeks later, he was in Dudley to be best man for Greg Stokes at his register office wedding; Greg thought he looked more nervous than at the Mandela gig. In September, he devoted another BBC *Lenny Henry Show* to Delbert Wilkins, in which Delbert is growing up and assuming responsibilities – specifically a girlfriend, of whom there had never been a breeze in earlier incarnations of Delbert. The girl was played by an actress Lenny had never met before, Mimi March. Delbert having a girl put Lenny again in a position he found embarrassing – having to do a love scene. 'When it came to filming the kiss in episode three I was racked with nerves,' he said. 'I kept puckering my lips up really tight every time we rehearsed the scene. But Mimi doesn't mess about. She just grabbed me round the shoulders and pulled me into this big snog. It was very good. Proper open mouths, but no tongues because that's not allowed. The cast and crew started laughing and cheering and I got very embarrassed.'

At the end of 1987, Lenny started up his own production company, Crucial Films, in a one-room office in Soho. Crucial's mission was both to encourage black talent in the film and television industries, and to help Lenny assume more control over his own work. It started in operation in 1988, although remained fairly low profile until the early Nineties. The germ of the idea for having his own company was planted in America, where he was told that film finance should be easy for him as a comedian; he had also felt unhappy for some time about the paucity of roles in Britain for black actors. 'I think casting directors would think a lot more seriously about using non-Caucasian actors in ordinary roles,' he told the *TV Times*. 'In America, they have a policy of positive discrimination. Here, we're way behind. I was interviewed in Washington DC recently and all the crew were black – lighting, sound, interviewer. And no big deal was made about it ... I'm sick and tired of waiting for the casting people to realise that I want to act,' he complained at the end of 1987. 'I'm sick of getting scripts in which I'm expected to play a black man who's a Rasta who is so stoned he doesn't notice there's a bank robbery going on behind him ... It was a small part and I thought, "What is this bullshit? I don't need this." The film company is very important to me and I will be devoting a lot of time to it next year. The emphasis will be on comedy and action adventure, but particularly comedy.'

At the time of Crucial's launch, there were several film projects in development, although none would provide Lenny with the eventual big movie break. There was a plan for *Coast to Coast Two,* another for *Theophilus P. Wildebeeste, The Movie.* Another project was for *What A Country,* featuring Henry as an immigrant in 1950s Britain. Another, dreamed up by Andy Harries, would be based in Zimbabwe. 'I'm not doing it for the money, I'm doing it for the challenge,' Lenny explained. He realised he had done fifteen TV series in five years, and that now the film world excited him more than television. British TV in particular was getting on his nerves; 'There's so much rubbish on – the only really good comedy comes from America, such as *Cheers* and *Golden Girls.*'

'The idea of *Lenny Live* was to record his stage shows, which were at their peak and had been well honed and built up over the years,' says Andy Harries, who directed the film, his popping out for a bottle of milk in Hammersmith just a year earlier having had far greater consequences than he might have imagined. 'I said to Lenny, "Why haven't you done a concert film?" which, these days, every comedian knocks out as a video, but then, nobody did.'

While a 'greatest hits' film may have sounded a little backwards looking, an attempt to squeeze some more juice out of Lenny's past triumphs, this project was instead closely linked to Lenny's intense desire now to make it in America. By making *Live and Unleashed* in full cinematic quality on thirty-five millimetre film, it was hoped to launch Lenny to an international audience. 'It was a specific idea of intriguing the Americans, of demonstrating that Lenny could show off the skills that he couldn't do in a live set,' Harries says.

Harries and Kim Fuller needed to coax Lenny back into doing impressions. They specifically wanted him to do Richard Pryor and Eddie Murphy, and more specifically still, as a way of wowing even the most sceptical Americans, to go back to Buffery Park basics and to impersonate a white man. All three agreed that Steve Martin, as an American, might be a better idea for this than the thoroughly English Tommy Cooper. 'He took some convincing to do that. He didn't want to do it, and was very resistant to it. He is a wonderful mimic, but he felt it was a bit unprofessional now to do impressions like Mike Yarwood; he was beyond that, didn't need it. But I thought doing Steve Martin as a white guy would intrigue Hollywood.' The impressions, that of Steve Martin done in a latex face mask, formed the beginning and end of the film, and were eventually instrumental in getting him a movie deal in the USA.

When Lenny's show, *Live on Tour*, opened at the Edinburgh Festival on 4 September, the plan was to edit the script as it went round the country, so as when the climax came in Hackney, it could be filmed almost seamlessly. Harries and Fuller went to one gig in three, and Dawn to many of the shows they could not get to. Although there were tensions, with Dawn often convincing Lenny to excise routines the director and writer were keen on, the process was undoubtedly creative. Unsafe, even dangerous material, within the unchallengeable no-sexism-no-racism parameters, was the theme that everyone was agreed had to run through the show.

But Lenny was no longer sure that the old 'you-know-what-it's-like-when-you're-having-sex' recognition humour that was so radical at the beginning of the decade was wearing all that well. Comedy audiences knew damned well what everything was like, because they had had their inner thoughts probed and exposed by alternative comedians for the best part of ten years. 'I think comedy has got very safe,' Lenny fretted in the *Independent*. 'It's one of the problems of the Edinburgh Festival. People do their stuff from their life experience, and really you are preaching to the converted. It's all jokes about the problems with plumbers and builders and the Underground.' Henry believed there was a need to be less comfortable and less middle-class. There would be, for example, a sketch on the new tour about animal experimentation.

On the other hand, what he was trying to achieve was very finely tuned and targeted. 'It can be a problem when you're trying to make people laugh and at the same time stay ideologically sound,' he admitted. 'With this kind of comedy, you're working in a very narrow area. Sometimes you wonder how far you can go before it's exhausted.

'Television is very restrictive, especially the light entertainment slot that I do. I'm before the watershed, I'm on 8.30 to 9, so a lot of the stuff that I do in that time slot is nothing like what I'm like on stage. You get a hint of what I'm like on stage, but with the stand-up and the sketches and with the characters you never get the full *thwack* that you do when I'm on stage ... we try and hit very hard.' Sometimes, he noted, this was easier said than done; 'Performing in front of a film crew is very off-putting,' he admitted. 'I don't think people realise they talk. "Oi Charlie, film's finished. Get annuver one over 'ere will ya. Doin' great Lenny, oi where's my sound?" Like, don't mind me, I'm just up here on my own trying to be funny.'

As the forty-one-date pre-Hackney tour continued in Swindon, Bury, Birmingham, Dublin, and Belfast, the question arose of how to get a substantial number of black people in the audience at Hackney. The choice of venue had been made with the area's strong Afro-Caribbean population in mind, but both Lenny and Harries were concerned that the advertised gigs might still attract a temporary migration of white middle-class fans from west London. Although blacks had been trickling into the stand-up gigs since about 1985, they were still resistant to what they saw as a white comedian's act. They often knew Lenny, liked him and admired him as the first young black man to make it in comedy; but, however much he changed his comedy, the perception remained that it would hold little appeal for black people.

The six Hackney shows changed all that, with up to a third of the audience black. 'It's added a whole new element,' Lenny enthused. 'It's exciting, riotous. It's great when they come; now it's the white audiences who might not get the jokes. They'll laugh, but they might not get all the other flavours.' They were certainly laughing, but it is arguable how spontaneous their presence at the Hackney shows was. Black people in the area distinctly recall being encouraged to attend by advertising at community centres and more direct methods such as complimentary tickets. It was a perfectly valid method of changing the profile of the audience – it was hardly bribery, after all – but its legacy has not been profound. In 1995, Lenny's live audiences remain predominantly white and middle-class, with only the odd black face.

Just how radical and unleashed Lenny's material was is also debatable. His performance was certainly magnificent, but there was still something unavoidably comfortable, homely and cuddly about both his persona and his jokes, even if his mother would not have approved of it. The film got a 15 certificate, and once again begged the great question of alternative comedy: just how dangerous can comedy be if performers avoid the taboos of racism and sexism? Is not a Bernard Manning or a Jim Davidson far more risqué by treading on conventionally thin ice? And is there any chance of being intellectually dangerous when your act is punctuated with animal noises exactly as it was when you were a children's entertainer? An opening number to *Live and Unleashed*, dazzlingly executed, saw Lenny in a sketch that would not have been out of place on *I'm Sorry I'll Read That Again*, the tame, mid-1960s BBC Home Service precursor to *Monty Python's Flying Circus*. The sketch, 'Bad Jokes', consisted of Lenny singing a series of deliberately pathetic 'A-bloke-goes-to-the-doctor-and-says'-type gags in the style of a funky black American singer.

There followed plenty of sketches involving sex and erections (could one be politically erect?), and cheeky attacks on members of the audience, little parries of riskiness (such as describing the Irish as white

Jamaicans). The film opened with Robbie Coltrane as a bigoted cabbie, driving Lenny to the Hackney Empire, while lecturing him on the art of telling jokes ('Well-rehearsed cruelty – that's comedy fer ya'). Early in the show, Lenny Henry stepped off the stage at the theatre and confronted a white girl in the front row to discuss her hairstyle. 'Freddy's back,' shouted Lenny, 'and this time he's got scissors and cutting gel!' Back on stage, he swaggered and grunted, then squealed, 'Why do black people *do* that?'

The truly dangerous bits of the act, however, were brief and separated by long periods that were extremely funny, quite traditional, and harmless to all but the most conservative; attacking animal experiments and fur coat wearers was certainly *unusual* for a comedian, but it is doubtful whether it risked offending a single member of any Lenny Henry audience since he left the northern club circuit. And while the large number of drugs and drunkenness gags in the Hackney show may reasonably have offended Lenny himself, with his deeply-held anti-drugs views, they will have sounded pretty safe to most of his audience.

Not for the first time, Lenny was reminiscent of a choir boy desperate to be thought of as a behind-the-bike-sheds smoker. 'I think I'm mature enough now and I think this film is a mature statement. I don't think there's an overly "please like me, please like me" element in the stand-up,' he said of *Live and Unleashed*; 'I think I'm a better comedian than I was six months ago.'

(This was not a view shared by a housewife at the Palace Theatre, Watford, where Lenny was playing shortly after Hackney. While doing his Theophilus, he took the woman, in her forties, on to the stage, miscalculating her keenness to participate. In front of her husband and fourteen-year-old son, he cuddled her on a scarlet bed and sang a raunchy song, 'Big Love'. She refused a 'thank-you' bouquet of flowers after the show: 'I felt I'd been assaulted. It had a devastating effect on me. I'm a reasonably strong person and not especially prudish,' she told the *News of the World*. Henry later wrote her an apologetic note: 'I'm shocked and horrified that the experience you had on stage was so traumatic. I've developed this character over four years to highlight the sexism of men of that nature. I've never received complaints before.

I've taken your comments very seriously – especially when you level the accusation of simulated rape. My wife is heavily involved in a rape crisis centre, so I don't take the word lightly. And I'd definitely not use it to describe anything that happens in my act.' He wrote the woman two further letters, elucidating the Wildebeeste philosophy; 'People shouldn't have to tolerate sexual knobheads and other sexist dickheads,' he said of the incident. 'That's why I invented Theophilus P. Wildebeeste. He represents all those sexist attitudes. He's offensive in the most extreme form, parading his studded cod-piece and thrusting his thighs. But in the end he is seen to be impotent . . . I've never intended to insult anybody, except men like Theophilus.' After talking the issue through with Dawn, he decided to eliminate Theophilus from his future stage acts.)

The world première of *Live and Unleashed* was at the Cannes Film Festival in the summer of 1989. Just before he left England, Lenny's mother had a heart attack, which meant Henry couldn't get to Cannes in time to open the British Pavilion. He did still manage to be in France in time for the Sunday screening of his film, arriving at Nice on the same plane as Joan Collins. However, not helped by having to sit tight while Collins disembarked regally, he missed the beginning of the film, and was left chewing his nails in a taxi instead.

Another purpose of the Cannes trip was to discuss – the Watford *affaire* notwithstanding – the proposed Theophilus P. Wildebeeste film, which was already scripted, and by the time of the festival, being rewritten. It did not work out. Additionally, to his dismay, Lenny was required to do a live show at Cannes to promote *Live and Unleashed*. He was worried that the audience would have already seen his material in the film, and confessed to a rare attack of nervousness behind the stage curtains at the hotel disco. He was unhappy with the small stage, and the show was not Lenny's best. He had a good joke about having no topless girls in his film, and needing consequently to pose topless on the beach himself. He did not like the rushed, tawdry, endlessly deal-making, Cannes scene, and the trip, overhung by worry about his mother, was not a happy one.

Back in London, another less than happy episode was, as they say in the film business, in development – a falling out with Andy Harries, who had played such a major part in Lenny's career, and to some extent in his personal life too, for a couple of years. Harries, who was an enthusiast of African music and had made several documentaries in Africa, had come up with an appealing idea and a story for a low-budget film, which Lenny was very interested in doing to exploit the terrific critical reaction to *Live and Unleashed*.

'The film was to be set in Zimbabwe,' Harries says, 'with Lenny as a taxi driver in Harare, who discovers a black pop band, The Bhundu Boys [a real Zimbabwean pop group, who had been known in Britain for three years at this stage] and who he thinks will be the new Beatles. It was quite a bad script done by a couple of writers who have actually gone on to do rather well, but it was a very early thing for them. It was a great idea of its time, a very pro-African little film in a country which had just become independent, and when African music was just coming up here.'

The Zimbabwe project was proceeding nicely when Lenny unexpectedly landed a movie deal with Disney in America. Harries was surprised that Disney had signed Lenny, but was assured that he was as keen as ever to make the British film as well as the three Hollywood movies he was now contracted to do. As if to prove the point, while Lenny was in the States, Harries was asked by the nominated producer of the Bhundu Boys film to come to a script meeting.

At the meeting, Harries recalls the producer saying, 'This is all rather difficult, Andy, but obviously you know Lenny doesn't want you to direct this picture any more.' 'I said, "No, I haven't heard anything," and he said, "Well, I am afraid that we are going to have to continue this picture, and obviously we want to pursue it more than ever, but we want to find a new director, I'm afraid. Lenny is the star, Lenny is the money, and Lenny is saying that you haven't got the experience to direct this picture." So I was beaten off my own picture, which anyway never happened in the end.

'The thing about it for me was that if I had received one phone call from Lenny, I probably would have backed down. As it was, in the end I stopped directing under my own steam and decided that I was a better producer. I am not one for conflict, and with stars I am very understanding of the pressures on them and their need to get things right. I would totally have understood Lenny's view on that. There was about six months, a terrible six months, when I was baffled by his non-communication and it was doubly unfortunate that this was prior to the première of *Lenny Live and Unleashed*.'

Just before Cannes, Harries and Henry had a lunch at which the ousted director says he 'threw a fit' and told Lenny how terribly upset he felt. 'It all rested upon the fact that I believed he had betrayed me. That's what I was tortured by, and I mean really tortured. This was not something I took lightly in any sense.' What he explained to me over that lunch was that he had made a film in New York with a first-time director which was never, or hardly ever, shown. This is a significant part of his film career which is not well known. He had agreed to be in this thing with Mariel Hemingway. It was a friend of a friend arrangement, and he agreed to do it. They shot it after *The South Bank Show* with some private money, and it was all a bit dodgy and had been a disaster. It didn't get a very big release, and it had a couple of bad reviews, and was dead, basically. So when Lenny sat down and talked to me, he said, "Look, Andy, I can't afford to get into that situation again," which I did understand, of course I understood. But a phone call might have been nice.

'I don't think he did it deliberately or with malice,' Harries feels now. 'It just came at a point when we had worked together very closely and I think his attitude was a bit sharp. He is very ambitious, and it was just perhaps a side of him I had never seen. His career was his driving ambition and obsession, and I think he sensed that he had got to the next rung and, by God, he wasn't going to make any mistakes. If there was any possibility that I might not have been up to directing that film then I needed to be got rid of. I think he was quite sure that if the offer came from America, he wanted to leave behind the team that in a sense had got him to that stage. I do understand that, but it was quite a shock how it was done.'

Kim Fuller also disappeared from Lenny's team at the same time, although his exit was more voluntary. 'I suppose *Live and Unleashed* was the last time I really worked with him properly,' Fuller says. 'It is quite consuming when you write for someone to that extent, and I just wanted to do my own things.'

Harries' memory of the period is less sanguine. 'There was a time when for at least two years when Kim and I would both meet and it was a case of who had last seen Lenny or who had heard of what Lenny was up to. We were both suddenly without him. I think we were all emotionally involved with each other. I wasn't married at that time, he was married but he didn't have kids and we were all quite young. We were all on the make. I have a reasonably good relationship with Lenny now, and we have lunch or dinner every few months. We maintain a very cordial, very polite relationship, but it is odd because ten years ago I really felt quite close to him. The whole episode was a bit of a lesson to me not to get too close to stars. I love working with talent, I get very excited by talent, and I get passionate about talent, but the truth is that it is much better to keep the talent at a distance. Having said that, I have absolutely no regrets. I am very proud to have worked with Lenny, and of the way I did it.'

In demonstration of the point, although Henry has in recent years resisted his old friend's entreaties for him to come over to ITV, Harries still keeps a large, framed *Lenny Henry Live and Unleashed* poster up in his big, river view office at the London Weekend building.

Fuller, who now writes for Tracey Ullman, still does odd characters for Lenny: 'I work with him whenever he needs anything – I am usually around. I've been good friends with him for a long time. It was just for the period after the film when I suppose we just went our separate ways for a few years. You need a bit of fresh input when you have been working with someone for a long time.'

As angry as Harries felt at Lenny Henry over this communication breakdown, there was never a hint of racial feeling involved in it, in either direction; it was a man-to-man disagreement. But elsewhere in British show business, Lenny was still sometimes shattered by the racism that he encountered. Incredibly, even though he was by now such an enormous star, some callous or clumsy comments of the kind he remembered from his early days on the road would still be directed at him. At a BBC Light Entertainment party in the late 1980s, 'a very well known comedian' came up to him and said, 'i knew you were coming because I heard the drums.' And, 'I know they said black tie, but this is ridiculous.' He would be expected to be amused by wags with lines like, 'I didn't see you standing in the shadows there,' and regarded as 'chippy' if he, as was now his way, challenged such behaviour. He said to the offending comic, 'I really like you. You never do this on stage. Why do you do it at me?' He replied, in effect, that Lenny was being humourless. Lenny resolved to mention him as often as possible on stage and in press interviews. 'I'm not going to mention your name, but you'll know who you are,' he said.

Another 'very famous' comedian on stage at Windsor enraged Lenny by picking on a black couple, saying, 'Oh dear, there's some teeth smiling on their own in the dark down there. I'd better be careful, it's our black friends, I might get a blow-dart in the neck.' Lenny approached the couple afterwards and told them they didn't have to put up with it and should have walked out. After the show, he told the comedian, 'How dare you? They've paid £10 or £18 to come and see you, and how dare you insult them like that?'

Lenny and Dawn were still having to fight racism if not on a daily basis, then at least more than a couple of times a week. Dawn, for example, had had a bizarre experience in Birmingham, going through Handsworth at carnival time in a taxi, on her way to see Lenny at a gig on the pre-*Live and Unleashed* tour. The taxi driver started sounding off to Dawn about 'sending all the bloody darkies home' after she commented on how nice the streets were looking decked out in bunting. 'Actually,' said Dawn, 'my husband is a darkie. Quite a well-known darkie, actually.' As she paid the fare outside the theatre, where Lenny's name was up in lights, the driver twigged and had the nerve to ask Dawn if she could get him a ticket for the show.

Lenny, as the driver of a late registration Jaguar, had his own experience of being pulled over by the police, on suspicion of being up to no good – until they realised who he was, when they would become matey. His sister Sharon, on the other hand, had been shown no such mercy when she was stopped leaving a London disco and insulted by a policeman; and Lenny's brother Paul had also been stopped and rudely questioned in Shepherd's Bush, coming out of a takeaway food shop late at night.

Henry's immediate task in Cannes in the summer of 1989 was to sell his completed film. He had signed distribution deals for New York and Los Angeles, but been stung by a remark one American had made about the black consciousness-raising aspect of his comedy being 'tedious'. Lenny tried to explain to Americans that in terms of both civil rights and their status in popular culture, British blacks were some way behind their Stateside brothers. He spoke at Cannes about Britain being 'a racist country in all the most important places', and said that comedy was just one way of educating people about their origins and potential. On TV soaps like *Coronation Street* and *EastEnders*, where were the black characters, other than in the background, he demanded? He wanted, he said, to see black business executives, jet pilots – and movies and TV programmes that reflect 'what life is really like in Britain today' – or at least, what it should be like. To do that, he wanted to encourage black writers by means of seminars he was planning. 'The ones I write with are great, but I get cheesed off that they're all white. I want to meet others who have the same life experience as me,' he said.

When Lenny had been a provincial, down-market comic, his self-deprecating jokes had not raised the interest, let alone the eyebrow, of the liberal white intelligentsia. Now, with *South Bank Shows* devoted to him and a film of his material showing at the cinemas, it was not surprising that he attracted the often critical attention of the more sombre newspapers. The *Guardian* took him to task over the Delbert Wilkins sequence in *Live and Unleashed*, as well as numerous West Indian take-offs elsewhere in the Hackney performances. But Lenny was equal to pointed questioning. He drew a comparison between himself and Spike Lee, whose film *Do the Right Thing* had recently come out; he said his act threw the spotlight on racism in the same way as Lee's film.

'If you don't allow me to make jokes about people in my own community, you're not allowing me to use my own sources of humour,' he told the *Guardian*. He invoked West Indian traditions of people sitting on their front porches and taking the rise out of passing characters. Why, he demanded, could he not, as a comedian in England talk about young black men wearing funny clothes? 'I think it's funny, so I want to talk about it ... If I watch John Sessions on *Whose Line Is It Anyway?* and he's told to do a West Indian accent or a reggae song, I know John Sessions is supremely intelligent so I'm not going to be offended by that. If, however, I see some bozo on TV with a bow-tie and a frilly shirt doing some stupid stereotypic West Indian gags that are sure to get cheap and easy laughs then I'm pissed-off and I throw a brick at the TV. There's a difference, and it's the intention behind the joke that counts.'

The launch of the *Live and Unleashed* film was another watershed for Lenny. In the summer, he and Dawn moved into their new house. The Wiltshire cottage had been on the market at £185,000 and not yet sold, but the house in Hammersmith had, albeit for a knockdown price. Despite the raging property boom at the time, the Agate Road house had dropped from the £415,000 the couple was asking in July 1988 down to its final sale price of £300,000 – a near 30 per cent drop – in the following spring. It was sold to Phillip Harris, owner of the Bahn Thai restaurant in Soho. The new Queen Anne manor house Lenny and Dawn bought, on the other hand, was also a bargain at £400,000. It was said to be worth £1 million when they had finished doing it up. The house has a long tree-lined driveway and a high stone wall surrounding the back garden, which has a swimming pool and tennis court, as well as a servants' cottage. 'The great thing about the country is that you can park your car,' Lenny joked.

He felt at this comfortable stage, aged just thirty-one, that he had achieved everything he wanted for himself, for the moment at any rate. '*Live and Unleashed* is the culmination of fifteen years work, the best stuff I can do. It's a benchmark,' he announced. 'I'm leaving stand-up comedy and certainly not doing any more gigs for at least eighteen months.'

He was now determined to turn his attention to helping other black people in the entertainment field, and he was deadly serious about it.

'In a lot of cases I will be spending my own cash. But I am in show business, which for some reason pays you a lot of money. And what else would I do with it? Buy lots more chocolates and suits?' he asked. In a joint initiative with the BBC, supported by Jonathan Powell, then Controller of BBC 1, he launched 'A Step Forward', a series of workshops for young, mainly ethnic minority comedy writers.

Lenny started talent scouting for Asian and West Indian comedy acts. 'It was very successful,' he said of the initiative some years later. 'But it was hard work at the beginning. Comedy is a very Oxbridge thing – black kids with a sense of humour are more likely to make a rap record than apply to the BBC for a job.' The workshops gave twenty-five young black writers a chance to learn from professionals. Some stayed the course, and are still making a living writing comedy. One of them was Paul, Lenny's little brother, who was writing professionally by 1991. 'I didn't even hear about the course through Lenny,' he said. 'I was doing various driving jobs at home in the Midlands before that, just earning a living. When I arrived, Lenny said, "What do you want?" I said, "I'm trying to get myself a job, man." The course was brilliant, it really helped everybody. Lenny hasn't helped me at all, though, I do all my own stuff. I know he's pleased for me but we don't go out of our way to complement each other. Our styles are totally different.' (As, of course, was Lenny's mother's style. In October 1989, when Lenny was being interviewed live on Wolverhampton's Beacon Radio, Lenny said to the presenter, Stephen Rhodes, 'Don't be such a silly bugger.' Winnie reportedly rang the station, demanded to speak to her son and then ticked him off for using bad language. Lenny apologised to her.)

In February of 1990, Lenny was named Show Business Personality of the Year by the Variety Club of Great Britain. At the presentation, clips were shown from *New Faces*, and *Tiswas*. Lenny thanked his mum, writers and 'Robert Luff, my manager, my mentor, who's always given me wise counsel in the past few years, who's never stopped me once from being a bit dangerous, who's never said play it safe.' He also thanked Dawn, to huge applause, and mentioned that she was doing three weeks at the Shaftesbury Theatre. Lenny was immensely touched,

Winnie a little less obviously so: 'I was asked if I wanted to say anything about it,' she said of the honour, 'but I declined because it is not my line any more.' Within a few hours of being presented with the award, Lenny flew to Uganda to make two more documentaries to show how Comic Relief money was being spent.

If more accolades were needed, one came in the summer of 1990. According to the *Sun*, in a survey of celebrities people would most like to live next door to, Peter Bowles came first, Terry Wogan second, Michael Aspel third – and the man who once used to threaten to move in next door to hecklers if they didn't shut up, Lenny Henry, came fourth.

CHAPTER 11

RE-MADE IN AMERICA

'I'm from Dudley in the West Midlands. Hollywood's a completely different world.'

Lenny Henry after the release of True Identity

Lenny Henry is not only a deeply English comedian, but one who is quite specific about coming from the Midlands, and furthermore, not just from the Midlands, but from the *West* Midlands, and even within that, he is resolute about being from *Dudley,* as opposed to Birmingham, Walsall or Bridgnorth.

None of this insistence on preserving in detail his provincial roots, much as a local, parochial performer might do, prevented him from having his sights on Hollywood from almost the start of his career. He says he started 'hammering away at Hollywood' – where the only Dudley they have heard of starred in *Ten* with Bo Derek – as early as 1983. It was 1987, however, before he performed in a major venue in New York (and then only in a contrived way, set up for *The South Bank Show*). By that time, however, Hollywood was starting to hammer away at Lenny.

The augurs were, on the whole, quite promising for his North American campaign. In the summer of 1986, Lenny performed at the Just for Laughs Festival, in Montreal, and received an unprecedented four standing ovations. The next year, his BBC 2 film *Coast to Coast* received rave reviews at the Washington Film Festival, 'The reaction blew my mind,' Lenny says. 'I went on telly to talk about it, and when we got down to the cinema, which was a little 200-seater, people were literally fighting to get in.' Back in London, David Wilkinson, the producer of *Coast to Coast*, said 'I have had phone calls and telexes from America from film companies who desperately want to contact Lenny. We feel there is a good chance of the film being developed as a series on American TV.'

On the other hand, as his first disastrous nights at Catch a Rising Star in 1987 amply demonstrated, America is a foreign country. In Los Angeles in 1986, Lenny had been several times, as a matter of curiosity, to a late-night Improvisation Workshop. On his third visit, he tried out his act, coming on in the small hours, immediately after a drunken wine glass juggler. 'It went really well,' he recounts, 'until I said "articulated lorry". They think that's a well-spoken vehicle.'

'I'm not salivating about doing America again,' he said after the trip. 'To get good in Britain is hard enough.' He may not have been salivating, but the idea was still burning inside him. After *The South Bank Show* trip to New York, he returned to Manhattan to make the 'dodgy' film with Mariel Hemingway that Andy Harries refers to.

The film was called *The Suicide Club*, and the role was a straight one, as a sophisticated seducer. 'You don't get the chance to act with someone as good as Mariel Hemingway every day,' he said when the film was shown at the London Film Festival. From Lenny's point of view, it was a good job that he didn't. The film was ignored in London, and bombed in New York when it went on limited release. Fortunately for Lenny, Lynn Darling, the reviewer for New York *Newsday*, barely mentioned his name in her (on the whole) less than enthusiastic notice in May 1988.

'Tedious drama about bored young rich people,' Darling wrote. 'Too bored to live, too dumb to die, ought to be the motto of young, unhappy Sasha (Mariel Hemingway), the heroine of this ridiculous movie ... Sasha gets picked up by Cam (Lenny Henry), a mysterious stranger with the profile of an aristocratic turtle. Cam takes her to a party back at his mansion, hosted by his half-sister/lover Nancy (Madeleine Potter) and populated by a number of unattractive people, all of them dressed up to look like bit players in Alice in Wonderland ... Mariel Hemingway, looking ghoulish in moonglow-white lipstick and with deep circles under her eyes, renders her lines with all the conviction of one of the people hawking perfume on the floor of Bloomingdales. Most of the dialogue sounds like it was recorded in an echo chamber. This being a debut feature on the part of director James Bruce, there are a lot of camera angles that make you feel like you've had one too many martinis in one of those revolving restaurants at the top of ugly hotels. *The Suicide Club* is based on a short story by Robert Louis Stevenson, but none of this is his fault.'

Yet still, the challenge mesmerised him. 'It freaks me out to see how much money there is available there,' he said. 'But it's not dosh. It's the challenge of translating my humour to them. In America, I stand in line like everyone else. It's just having the bottle to get up and do it. It's petrifying. You go to a club every week and see the same people getting up and doing the same material night after night, but inserting three or four minutes of new stuff. In Britain, there's no way you can go and do that.'

He kept going over to the States. In late 1988, the Bravo cable system launched a nationwide campaign to introduce Lenny to America by showing *The Lenny Henry Show* every other Tuesday evening at seven, but kept him so low profile that he was barely noticed by the press. Bravo sent out a promotional video and arranged a single gig at Crackers Restaurant and Comedy Club in Anaheim, Los Angeles, which did not raise much dust.

The LA *Daily News* nevertheless responded enthusiastically to the series. 'HENRY IS HIP TO AMERICA: Pop culture inspires comedian's switched-on humor,' announced the headline over an article by Jody Leader.

Lenny immediately impressed Leader with his love of American TV programmes, citing *Oprah*, *The Jetsens*, *Scooby-Doo*, *The Flintstones*, *Hill Street Blues*, *Cheers*, *Twilight Zone* and *The Golden Girls*. 'This obsession with American television filters into his stand-up act,' she wrote, 'and makes his character impersonations immediate and slick. There's American soul singer Theophilus P. Wildebeeste, street hustler Delbert

Wilkins, reggae Rastaman Razzmatazz, the low-key Fred Dread and the Rev. Nathaniel West ("You can just call me Nat West"). They're hilarious, these too-cool-to-be-hip con men, because they are reminiscent of the used-car salesmen who flicker across our TV screens after midnight. Henry has keyed into the American mass consciousness as if he were born and bred in Middle America.' (Can Leader possibly have understood the exceedingly English reference in the show to the National Westminster Bank? And, if she did, was the knowing parenthesis at all helpful to her readers? We shall never know.)

He said of his attempt to establish himself in the States, 'In England, at the moment, I've reached a certain point where I can go on stage and do virtually anything and get away with it, whereas here I've got no history. They don't know who I am, and they don't care who I am. They care whether I'm funny or not, and that's it, so it's right back to basics. Being famous in America isn't the most important thing in the world – but on the other hand, it would be nice.'

The more upmarket Los Angeles *Times* was far less excited about Lenny, however. Their writer Lawrence Christon went to Bravo's Anaheim showcase, and his ensuing piece crystallized every problem of perception Lenny had already suffered in America and would, sadly, continue to. By the article was Lenny's photo, with a caption, 'Is he England's answer to Eddie Murphy?' which made it plain that the answer would be 'not really'.

'BRITISH COMIC HENRY SUFFERS CULTURAL JET LAG,' ran the headline. 'At 30, Jamaican-born Henry has co-starred with Tracey Ullman on British TV's "Three of a Kind," as well as a number of shows,' Christon wrote. 'Two of them, "The Lenny Henry Show" and "Lenny Henry Tonite," have been running for five years on the BBC. Every outward indication is that he's a major British talent; he's even been touted as England's answer to Eddie Murphy.

'The comparison is overdrawn. Murphy is a lousy stand-up comedian, but he's a brilliant character actor. Henry's people (of whom we saw only a couple) are not as sharply drawn, and his stand-up routine falls into that generic Interzone that characterizes stand-up everywhere when it sacrifices point of view for the easy laugh. Henry is a powerfully built 6-footer with a heavy Paul Robeson voice who, in his appearance at Crackers this week, wore a pinstripe suit with stripes so wide they looked like a parody.

'He talked about what it is to be black with an English accent; about 17th-Century British blacks wishing the departing Pilgrims well and hoping more whites would join them. He joked about chasing scared white folks on New York's 42nd Street. He did an evangelical preacher. ("Say 'Ah!' Say 'Ah! Ah! Ah!' Say 'Get down, you funky sex machine.'")

'He talked about the Flintstones in the White House, not realizing that evangelical jokes and Reagan jokes have been pretty well used up by now. He spoke about how much more clever women are than men. ("When we were outside playing marbles, they were inside watching 'People's Court' and 'Perry Mason' and taking notes.")' [Lenny had used the identical gag in *Live and Unleashed*, with *Crown Court* in place of the American programmes.]

'As soul singer Theophilus P. Wildebeeste, he played up the old Barry White stereotype of the black super-stud. ("I'm so sexy, I got up in the morning, went to my dresser, and my underwear said, 'Me! Me! Me!'") He brought up an attractive woman from the audience, and played a bit of his routine off her. Then he was gone. There's an awful lot a foreign comedian can bring us by way of cultural perspective – or even ethnic idiosyncrasy – that an American comedian cannot, and the British Isles have furnished us with a number of bright talents over the years – Scotland's Billy Carrol comes to mind.' [The *Times* man may have meant Billy Connolly.]

'But Henry is clearly in search of an American success on American terms instead of his own . . . he has a strong presence, but his routine seemed culturally jet-lagged, out of focus. If Bravo had let him settle in for an hour or so, we might have seen what all the promo fuss has been about. But he was gone before we had a chance to see anything out of the ordinary.'

Lenny, to be fair, was not seeking American success on American terms. He had often made it clear in England, for example, that although he admired Murphy and Richard Pryor, he disliked a lot of what they did. 'I like Murphy as an actor, but it's different with his stand-up routine. Richard Pryor is very sensitive. he's been through a lot, and he uses his personal tragedies to enlighten you; he's not just grabbing his crotch and telling you about chicks and how much money he's making . . . With Murphy it's completely different, it's all very macho. There's a lot of hatred there, which I find disturbing. In *Raw* [a film of Murphy's live show], he spent forty-five minutes denouncing women; my chin was on the floor, because you could tell that that's what he really thinks. The kind of comedians they're moving towards in the States – and here, to some extent – are the ones who couldn't give a monkey's about anything. They grab their crotch and say "Hey, up yours!" or, "We don't like rubbers, do we guys?" It all seems to be about getting crowds of sixteen- to twenty-four-year-old men to cheer very loudly.'

In November 1989, still on a high from the success of *Live and Unleashed* in Britain, Lenny and James Hendrie, a scriptwriter, worked in American clubs to try to get to grips again with the kind of humour that might work with audiences there. They wrote during the day and performed the same material at night. Lenny observed that, 'All your references have to be "bi-oceanic", as they say – which means *EastEnders* and *Coronation Street* jokes are out. My aim is to put together an act that anyone who speaks English anywhere in the world will find amusing.' It was on this trip that he and Hendrie heard that Jeffrey Katzenberg, the chairman of Disney Pictures, was interested in Lenny. He was summarily flown out to Hollywood to meet studio executives.

Slowly, Lenny's star was making it into the ascendant. The thing that fascinated Disney about Lenny was, as Andy Harries and Kim Fuller had predicted, his Steve Martin impersonation. The head of Touchstone Pictures, the Disney subsidiary that eventually signed Lenny, David Hoberman, said: 'When we saw the video clip we thought he was a very talented white comedian. It was only later when someone showed us some other sketches he had done that we realised his true colour. We knew then he would be just great for our own new film which involved a black man disguising himself as a white guy.'

Lenny perceived that they thought, as he put it, that 'I was cute.'

Meanwhile, in England, as everyone waited hopefully for news on the Disney front, Lenny and James Hendrie cooperated on a short film, *Work Experience*, which almost immediately won an Oscar in the Motion Picture Academy's low-profile 'shorts' category. 'I was so excited when I heard the news in London that the dogs in Sweden could hear me scream,' Lenny says. A vignette of less than twenty minutes about Lenny as an ingenious but unemployed man, who gets a job as a department store sales assistant, the film's timing could not have been better.

Lenny was getting to like America very much indeed. In a New York night club, he bumped into Prince and went up to him to say, 'I saw you last year in London.' The singer, one of the pantheon of Henry's heroes, looked at him and said, 'You're Lenny, right?' In 1981, Lenny explained in an interview, he came to America, and 'for the first time I realised there was much more I could do that was much more real; I could use my blackness in a much more positive way.' 'America makes me feel more black,' he told the Chicago *Tribune*. 'In Britain, you just get accepted. In America, I really blossomed into blackness.' He was so confident as a black man in America, that he floated the idea of calling a film *International Negro*, negro being a semi-reclaimed word in the States, and a phrase he had toyed with at home in *Live and Unleashed*. In Britain, however, using negro was still a bit risqué; the term was all too often to be heard in its original derogatory, or patronising, Sidney Poitier sense.

The good vibe in the film industry about the short film, combined with a trend towards mainstream movies featuring black actors in positive roles, finally prompted Touchstone to sign Lenny in the spring of 1990 to a three-year deal worth up to £1.75 million to him. It was not, significantly as things turned out, to be a three *picture* deal; if the first movie didn't work out, the contract all but spelled out, well, hey, that's show business. But Lenny is not one for pessimism; the long process of making *True Identity*, his one proper American film, and the cathartic experience that finally stopped him from chasing American success, had begun.

Problems over *True Identity* started early, when the old Hollywood tradition of sorely messing about any actors other than the top home-grown talent, reared its head. Lenny and Dawn had an agreement that if a long stint abroad were required for one, the other would accompany them. Filming of *True Identity* was to start in April; when the couple arrived at their rented house in Malibu (Dawn, brought up in Plymouth, relished the idea of staying by the sea) they found the script for the film (by Andy Breckman, whose previous scene credits included Richard Pryor's unmoving film *Moving* and Dudley Moore's disappointing *Arthur 2: On the Rocks*) was being rewritten for the nth time, and no decision had yet been taken on what Lenny's white mask would look like. Dawn had cleared the decks of work from April to August, and was looking forward to the novelty of spending time as a Hollywood wife. As the weeks went by, Lenny would rehearse on the balcony when he wasn't at the studio, and friends from England would come to stay. Dawn took most of them on the hour's drive to Disneyland. Otherwise, she watched television, cooked bangers and mash and, boredom overcoming her, went native and wrote a treatment for a movie. The filming of *True Identity* did not begin until November.

All this hanging about, away from their beautiful new home and old friends (and without income) evoked in Lenny an almost immediate, and understandable, desire to be in Dudley. He had only had limited experience of America, but he was already more sure than ever that he never wanted to leave England full time. 'It's where I belong. My mum's here and it only takes me an hour-and-a-half to go and see her any time I want ... I know what they're selling over there – and it's not real.' In the midst of going back and forth to Los Angeles, he helped organise a huge Henry family party at Dudley Town Hall to celebrate Winnie's sixty-fifth birthday. More than seventy close family members took over the civic banqueting suite, and the Town Hall catering staff was sworn to secrecy over Lenny and Dawn coming. There was a gospel choir, and each child made a speech about Winnie, mentioning Winston respectfully, but only very briefly.

A barman at the party, who was a great Lenny Henry fan, noted a *faux pas* by Lenny that gives some indication of the strain he was under. 'At one point,' recalls the bearded council worker, 'Lenny, who was on the top table with his mother, wanted something from the bar and snapped his fingers in my direction without even looking at me. I was furious – I don't take that from anybody, and I think my look gave away my feelings because, to my surprise, Dawn sprang across and apologised for him. She said, "Please, just ignore him," and I said, "Don't worry about it." You have to keep smiling in this job and not let your anger show. I'd have got into trouble if I had got annoyed, anyway.'

Such was the stress of being constantly recognised that Lenny was becoming much more cagey than he had been in the past about his Dudley connections. Although even now he goes back to the town and is seen a celebrity who has not lost his roots, he would by the late Eighties avoid filming in Dudley. At the beginning of *Lenny Go Home!*, a video released at this time, he is seen apparently showing the site in Dudley where his primary school, St James's, used to stand. In fact, he was filmed in Walsall, several miles to the northwest; when the video was seen by fans in Dudley, it looked distinctly odd that he was claiming to be in his home town.

With Dawn by his side again, Lenny returned to America in July. Neither LA life, nor Hollywood working practice, turned out to be to Lenny or Dawn's taste. The superficiality of LA life is famous for either turning the brains of left wing English people to mush – or, as in Lenny and Dawn's case, sickening them. The guns and violence were one thing. The social side was more immediately cloying. They would be out at restaurants and people would come over to do the Hollywood thing, saying how great you are (usually followed by, 'Who are you?'). Lenny, as a gregarious sort, initially thought this was rather friendly of them; Dawn would then give her husband a stony look. 'She's very shrewd and she sees right through the falseness of the place,' Lenny commented.

'I think it's an evil place,' she said. 'It seems to me that everybody lies to you. It is taken for granted that people are going to lie, but nobody warns you. You should be issued at the airport with a document that tells you not to believe what anybody says.' The industry gossip about nothing but movies, who was earning what and who was wearing a toupée got on their nerves. Hearing a woman in a restaurant announc-

LENNY HENRY

ing to her friend, 'I'm dealing with my ego right now,' made Lenny
pine for a quiet drink with an old mate in a pub in Dudley.

At the studio, Lenny's work was more circumscribed than he was
used to. 'In light entertainment here [in Britain] it's left to you,' he said
on one of his trips home before filming began. 'They simply say:
"Darling, you're funny, so go ahead and do it your way." But with
Charlie Lane, my director in *True Identity*, it's going to be different.
He'll tell me that I've got to be angrier and that's the challenge ... I've
taken the king's shilling, and I'll try and make sure that the spirit of me
is involved and that I don't just become a cipher for someone else's
jokes.' He felt tremendous pressure as an actor, a foreigner, and even as
a man, to justify the dollars Disney had poured into him. To do this
was not simply a matter of smiling through the long days, which could
stretch from a 4 a.m. call to ten in the evening. It felt, he said, 'like
doing a Rubik cube every day blindfolded'. Dawn would discuss acting
details with him every evening, and at lunchtimes too, when she would
often come to the studio.

The period was not without its enjoyable moments, or at least,
experiences which would become fond memories. 'In America they
have a completely different thing to the set up in English films,' Dawn
explained in interview with Michael Aspel. 'In English films you break
at 11 o'clock for elevenses which is a bit of a Kit Kat, a nice cup of tea,
a scone if you're lucky; and then you break in the afternoon for sticky
buns ... So in America I went along to visit him and, of course, there
they have this thing called the Craft Services, which means a running
buffet the entire day. I couldn't believe it. I thought I had died and
gone to heaven. They put lollipops out and there were rows and rows
of peanut butter and jelly sandwiches for whoever happened to be
visiting. So obviously I spent about seventeen hours a day there.' When
she went to the studio, however, she was ignored as she was not the
star. When some people discovered she had her own TV series, they
thought she was mad for not mentioning the fact.

In October, on their sixth wedding anniversary, which fell on a rare
Saturday off for Lenny, he and Dawn went to Las Vegas for a semi-
spoof remarriage ceremony in the Silver Bell Chapel, where Brigitte

Nielsen had recently had her real wedding. Lenny wore glasses, a white T-shirt and red waistcoat, Dawn, a loose white cotton suit. They arrived by rented limousine, crossed a little bridge, and were serenaded with 'Love Me Tender' by a rented Elvis lookalike with stains down his front and black hair-dye running down his face. Vegas's only black minister, George Cotton, conducted the service. As they approached, Mr Cotton said, 'You have now crossed the river of life. Welcome.' 'I pissed myself, basically,' Dawn recounted later. 'It was very funny.'

True Identity, which co-starred Anne-Marie Johnson, was directed by a young black film-maker, Charles Lane, whose previous silent black-and-white film, *Sidewalk Stories*, received international acclaim. The screenplay was originally an expanded version of a sketch Andy Breckman (the writer of *True Identity*) wrote for Eddie Murphy for *Saturday Night Live*. Lane liked the movie's premise but not Breckman's treatment and tried to make it more socially responsible. Lane called the film, 'an action comedy that is also a tender love story'. Lenny played a struggling New York actor, Miles Pope, on the run from the Mob and forced to masquerade as a white man. It starts on a plane about to land in New York from Florida, that encounters horrific turbulence and everyone thinks is about to crash. The man next to Miles, Frank Luchino, confesses, as you do, that he is a Mafia boss the FBI think is dead, but has changed his identity. Then the plane lands safely. Miles knows that he is doomed for being unlucky enough to be in receipt of the Mafia man's confession. Terrified, Miles adopts the white disguise (applied by Charles Lane, playing a part in his own film) and ends up being a hired by Luchino as a hit man under orders to bump off ... Miles Pope. Somewhere along the way, he also falls in love with Luchino's interior designer, played by Johnson.

Henry was made to lose two stones as soon as he arrived, and also had to get into shape as he had a lot of running to do in the film. He was assigned a personal trainer called Doug. However, because Lane was shooting out of sequence, Lenny said you could see his bottom shrinking and expanding as the film progressed, depending on which part of his diet and exercise regime he was on at the time of shooting. He became so fixated on losing weight that on his birthday, Dawn had a cake made modelled on him lying on the floor, holding a pair of dumb-bells and gazing at himself in a mirror.

The Miles Pope make-up, in which Lenny looked oddly like Jackie Mason, the Jewish New York comedian, involved taking a cast of his face, cosmetically reshaping his lips, chin, forehead and nose, then covering his face with thinnest layer of rubber possible. Details such as veins, freckles and stubble shadow were then painted in. The mask took several hours of indescribable boredom to apply each day, and Lenny had to spend most of the movie – up to twelve hours a day, seven days a week – swathed in its rubber.

'It was very claustrophobic,' he says. 'Then all these people kept peering at you from, like, an inch away. But the most alarming thing was when you were on camera during a scene and you'd notice out of the corner of your eye that Michelle Burke [the constructor of the make-up] is looking at your face through binoculars to make sure that half your nose hasn't dropped off.'

He was fascinated and a little horrified by the effectiveness of the mask and make-up. He tested it by going in it with a black friend to a record store in New York, where no one batted an eyelid. White people ignored both of them, while blacks would acknowledge his friend, but not him. 'It was strange not to be a part of that "brother" thing,' he said. The funniest time in the make-up was when he was in the Disney canteen, when people saw that he had a white face and black hands, and, he says, would put their trays down to stare. He even went out to a smart restaurant wearing the mask and make-up, minus the latex top lip, which during filming prevented him from eating anything.

On the whole, Lenny found the experience of turning white very disturbing, and not particularly funny. Dawn hated seeing him in the mask, feeling like she was with a stranger, and when Sharon, his sister, visited the New York set in the East Village, she burst into tears because she couldn't recognise him, and thought she had somehow lost her brother. 'The only way you'd know it was me was that I bounced when I walked,' Lenny said.

There was, of course, supposed to be a serious message about racism implicit in the film. At one point, Miles tells his girlfriend, 'I've learnt some really important lessons from all this stuff we've been going through ... There's black, there's white and there's meaningful shades of grey.' At the beginning, he is told by a playwright that he is 'not black enough. You need to be more Afro-American, more Harlem-esque. Miles, feel your roots, get down with your bad self.' To which Henry replies, 'I'd love to get down with my bad self, Mr Grunfeld, but black people don't talk like that any more.' Lenny was tutored in the variety of American accents he employs in the film by Richard Ericson, who had coached Sir John Gielgud. He was also taught to rid his walk of its characteristic, jaunty Buffery Park bounce. So effective did a combination of Lenny's uncanny imitative gift and a team of Hollywood specialist teachers prove, that at a Chicago screening of the finished film, someone asked Lenny, 'How much did the white guy get paid?'

One of the many requirements of Lenny in *True Identity* was for him to do, as the climax of the film, a soliloquy from *Othello*, and, what was more, to do it absolutely straight, albeit in an American accent and wearing body armour (as he was expecting to be assassinated by the Mob while declaiming). He did not at least, for obvious reasons, need to wear his white-man disguise for the *Othello* sequence. Lenny worked on Shakespeare every day for three months to train for the scene, but, true to their capricious form, the studio did not tell him which passage he should be revising for until a week before – a replay for Lenny of his English Lit. O-Level of six years earlier. There was a sense from Disney that they assumed, because their star was English, he would be genetically programmed with the entire works of Shakespeare, and that doing it in an American accent should be no sweat. In fact, he was very nervous about it, convinced he would forget himself and lapse into a Dudley accent in the middle of his big, climactic scene.

Both Dawn and Lenny had an inkling that the film would bomb when they returned to England in January 1991. She assured Lenny that the film, and more especially his performance in it, was good, but said publicly that the Americans had 'not yet fully tapped into her husband's strengths as a performer'. He told a journalist who asked how he thought *True Identity* would do, 'Could be a blockbuster, could be in the video shops next week. We'll have to wait and see.' Privately, Lenny was more certain than ever that his future lay in projects where he had control over his material – even though at that stage, he was aware that he was contracted to do a further two Disney films.

Promoting the film, Lenny flew from venue to venue and did as many as twenty interviews a day. He made a promotional film, *Lenny in Hollywood*, which involved a lot of joking about him having a star on the sidewalk (in fact, his fake one was obscuring Julie Andrews' real one). He was said to have been inundated with further film offers, including one co-starring Harrison Ford, but pointed out that he was still under contract until 1993. The vibe again was good, and when the reviews turned out to be average for the film, but excellent for him, it really seemed that there was a new star in the Hollywood firmament.

The story that *True Identity* failed is obviously true, in the sense that nobody went to see it and Lenny was dropped from the contract in June 1992, nine months after the film's opening date. For the purpose of historical accuracy, however, it is worth noting that the reviews for Lenny himself were not at all bad, and that in the interviews he did with American journalists, he made a very good impression. The way Lenny presented himself in a different setting, and how the Americans reacted to a British black man, were fascinating.

The Los Angeles *Times* ran their interview prominently a fortnight before the launch. 'The idea of racial transformation is not new to the movies,' Karen Grigsby Bates, a black writer, started her authoritative piece. 'In the '40s and '50s, "Pinky" and "Imitation of Life" explored the myth of the Tragic Mulatto, and in director Melvin Van Peebles' 1970 "Watermelon Man," Godfrey Cambridge starts the movie in whiteface, but awakens one day to discover he's black. He begins to realize, with painful rapidity, that the world treats him differently.

' "True Identity," ' it continued, 'taps the same metaphoric vein ... "Putting on your professional face, I think that's what blacks do when they go out into the world of business – particularly in the media," Henry says. The tall actor furrows his brow for a moment. "I know there's another film, 'Living Large' (directed by Michael Schultz), that addresses this, where the black guy becomes a newscaster, and finds himself becoming more and more Caucasian as he goes along. I think that's a legitimate fact. Black people do kind of transform themselves when they're going out into the wide world, where they have to come into contact with white people on a daily basis."

'In fact, that's not so very different from life in Great Britain, Henry acknowledges. "You know, there's that thing they tell you when you're little: 'If you're black, you've got to prove you're twice as good as the white guy just to be accepted as usual' ... didn't your parents say that to you here?" Whenever he heard that admonition, Henry says, "I always wanted to say, 'Why?' Just let me try to be twice as good as I am, and maybe they'll accept me." ' Lenny ended the interview saying he would 'love to do another U.S. feature.' 'For now,' the writer concluded, 'it's enough that people are beginning to recognize him on the street from "The Lenny Henry Show." '

In the LA *Daily News*, the film writer Bob Strauss started, 'It's unlikely enough for a black man to become one of England's most successful comedians. Now, Lenny Henry has to convince American audiences that he's from Harlem – and in whiteface, no less.' Strauss made note of Lenny's 'melodious, Midlands accent' (a first for Dudley, this description of the local intonation) and how he had adjusted to Hollywood.

' "It was just like the movies," said Henry, a tall, friendly sort in a white cotton shirt with the word "freedom" embossed across it. "But bigger, more intense and just very exciting. It was work, but it was fun. A real stretch. What I'm most proud of is the sustainment of Miles Pope. That was always going to be the hardest thing, convincing American audiences that this guy is a young, living, breathing black New Yorker, who's a theatrical actor. That was the challenge. I didn't want brothers saying, 'Wait a second! I'd never say that like that!' I wanted them to believe that Miles was cool, that he was down." '

Susan Wloszczyna in *USA Today* wrote, 'Already dubbed the British Eddie Murphy, Henry doesn't need to be compared to anyone. He is a limo-sized talent.' John Anderson, in New York *Newsday*, said 'Henry displays a large talent for mimicry,' and Harry Haun, of the New York *Daily News*: 'Henry doesn't miss a beat.'

In the more provincial cities, the response to Lenny and *True Identity* was the same. '"TRUE IDENTITY" TOO CONTRIVED TO WORK,' pronounced the Kentucky *Post*. 'British comedian Lenny Henry is a gifted impressionist, and during the course of "True Identity" he gets to impersonate James Brown's brother, a gay realtor and the Italian-American hitman Luchino hires to kill Miles,' the paper said. 'Henry is fine; Andy Breckman's script is not.'

The New Orleans *Times-Picayune*'s movie critic, David Baron, judged *True Identity* was, 'an ingratiating piece of whimsy that introduces a performer well worth getting to know. He's Lenny Henry, a black actor who has built a reputation in England, but is almost unknown on this side of the Atlantic. All that should change after Henry's winning turn in "Identity," a showcase for his versatility as an actor, comedian and mimic ... Henry responds generously to the challenges implicit in the part, even doing a credible scene from "Othello" at the film's climax.'

In England too, reaction was quite good. Shaun Usher in the *Daily Mail* called film 'gossamer-thin but amiable'. 'It's not a disaster, just another of those mildly entertaining very silly pieces offering no pressing reasons for going out and queuing in the rain to see it.' Usher concluded that Henry 'deserves better luck next time.'

There was, however, not to be a next time, not in Hollywood, anyway. A few months before *True Identity*'s release, there had been talk of another film, *Lloyd of London*, about a British police inspector assigned to a case in the States. But neither the American nor the British public, as Usher perceptively forecast, could see any point in going to see it. It was nothing personal; everyone – critics, audiences, Dawn French, Disney, Lenny's friends – agreed that it was a nice film, and Lenny a rather good actor.

In June 1992, Touchstone dropped Lenny Henry, just as he was planning his follow-up film and arranging to rent a house in Los Angeles again. He had already received £1 million for *True Identity*, so the episode had not been completely pointless, but Disney was not obliged to let him make another film. As it was a three-year contract, he was obliged to let the studio know if he had any other ideas over the next couple of years, but they were not waiting on the call. 'A friend of Lenny from his home town' told the *Sunday Mirror*, 'Lenny is devastated. It was his dream to become an international movie star.' A spokesman for the star said, 'He is not planning any more Hollywood films. His new BBC series is still being planned.' Lenny said to Clive Anderson, 'I made a Hollywood film which we won't mention – currently in the bargain bin of your local video shop.'

'It's their loss, really,' he says today. 'Unfinished business, because I'd like to do a brilliant comedy film and have them go mad over it.'

CHAPTER 12

SAVING THE SOUL

'It's what I listen to the whole time, in the car, the bath, wherever.'

Lenny Henry on funk music

To try to understand Lenny Henry without appreciating his love for black music would be to miss one of the dimensions of the man; music for Henry is more than a hobby. It is his strongest tie to blackness. It is what reminded him sharply that he was rooted in a different culture from his predominantly white school friends; he would listen politely to Dylan and Donovan in their bedrooms but, try as he might, it failed to move him as it did them. Later, black music is what deepened up his awareness of his own culture and, to a considerable extent, kept up his morale during the bizarre period when he was the first black Black and White Minstrel, taking part in a show that was, whatever its innocence, deeply racist. Uncomfortable as he was with the Minstrels, knowing that simply by going to the right kind of record shop, or closing out the world and listening to music, he could immerse himself in something a little more respectable was a great comfort.

Today, freed from the restriction of having to fit into anybody else's conception of what makes suitable comedy material, a large section of his stage set dwells on the influence of music on his life; as the *Daily Telegraph* commented recently, 'He celebrates the virtues of funk and other related syncopated rhythms in an autobiographical 10-minute routine that goes back to a childhood being force-fed ska and blue beat.'

The Seventies, in which Henry grew from twelve to twenty-two years of age, was the decade of his musical education. His adolescence was accompanied by a soundtrack that saw two main types of music, disco and funk, dominating the dancefloors. When Lenny started to go to clubs, he was far more interested in the music than skirt-chasing. And he lived through some great – not to mention greatly pastiche-able – movements in popular music, from the kitsch – Travolta strutting to 'Saturday Night Fever' – to the sublime – the golden years of the Godfather of Soul, James Brown. Being young when such stuff was happening was to influence Henry's career, his ambitions, his life, and his living space – his love of music adds up to a record collection of over 3,000 albums and 6,000 singles. Henry's ghettoblaster is a constant companion in the dressing room – it was noted by a journalist that Lenny was playing a Prince tape during an interview on his 1993 tour, and he plays funky music to get him in the mood at photo sessions. He even keeps at home an amazingly tacky stage costume and silver platform boots, as worn by one of his great black musical heroes, George Clinton – and named his cat Aretha after the soul singer, Aretha Franklin.

Lenny's brilliant impersonations of white stars from Elvis Presley to Noddy Holder were a short cut to acceptance by his school friends, and eventually, the show-business world. But musically, Lenny was really in a different place altogether, hunting round Dudley's second-hand record shops for rare singles and albums. He has described how he bought the Stevie Wonder album 'Songs in the Key of Life' in 1975, and treated it with an almost a religious reverence: 'I remember buying it and keeping it in a wrapper for about two weeks because I was so scared to play so great an album.'

The mood of the 1970s was to bring black music almost into the mainstream. But, as with all cultish tastes, it was never so mainstream that a dedicated enthusiast could not have his own, esoteric musical corner of it into which he could secrete bands nobody had ever heard of. The growing plethora of radio stations were playing black music but there was one sound that the white mainstream simply could not fathom – funk. Related to soul, but much, for want of a better word, funkier, it was to become Lenny Henry's favourite music.

Defining funk is not simple. As Lenny told Melvyn Bragg in a 1991 *South Bank Show* called 'Hunting The Funk', in which Bragg let Henry scour the USA for information on his two funk heroes, James Brown and George Clinton (Bragg had originally asked Lenny to do a film about *Marvel* comics but had been persuaded that funk was a better subject), funk is 'about sex, clothes, language, attitude – what you people call "lifestyle".'

James Brown, otherwise known as 'The Godfather of Soul', 'The Minister of New New Super Heavy Funk', 'The Ruler of R&B', 'Mr Dynamite' and 'Mr Superbad', was raised in a Georgia brothel. Whereas the likes of Nat King Cole brought black sophistication to crooning the likes of 'Unforgettable', Brown developed R&B to a more raw, sweaty, sound, punctuated by grunts and yelps. As early as the end of the 1950s, he was packing them in at the legendary Apollo in Harlem with his band, The Famous Flames, earning $12,000 per night, selling millions of records and being mobbed in the street. But white Americans other than those employed in the record industry were oblivious to him.

The late 1960s saw Brown making sure no one could ignore him. While in Britain a band called Blue Mink were calling in their lyrics for racial integration with their no. 2 hit 'Melting Pot' ('... all we need is a great big melting pot ... take a pinch of white man, wrap it up in black skin, add a touch of Red Indian Boy ...'), in America, with Martin Luther King still on the march in the South, Brown was producing songs with titles like 'Black and Proud'. And, by the time, Lenny Henry was old enough to get into Dudley discos, James Brown was established in Britain, and inspiring the young blacks with his success.

Brown was still, perhaps oddly, a great American patriot, described by a journalist, Nelson George, in Lenny's film on the *South Bank Show* as having a Booker T Washington philosophy – a 'pull yourself up by your capitalist bootstrings' ethos. This ended with the spectacle of Brown endorsing Richard Nixon and visiting the troops in Vietnam. James Brown was also notorious for his stringent managerial methods, regularly firing members of his band for being late, or missing just one note in recording sessions.

But while Brown may have personally been the embodiment of a poor boy made rich fairytale, the music, funk, was not embraced by the youthful population as a whole. Though the pay-off from Brown's success was the American ideal – money and political power – Brown's persona and his sound stood for uncompromising blackness; it was bloodstream rather than mainstream music, with more than a touch of gospel in it. It was also overtly sexy; a 1970 James Brown single was called, 'Get Up I Feel Like Being A Sex Machine'. 'It's like speaking in tongues,' one aficionado has said of funk. 'Those who have ears hear and those who don't, get funked up.'

To the young Lenny Henry in Dudley, Brown's sound and sexed-up strutting performance raised both the temperature on the dance floor and his consciousness. As the black writer Lloyd Bradley, who used to write Lenny's Delbert Wilkins monologues, has said, 'A vital part of the function of soul music (and the similar black expressions that preceded it) is as a saviour of self-esteem within its own community.' Lenny could hardly have imagined that within not many years he would meet and become friendly with Brown and his other heroes, George Clinton, and MC Hammer.

George Clinton made Brown look and sound relatively establishment. Clinton's brand of funk was termed P-funk, the P standing for pure. 'Clinton has been a great influence on me, proving that you can combine funk with comedy,' Lenny has said. Clinton certainly knew how to jazz up a stage act – in fact, he filled it so full, you could barely see the stage. His band looked as if they had just been to a futuristic bring and buy sale. His crew included a few key members of James Brown's former musicians who, fed up with his autocratic regime, or fired, went to join Clinton in the mid-Seventies. This was the look of the band, as described by Lloyd Bradley, in his book *Soul on CD*: 'The lead guitarist is wearing a nappy, the keyboard player's just brought his mum on stage to take a bow, a man in a pimp suit and long rubber nose is skulking in the corner of the stage, and in a few minutes a middle-aged black man wearing a three-foot blond wig and a white fur coat and sunglasses will step out of a space ship and shine an enormous torch on us. It's a bit like trying to explain smoke to someone who's never seen it.'

Naturally P-Funk had its own terminology, easily learnt because the key to it was simply using the funk prefix, so followers of the funk army would refer to Funkcentral, Funkativity, Funkmobile. They also termed the followers of funk 'Maggots', and Clinton called himself Maggot Overlord. To teenagers like Lenny (and anyone else with a sense of the theatrical) it was another world, and a perfect example of stage performance. One Clinton lyric sums up the attitude of funk fans brilliantly: 'Free your mind and your ass will follow.'

Musicians kept on joining Clinton throughout the Seventies until, by the end of the decade, Clinton was touring with around seventy singers and musicians who would wander on and off stage, seemingly as the fancy took them. The definitive album by Clinton and his band Parliament, which was released in 1975, was called The Mothership Connection; its theme was the band envisaging themselves as aliens and hi-jacking the airwaves to bring P-Funk to the world. The title track of his 1978 record, 'One Nation Under A Groove', was one of Lenny's *Desert Island Discs* choices in 1989.

Meeting his funk icons for his *South Bank Show* film sparked in Lenny his old ambitions to be a singer. As far back as 1985, on an Easter Channel 4 live special, he sang a verse with the Style Council, fronted by Paul Weller. (The *Guardian* wrote that Henry's performance, 'would have done credit to Luther Vandross'.) In 1991, sixteen years after recording 'Boiled Beef and Carrots', he signed up with Island Records and recorded his first track with James Brown's backing band, the J.B. Allstars. This he described as, 'one of the greatest experiences of my life'. A few months before being signed, Lenny appeared on *Tonight* with Jonathan Ross, singing a song called 'A Little Bit of Love', backed by J.B. Horns, who used to work with Brown.

Dressed in a black leather jacket and trousers which made his bottom look enormous, Lenny's voice was much lighter than might be expected, and not terribly powerful or exciting. It begged the question of whether Ross, as his show's style dictates, was almost letting Lenny make a fool of himself. Lenny had recently performed as Theophilus in a duet with Tom Jones, on Comic Relief 1991. ('Tom Jones was brilliant. It was like he had a primal energy, this great force. It was like trying to catch lightning in a bucket.') Lenny explained to Jonathan Ross: 'I remember saying to you a few years ago on the *Last Resort* that I wanted to sing, and it's difficult to be taken seriously if you're a comedian in this country.'

He went on: 'You can do a crap cover version and it gets in the charts – but to do anything with any integrity, you've got to work with the right people and the right songwriter, and over the past few years I've been trying to find songs that I like, and also trying to find people who I like writing with, and eventually I'll do something.' Meanwhile, when it started up in 1992, Lenny became chairman of the London music radio station, KISS FM, which is renowned as a platform for black music.

Many of Henry's musical heroes come from the Seventies funk era, but, as his *Desert Island Discs* choice showed, his tastes are eclectic. The first thing he remembers wanting to be at the age of eight was a Beatle. And his appreciation of music is heartfelt; he melts at the most melancholy songs. 'Oh God, just scoop me out of that bucket,' he said after playing 'Company' by Rickie Lee Jones (a white singer) on *Desert Island Discs*. 'I used to put this on and get incredibly . . . sad just because she's got such a brilliant voice, a very plaintive voice. And it's still my favourite album, the first album.'

Lenny only really got into black music when he was fifteen, and started having a relatively large amount of cash in his pocket, earned by his early gigs at venues like the ballroom at Dudley Zoo. And once he discovered black music, he still kept an open mind, buying a wide range of different kinds. Alongside funk, he also has a soft spot for Gladys Knight and the Pips, especially their song, 'Midnight Train to Georgia' ('I loved the Pips because it seemed to me they had the easiest job in the world,' he says), and Stevie Wonder, whose soppy hit, 'I Just Called To Say I Love You' he picked as the record he would most like to take with him on his desert island. (This was, of course, the song he used to sing down the phone to woo Dawn when they were apart, he in Blackpool doing summer season with David Copperfield, she in London working on the alternative comedy scene.) He is less keen on rap, the musical form that, as musicians often say, accidentally lost its initial 'c'. Lenny has confessed that he, too, wonders what rap lyrics mean; 'I'm a black man and I don't know,' he says.

Discussing Stevie Wonder, Lenny explained, 'He's a brilliant artist, and the fact that he doesn't have his sight and can see things so clearly in his lyrics and the way he performs his music is brilliant. He's also a very funny person. I've met him and he's hilarious ... He's got a wicked sense of humour ... I went to see him at Wembley and some friends of mine said, "Do you want to meet him?" So I went backstage, and he touched my hair and said: "Hey man, your hair's nappy." And I thought thanks a lot. He was really nice, though, very funny, always cracking gags.' (Lenny was not quite sure what nappy meant in this context, but was far too polite to ask. It actually means 'fuzzy' or 'downy'.)

Henry's passion for music has also contributed to his characterisations and career choices. Delbert Wilkins and Theophilus P. Wildebeeste were both direct descendants of his musical knowledge, Delbert of funk, Wildebeeste of soul. One of the cleverest aspects of these characters was that, by their creator knowing music intimately, they were lent an extra measure of authenticity. Their wicked accuracy made them funnier than had Lenny simply been posing and swaggering for the sake of it. However; when Theophilus strutted his stuff in leather trousers, the effect was not so much reminiscent of Prince, whom Lenny describes as 'a penis on heels,' or even of the tubbier Barry White, but of a sausage straining to split its skin.

By keeping his finger on the pulse, Henry has also been able to characterise the ever-changing men of the moment in music. His range includes takeoffs of Michael Jackson and the dance steps of the rapper MC Hammer (now known as just Hammer), whose voluminous trousers in Lenny's parody seemed to have a life of their own. Lenny's musical taste also seems to have influenced his wife, who with Jennifer Saunders once did a parody of the band Public Enemy, one of whose members, Flavor Flav, is renowned for wearing clocks round his neck.

But even though Lenny keeps track of new music, that pop-music's-passing-me-by feeling that comes to us all in the end, started to affect him eventually. At thirty-four, he admitted that he felt like an old man when he watched *Top of the Pops*. 'Whatever,' he complained, 'happened to songwriting?'

CHAPTER 13

COMIC RELIEF

'I'm not out to be Crusading Len. But I can communicate and I
can make people laugh a bit.'

Lenny Henry on his charity work

The first Comic Relief Red Nose Day was held on 5 February 1988,
a six-hour telethon in which Lenny played alongside the likes of Griff
Rhys Jones, Ben Elton, Cannon and Ball (Lenny's path crossing with
the duo once again, but this time with him as the star), Ronnie Corbett
and Roland Rat. Oxfam was to receive forty per cent of the proceeds
for famine relief in the Sudan, Save the Children forty per cent for
Ethiopia, while twenty per cent was to go to home charity projects for
the homeless, disabled and ex-drink and drug addicts. The money was
harvested in by 2,500 volunteers on 400 telephone lines.

The awesome money-raising power of comedy combined with
compassion had been foreshadowed ahead of the show; stunts such as
the 1985 release of a single of Cliff – now Sir Cliff – Richard and The
Young Ones singing 'Livin' Doll' and a Holborn Great Investment
Race (for City types) in 1986 had raised £250,000 and £809,000
respectively. In 1988, Comic Relief collected £2 million before the
TV special began. Lenny, extraordinarily motivated by his trip to
Ethiopia and having first-hand knowledge from that of the real benefits
money could bring to the desperate people he had seen, spent the
weeks leading up to Red Nose Day working long, tiring days publicising

the cause. He would eat in his car as he went from meeting to meeting, and get home exhausted to relax, grumpily, he admits, in front of the video. By March 1988, he had helped raise more than £13 million; the total for 1988 was £15 million. Comic Relief has since consistently raised around £20 million (and as much as £27 million) a year.

On top of official Comic Relief projects, Henry was also putting his own money into helping the poor in Africa. He has personally financed a ten-year water and agriculture project in Burkina Faso, having seen how a well, dug in twenty-four hours with the right equipment, can give 10,000 people clean water for life. As just one other instance of him putting his hand in his own pocket, he dedicated the proceeds of the première of *Lenny Henry Live and Unleashed*, at the Odeon Haymarket, to the charity. 'Brilliant isn't it?' he chuckled in a 1989 interview, 'knowing that one individual in this country can help alleviate the sufferings of another human being halfway across the world.' (He was referring not to himself, but to any individual who gave to Comic Relief.)

He has become progressively more serious about third world issues. In 1993, he wrote a long letter to *The Times*, very politely asking the Government not to cut Britain's overseas aid budget: 'When there's an earthquake in San Francisco 70 people die – when there's an earthquake in India, 30,000 people die. When there's a drought in Ethiopia, half a million people die – when there's a drought in Britain, it's our roses,' he argued. 'Of course we at Comic Relief, and the millions who support us, aren't politicians – we don't have to face the Treasury's tough choices. But, readers of *The Times*, if you bump into Ken Clarke, or find yourself sitting next to Michael Portillo in the canteen, please pass this message on – "Don't Cut Foreign Aid." '

Henry is no fool, and was perfectly aware that, like Bob Geldof, he and his comedy friends could be accused of vainly using charity to keep themselves in the public eye, of developing an unbecoming earnestness and all the slurs often heaped on performers who try to spread some of their wealth around. 'I'm not too good to be true,' he insists. 'I know that people look at things like Comic Relief and say, "Oh, he's doing it for a reason." I want to help, and because I'm on the telly, people will listen to me more than they will to a guy in a safari suit.

'Time and talent are what performers have to give. I don't want to sound too worthy, but if, because of who I am, people will listen to me, I might as well go ahead and use it to help those who can benefit. That's why charity work is so easy to do. I might be involved in films, television and music but you can't keep it all to yourself ... I don't think there is anything unusual in wanting to help people who are hurting. If you saw someone in trouble on the other side of the street, you would go over and help. Most people would, anyway. Maybe it's because of my own good fortune that I want to help.

'It would be very arrogant to say a TV programme about a chef could stop a riot,' he willingly concedes, but adds, 'People look down on show business as something that can't influence, but Comic Relief has raised about £92 million in the past ten years so obviously comedy, if used correctly, can be useful.'

While it became fairly plain from 1975 onwards that Lenny Henry was going to go into show business – the only area of doubt being just how big he would make it – a betting man would have got longer odds on the clown of Blue Coat secondary modern school becoming by his early thirties an old Africa hand who would get a letter on overseas aid published in *The Times*.

He was, by his third trip in 1991, an experienced traveller in different parts of Africa. In that year, he went to Burkina Faso (previously Upper Volta), the second poorest country in the world, with a *Daily Mirror* photographer, Kenny Lennox, in the small party to take photos for his newspaper and Comic Relief. The *Mirror* had been very keen on supporting Comic Relief, but Lennox, a renowned and widely travelled photographer, had not met Henry previously. Lennox had been warned by the TV crew with the star that Lenny did not care for press people these days, having had 'a bad experience with a tabloid journalist.' The Scottish photographer therefore made a thoughtful decision to steer as clear as was possible of Lenny – not easy when you are together in a Landrover heading into one of the most remote inhabited desert regions in the world.

'When we first got to Ouagadougou, the capital, Lenny was virtually invisible,' Lennox recalls. 'He spent the first twenty-four hours on the phone, and then we set off on a convoy up to a place called Gorom Gorom, which is on the edge of the Sahara Desert. Lenny was on his own, virtually. He had no agent with him – just the TV crew and a producer.'

Travelling over roads that were like corrugated iron, the driving was exhausting, and about seven hours were all anyone could stand. The party would stop at filthy truckstops and sleep outdoors. 'It was becoming difficult not to speak to Lenny,' says Lennox. 'I shook hands with him on the second day and he was polite, a bit distant. Then that night, we got to this truck stop, and as we lay in our sleeping bags, or on top of them, in the compound in the middle of the night, Lenny started to tell stories.

'I don't remember the words, but he had to get up and wander around to tell them, and we were in tears laughing with this guy who we could vaguely see when he cut the stars out, lunging around and waving his hands about. He was very funny, but he was like a caged animal. He is a very big man and he was charging up and down in this compound with just a sand and muck floor. Other people would chip in, and we all sort of added little bits. I told a couple of fairly dodgy yarns about being on trips with various personalities and so on, and he would turn the story into a production. You know if you are in school and you are up in the dorm late at night and someone tells a story, then someone else enlarges upon it and goes on and on. Well, he was doing that to his own stories. He was virtually building his own script.

'He wasn't exactly competitive, but nobody could top him because he had this sense of the surreal. He wasn't being silly in any way, but just hugely entertaining and funny. It was like he couldn't catch up with his mouth because there was so much happening inside him that he couldn't get it out fast enough. We didn't get to sleep until about three in the morning.

'The next day, we trundled on a bit, and when we stopped, he said to me, "When are you going to talk to me?" and I said, "Whenever you feel like it." He said he wondered why I was standing back, and didn't I want to take photographs? I said, well yes, but I don't want to be snooping around taking photographs. I want you to feel comfortable with me. He said that he knew some of my history and he had spoken to Bob Geldof, who said I was all right. Which was a little odd, as a matter of fact because Geldof had called me "a cunt" in his biography. I said to Lenny that it was reassuring he was now recommending me, and I hope he hadn't read the book.

'One of the most amazing things that we saw was the reaction of these little kids in the villages to Lenny Henry,' Lennox continues. 'They had never seen a black man like him. He is physically huge, and he has this huge all-encompassing personality that made kids flock to him like he was the Pied Piper of Hamlin. They had seen white men who were gregarious and noisy and commanded attention but they had never seen village elders or chiefs of the local villages who had anything like the presence that this man had. Now normally, as a photographer, kids in places like that are fascinated by you. But when I was with Lenny, I was completely ignored. He totally consumed them. Neither could understand a word the other was saying, but he didn't need words. He made jungle noises like he does on his shows, and funny faces. He just encompassed them in his arms. He could pick up five of them at a time – these are skinny little runt kids who weigh about twenty-five pounds a piece. He sat in on an English lesson, sitting at a tiny kiddies' desk, that he couldn't fit in behind. He was wearing big baggy trousers and an odd sort of hat like a pork pie and a red T-shirt, and the kids were so small and so skinny that the red noses wouldn't stay on their faces.

'Even when he was totally serious, the kids were fascinated by him. All he had to do was speak Brummy and they would laugh. If we find him fascinating and larger than life, can you imagine how these children found a black man with a squad of white men – and him the centre of attraction.'

One of the cheap but effective medical treatments for diarrhoea – the greatest killer in these parts – are rehydrants, a simple salt and sugar solution in water, that can mean the difference between life and death for malnourished children. 'There was a funny scene where Lenny was in a classroom in the middle of nowhere with this little kid, this urchin weighing half a bag of rice, beside him,' Lennox says. 'They had both had glasses in front of them. Now, for you and I this stuff is disgusting. The cameraman had to film him talking about rehydrant and saying, "If you donate only 6p you can save one child's life and this is what it is; one spoonful of sugar, two spoonfuls of salt into the glass stir it round." Then he had to drink it down and turn to this kid who was looking at him and encourage the kid to drink his.

'Well, as usual it took five or six takes, but he never blanched at this and he continued to drink it. But in between takes, he had one bugger of a struggle to keep this stuff down. The kid beside him was the only reason that he did. Every now and then, Lenny would say, "OK, great how does that look?" and the cameraman would say, "I'm sorry but as you did that, one of the teachers popped her head round the door." The kids would walk for two hours pre-dawn to get to the school, and this sort of thing impressed Lenny terribly.

'But he was also a very serious man. He would absorb what was going on – he wasn't just flip all the time. He is this manic personality who is obsessively funny, but at the end of each day, I would sit there and talk to him, and he would give me his impressions of what he had seen. He had been deeply affected by this village chief who had said that God would decide if they were going to get any water in this dam and God would decide if they were going to survive. They had been building a village earth dam for three years, and during this time there had been no water.

'When he was asked what he wanted in life, he said you don't ask for things like that because God will decide, and this really hit home to Lenny, the humility of that. He said that that had brought him close to tears on that occasion.

'We got to this clinic at Gorom Gorom, just a mud and lath building. It was devoid of anything that made it look like a hospital. I think the staff had given up and legged it because there hadn't been any supplies for months and months. But they still called it the hospital, and the locals were very proud of it. The equipment on what you might call the ward consisted of one iron bedstead and a weighing device for babies. The main medical room had a bed and a chunk of wood about six foot high with little feet on it that kept it upright. That was what they used to hang their IV bottles from, and the walls were covered in blood, from people squeezing syringes and just letting it run on the walls. It was just like a slaughter house. Lenny walked into this room. It was very dark, and he looked at this and you could just see his shoulders dropping and his face became utterly bleak. I took a photograph of him; I didn't say I was taking it, I just took it. By this stage, I was taking photographs and he had forgotten about me.

'He also witnessed a baby hanging up from this weighing machine, and it looks like a new born child, but is actually two and a half years old. The reason you can tell it is that old is that it is crying, and it has got a full set of teeth. Lenny said nothing in the hospital. He just looked at that and absorbed it. The Lenny Henry that is full of bounce and noise and fun and opinions was silent. He sat, perched on the edge of this iron bedstead looking at this wooden thing and the walls all splashed with blood.'

The practicalities of life in Africa affected Lenny as much as the rest of the party, meanwhile. 'We all got terrible shits, by the way,' says Lennox. 'Every half hour, one of us had to get out and disappear. Up there, there are no bushes so everything is very public and you just sort of wander off with a spade across the hill and you get 100 yards away and you just squat and dig. This included Lenny. He didn't complain – he is too smart a man to do that, he is a highly intelligent man who didn't at any stage tell us that he was a big showbiz personality, except in a fun sense. He's a very, very nice bloke.

'Recently, I was asked by the British Journal Of Photography what I thought was my best photo and it upset them terribly because they wanted me to give them the photo of Margaret Thatcher leaving Downing Street in tears, and I didn't reckon it was my best by a long chalk. The one I reckoned I was the best was Lenny Henry in that hospital in Gorom Gorom, with this expression on his face of having reached the level where he'd seen what he reckoned is the lowest point of the whole trip, and how it got to him.'

CHAPTER 14

TO BE CONTINUED

'I tried in the past to please too many people, and there was a time when I was in danger of spreading myself too thin, but you learn.'

Lenny Henry in 1994

In February 1995, twenty years after his debut appearance on *New Faces* – the bus to the Birmingham audition, the bow tie, the advice to talk to the camera as if it were a box of groceries (whatever that had meant) still relatively recent memories – Lenny Henry did a run of shows at the Riverside Studios Theatre in Hammersmith. The title of the set was 'Raw Material', and he was indeed trying out some new stand-up routines prior to recording a BBC TV series. The fact that it seemed natural to him to do this semi-experimental gig at a cool, fashionable, arty venue in west London's media gulch, rather than in Birmingham, or Swindon, to gauge the reaction of the bulk of popular television viewers, or even, for convenience, in Reading, at the closest theatre to his home, says a lot about how your horizons change in a couple of busy decades.

Any suspicion that Lenny's career had gone a bit flat, that he had calmed down into his mid-thirties more as if it were his mid-forties (what with family life, letters to *The Times*, the country house, the chauffeur-driven Jag, the company of his own and the rest of it) was quickly dispelled. Or so it seemed, once he was stripped of all the accessories and there with a large, intelligent, impatient live audience waiting on a wet winter's night to be entertained. He was exceptionally good.

The Riverside is the kind of venue where trendy Londoners come to catch experimental theatre, obscure art-house movies and spend the interval sipping their cappuccinos and chilli-flavoured vodka. The audience for Lenny was a mixture of such Riverside regulars plus the very occasional black person from south and east London, plus Dawn, wearing dark clothes. Lenny introduced himself from off stage as 'Mr Showbiz Himself', urging the audience to 'give it up' – i.e. to clap loudly. After apologies for the half an hour late start on this particular night, which Lenny seemed to be genuinely sympathetic about, he advised all those who were annoyed to spank him very hard.

The set, in suitably experimental theatre style, was for a different show, the on-going play which Lenny's show had supplanted for the night, *Hancock's Last Half Hour*. The stage contained all the elements of a tatty flat – a bed, fridge, wardrobe, telephone and general tat like a stuffed moose head, all of which somehow seemed to fit in to the extempore nature of the gig. Lenny's warm-up routine was an audience/comic ice-breaker, Lenny's own stylised version of the Mexican wave.

When a Barbadian lady in the audience piped up to ask what Lenny had between his legs (he was gripping his mike whilst drinking water), he recognised her comic potential and led her round the set introducing her to 'his' room. Although there was the obvious comic exploitation there (he said her spangly jumper would make her a good sparkly ball at a disco) there was also something very gentle there, a chance, in a way, to make a fuss of a 'sister' in a room full of white people. 'Are there any black people in the house?' Lenny asked, surveying the theatre, then adding with a smile, 'Good about four . . .'

Lenny was obviously nervous, and strangely and endearingly vulnerable. He made jokes about fellow black personalities – Chris Eubank, Bruno, Trevor MacDonald etc. – but never really to their detriment. The PC idea that jokes can't be made about ethnic groups, it seemed, had now been pushed one stage further, to the point where jokes are being made but with a completely different motivation – one of celebration of black stars.

His material was almost entirely autobiographical. 'I started doing the clubs when I was sixteen,' he began. 'They were all called things like the Talk of The North and The Talk of The West. I don't know why because nobody went there to converse. Why not call them The Grope of The North, The Feel of the West, The Snog of East Anglia, because that's what those clubs were about.' It was a kind of wise, knowing, quiet and very sophisticated humour that was a tangible step on from the concentrated energy of *Live and Unleashed* six year earlier; he talked about being a black performer out and about in provincial England in the Seventies; 'Can you imagine me in a club in Somerset in 1975? They didn't watch, they stared. I shouldn't have played the clubs in Somerset I should have played the museums.'

Lenny was mature, affectionate, clever and funny; it would have been obvious even to someone who had not kept track of Lenny's life that things had changed fundamentally, not just in the twenty years since *New Faces*, but very recently. As indeed, they had.

Lenny and Dawn's adoption in 1992 of a mixed-race baby, whom they named Billie, became, for reasons never quite clear, an enormous media event. Kept deeply secret for reasons that appeared at the time vain and 'luvvie'-ish in the extreme (although there was actually a perfectly good explanation for the furtiveness over the adoption), the effect when the egregious *Hello!* magazine broke the story on its front cover was close to a tabloid sensation.

Lenny and Dawn had decided in March 1991 to adopt, and Billie was two months old when she came to her new home in September. They underwent nearly forty hours of probing questioning by social workers, who needed to establish whether, as show-business per-sonalities, they perhaps led too wild a life to be adoptive parents. The social workers also interviewed Jennifer Saunders as part of their inquiry. For six months after the adoption – up to the point when Billie was legally adopted – a minder was said by the press to have been hired to check all cars in the lane leading to the Henry house.

The disproportionate attention paid to the adoption was so puzzling that the event, supposed minders and all, almost seemed like a public relations man's contrivance to gain publicity for Lenny and Dawn, which it was not. Well-known show-business stars have children all the time, and the fact that the couple adopted Billie should not have been seen as a major news event. The attempts to keep Billie's existence under wraps, however, paradoxically turned a middling-interest personality driven tabloid story into something which looked like a real story.

Lenny and Dawn's choice of *Hello!* as a vehicle for letting the world know about Billie also goaded the more conventional newspapers. Dawn confessed to being an addict of the magazine, and a lot of show-business people continue to have a soft spot for it, but Fleet Street was collectively irritated. The suburban naffness of *Hello!* was one thing; its virtually fascist theology was another (*Hola!*, *Hello!*'s Spanish parent, was founded to publicise the late Generalissimo Franco's cronies in the most favourable possible light, and continues the same unquestioning, uncritical PR puff tradition with the royal and showbiz celebs of today); Lenny's prickliness towards the press had also got on the newspapers' nerves – what, after all, was little Len of *New Faces* fame doing requesting, as he now did, samples of a journalist's previous work before he would speak to them?; but perhaps worst for the tabloids was the fact that they had missed out on quite a good little story.

Its genesis had been in 1987 when Dawn became godmother to Jennifer Saunders' first daughter Eleanor. 'The time has arrived when we are thinking of starting a family,' Lenny was quoted as saying. 'Married life is fabulous and we want to have a baby. We're still practising. At the moment, I'm still trying to get her dressing gown off, but I'm sure we'll have a baby soon.'

The couple have consistently denied rumours that they had any problem conceiving their own child, explaining that they made a positive choice to adopt at the beginning of their marriage. Lenny's experiences in Africa reinforced his conviction that having a child of your own in the west can be seen as a little selfish. 'When I came back from visiting Ethiopia in 1987, I told Dawn I wanted to adopt a whole orphanage. People are wrong when they say we can't have our own children . . . we don't know we can't,' he told the *Daily Mail*.

With the benefit of hindsight, some journalists claimed the great exclusive in retrospect. A fortnight after the *Hello!* story, *Today* reported that a 'BBC friend' said Lenny nearly let slip about Billie: 'He turned up for a party at the BBC and when the conversation turned towards children he got very excited and started talking about some "news" he might have for everyone soon. We all thought that Dawn was pregnant. He just laughed and waved his arms around and told us his lips were sealed. He was in a terribly good mood.' Neighbours in Berkshire also claimed to have been in on the secret all along, saying they had spotted prams being wheeled in and out of the house.

The *Hello!* spectacular was perfectly informative, and quite revealing, given that the magazine would have published whatever the couple said, even if it had been complete drivel, and still said thank you. We saw the Henrys' house from the inside (pictures of the three of them, pictures of cars, a photo of Neil Kinnock and one of Lenny meeting Nelson Mandela). Dawn parried attempts to find out where Billie had been born or in what circumstances, responding to the obvious thought that she might be from Ethiopia or Romania. She refused to name the adoption agency to protect Billie. 'It wasn't Romania, but maybe it wasn't this country either,' she unhelpfully hinted, suggesting, perhaps, that she was from Britain after all. Even some members of the family, Dawn said, had not been told until the adoption was made legal.

She explained that Billie's first six months with her and Lenny was kept low key because Billie's natural mother might have changed her mind: 'It was tense which is why we kept it very quiet. Maybe we also wanted to get to know her before anybody else did. We wanted some time with her on our own.'

Getting Billie's baby things into the house had required a measure of dissimulation that would have been worthy of Miles Pope in *True Identity*. The nursery had to be prepared in complete secrecy; going shopping on her own for all the baby equipment at once would invite comment; going with Lenny would be impossible. So she went with her best non-show-business friend, who stuffed cushions down her front to appear pregnant. In Mothercare, a kind assistant even sat the 'pregnant' friend down and got her a reviving cuppa; an embarrassed

Dawn thoughtfully apologised in retrospect to the shop girl for the trickery.

Once Billie was home, Dawn was still precluded from wheeling her out in the pram. Friends would take her to the shops to acquaint the baby with the general layout and atmosphere of the world. Even once she was public knowledge, Billie's arrival still had the effect of slowing Lenny and Dawn down. 'Dawn and I were really pushing our careers until she came to us,' Lenny said. 'We were ambitious and career-minded. Now our favourite pursuits are of the family kind.'

They were model parents, talking to Billie all the time, and playing with her endlessly. Lenny, who has jokily called her Little Miss Motivator, started to include glimpses of the joys of parenthood in his comedy material – 'what happened when your kids throw a tantrum in a crowded shop, and when you take them to the playground, why they want to go on a slide twenty-seven times,' as he put it. In 1995, Lenny pulled off the ultimate celebrity dad coup, and published a children's book for three- to seven-year-olds, featuring a little girl called Charlie (a thinly disguised Billie) with a mother who has a remarkable resemblance in the drawings (by Chris Burke) to Dawn French. Called *Charlie and the Big Chill*, it had indeed started out as a bedtime story for Billie, which Burke had seen as perfect for illustration.

Billie's coming on to the scene meant both Lenny and Dawn curbing their workaholic tendency and rushing home to be with her whenever possible. Whereas in the first half of 1987, they spent one full day together in six months, they now avoid evening appointments in so far as they can. More often than not, however, their work schedules would mean only one could be home at a given time. This lifestyle had its tensions, which even the public was made privy to at one time. In September 1993, Lenny was appearing on ITV's *This Morning* show, when a 'Dawn from London' phoned in demanding, 'I want to speak to that handsome man.

'This is the only way I get to see Lenny these days – and jolly nice he looks too,' she said sarcastically. 'Do you fancy a date?' Henry answered cooly. 'What about your birthday in October?' She then said she'd reveal how he steals jokes from other comics if he didn't stick to the date. Henry pretended to try to buy her silence. French: 'Don't call those sexual favours your payments – I want hard cash.' She also inquired: 'What was in the baby's nappy this morning? Was there poo or just wet? . . . Is everything fine at home? Did you feed the cat?' She even discussed what they'd have for dinner that night: 'I expect there'll be pasta again. It's the only thing I can do.'

It was a sweet incident, and Dawn's reference to her cooking became a matter of minor interest as Lenny was already famous as the chef in his comedy series *Chef!* They were both obliged to spill the beans on their kitchen habits. Lenny, it turned out, was the natural cook of the family, the maker of a famous chilli (that Dawn found too hot), cauliflower cheese and spaghetti bolognaise – 'I cooked that for my mum once. She liked it!' he says. Dawn, apparently, could only make vegetable soup and pasta. Dawn's suggestion that she would be cooking pasta the evening of their complicated public joke on *This Morning* did not quite reveal the whole picture, however; 'We've actually got a housekeeper who does the cooking,' he confessed later. 'I've got a kid, a life . . . But if I had more time, I'd love to learn.'

Domestic life, Lenny has often said, is normal and undemanding at his house. 'We've both got irritating habits,' he admits. 'Dawn can't seem to live without the TV being turned on night and day . . . I do tend to spend a lot of my time in the bath reading comics.

'I think Dawn and I live as normal a life as we can: we do the things that other people do, see friends for a drink, go to the supermarket, change light bulbs. The minute you start to assume you're a god or something, you're going to be messed up.'

Apart from cooking when he can, which he still describes as his hobby, Lenny has also become interested in good clothes. His taste in these has often excited the interest of journalists sent to interview him. 'I love trousers,' he enthused in 1988. And it, seemed, he was no dilettante, but a man who really *knew* his trousers. 'These are by Lucy Robinson and the ones I wore on Mandela Day were by Shimel,' he said. 'My suits are by Mr Eddie and my shoes are by Shelley. I have to go to these places because I'm a big bloke and I can't get things off the peg.' Mary Riddell of the *Daily Mirror* described his 'beautifully-cut trousers, suede loafers worn without socks, and a burnt orange silk jacket given to him by his wife.' Henry admitted to Riddell, 'Yes, I am vain. I still break my neck looking at myself in mirrors.' In another interview in 1991, he wore a shirt by Betty Jackson and Italian shoes: ' "I'm not usually Mr Labels," he says, his voice rich and resonant. He used to wear corduroy trousers so massive that he looked like a ship coming down the street. "So huge you couldn't get anybody else on the pavement ... I like to wear clothes that fit." ' Hair-wise, he described what he had as a 'laid-back flat top'. In 1993, his clothes were still fascinating those he met; a *Radio Times* writer described him 'wrapped in fashionably capacious and baggy clothes, with a tiny, brim-up straw hat'.

Lenny's radical politics have not been diverted by success as much as the views of other left-wing people coming close to forty. If anything, he has drifted leftwards over the years; asked by the *Guardian* about his political outlook in 1988, he replied, 'It's fairly obvious isn't it? I don't get invited to parties by the Conservatives any more. I was once invited to a golf dinner with Denis and Margaret. What do you mean did I go? Of course not! You think I turned up and said, "Yeah Maggie, what's going down? This music's useless Maggie. Haven't you got any Public Enemy?" '

'I get a lot of letters from political people who want me to show up,' he said, preaching to the unconverted, in a *Sunday Telegraph* interview the following year. 'It was nice to be asked to do Mandela Day, but a lot of the other stuff just leads you into party politics. I end up thinking, "What's this got to do with me?" I'm just a guy who comes on TV and makes you laugh and says something meaningful every three weeks. That's all.'

In January 1992, Lenny re-emphasised his commitment to politics in the broad, but not the party, sense by leaving the Anti-Nazi League because of a suspicion about its extreme left-wing tendencies – it shared premises with the Socialist Workers' Party. His agent said: 'Lenny no longer wished his name to be used on their list,' adding, 'he never wanted to be actively involved, anyway.'

Chef!, first aired in January 1993, has been Lenny most high-profile

TV series in the Nineties. Henry played Gareth Blackstock, who has a beautiful (black) wife (played by Caroline Lee Johnson) and is chef-patron of Le Château Anglais, a gourmet restaurant in Oxfordshire.

The series was about as bourgeois as a sitcom could be, but was famous for employing several black people in the production crew, thanks to the philosophy of Crucial Films, Lenny's own company, who were co-producers. *Chef!* had a black, female sound recordist, black associate producer, several young black trainees and assistants and a black director of photography, Rimy Adefarasin, who did the lighting for the vogue British film *Truly, Madly, Deeply*. Lenny was sick, as he explained repeatedly, of walking into TV studios and being the only black face on either side of the camera: 'It can be very lonely when you are out there and everyone else, including the audience, is white. I get a bit cheesed off if the only black people I see are my family, and even if there is a black stranger, it's probably a security bloke on his tea-break.'

He even approached the BBC ticket unit, which gets audiences in place for shows that require one. He suggested that it might be sensible to approach organisations other than the British Legion, who tra-ditionally were first in line for tickets. 'It was only when I suggested that my stuff might appeal to people who hang out in social clubs in Brixton and Willesden that anyone thought about the imbalance. It wasn't particularly racist – it just hadn't occurred to anyone before,' he said.

During the planning of *Chef!*, Lenny worked intermittently at L'Or-tolan, John Burton-Race's two-Michelin-starred restaurant outside Reading. 'They gave me this tray of rabbit and said, "Sort that lot out." I had to take the insides out and chop off the little bunny wunny tails.' He was proud of his Roux brothers gigot: 'It's like defusing a bomb. All those instructions and if you get one wrong you'll blow the whole thing up.' He had talent as a cook, with the help of this training, even managing to make a mille-feuille for his family. I'm quite good at eating, too – witness my ever-expanding bottom,' he commented.

The rather stuffy, even middle-aged, idea for *Chef!* came to Henry when he made the not-very-original or strictly accurate observation that, 'Chefs were becoming the new showbiz figures that everyone talked about.' 'It was really tough researching the role. I had to go and eat in all Britain's top restaurants,' he said. 'Marco [Pierre White] said running a restaurant is like running a theatre. You've got to be larger than life otherwise people might as well stay at home and eat a TV dinner straight out of the microwave.'

Gareth Blackstock was a bit of a Marco character in consequence of these arduous research expeditions, an updated Basil Fawlty. (The restaurant/kitchen-based Fawlty Towers episode, 'Basil The Rat', is one of Lenny's all-time favourite sitcoms.) 'Gareth does lose his rag sometimes,' he said. 'He doesn't like people in banks. He doesn't like suits. He doesn't like journalists at all, especially ones who want to know how he met his wife or what his star sign is. He wants them to ask about the food.' Like Basil Fawlty, Gareth would rant at customers too cretinous to enjoy his creations.

The TV critics' reaction to *Chef!* was muted. *Today*'s Pam Francis wrote of the first episode: 'Thirty minutes of him bitching about the quality of the Hollandaise sauce is not my idea of a good time.' Another critic looked at the series differently; 'It may be 1993, but it is still unusual to see a black family portrayed so positively on British television,' judged Steve Clark in the *Independent*, 'But compared with some of Lenny's earlier small-screen roles, isn't *Chef!* perhaps a touch bland?'

Lenny could not see it that way. 'Although he doesn't come on with a Malcolm X reader under his arm, he does have a lot to say about the ways of the world,' he said. 'I think it's pretty spiky. Black people come up to me and say it's great to see black people doing this stuff, standing up to people and not being scared. So the whole thing about "Lenny trying to be Bill Cosby" is nonsense . . .'

Blandness, if it were such, clearly paid off, anyway. During the first series of *Chef!*, Lenny was named BBC Personality of the Year by the Television and Radio Industries Club; Des O'Connor was the simultaneously anointed ITV Personality of the Year. Two months later, Lenny was voted the top role model for teenage boys for the second time in a TSB-sponsored young people's survey; Anita Roddick was the exemplar for teenage girls.

If Lenny's spike was blunted, as some felt, it was revived by a shocking incident of overt, in-your-face racism he suffered on a 1993 trip to Australia. In a taxi with a white female promoter, on the way to a television studio to appear on an afternoon show, the driver pulled up at the television centre and asked, 'Which studio are you in?' Lenny replied, 'We're on the *Midday Show*,' whereupon the driver snapped, 'I'm talking to the lady.' 'Nobody's ever talked to me like that. Not even my mum,' Henry said later. 'My chin hit the floor. And it took all of my dignity and intelligence to get out of the cab and ram a lamp post up the guy's arsehole.' He later found he had to wait half an hour with a black DJ at a radio station before a cab would stop for them.

Back home, Crucial Films, which had been a little chrysalis-like for some years, was starting to fly. Lenny redefined its policy of pursuing black talent in black films. 'I want to make quality programmes, not quality black programmes because that way lies ghettoism,' he insisted. Even today, the company, which has four employees – two black, two white at its Notting Hill Gate offices – professes to have no idea what proportion of its output is by black or ethnic film makers; the majority of its projects to date have involved Henry in some capacity.

Like most film companies, it tends to have far more projects in development than being made, but the list of its completed works is growing; it currently includes *Chef!*, *Funky Black Shorts* (a series of six films for BBC 2, including one submitted by Lenny under the pseudonym Chris McGinty and accepted by the BBC on spec), *The 1995 Lenny Henry Show*, *New Soul Nation*, a film by Lenny on soul music for Channel 4, and another *South Bank Show* by Lenny, this time called 'Darker Than Me', which explored the roots of black American humour. In 'Darker Than Me', Lenny was filmed sheepishly confessing his *Black and White Minstrel* past to a black comic, Paul Mooney, who is Richard Pryor's co-writer. Mooney was understanding. Polly McDonald, Crucial Films' managing director, said, 'It's by a long margin the most serious thing Lenny's ever done. It's a painful and disturbing film.'

For a man who had almost literally done it all before he was thirty, the future poses a problem that perplexes those close to him. Kim

Fuller, who was by his side as a writer through the Eighties and is still a good friend, explains, 'I think it is difficult that he had so much success when he was younger. He is a brilliant stand-up performer and I don't think that comes over on television as much as it should do. He is a phenomenal live performer, but I think, as with all stand-up comedians, they eventually need more than stand-up.

'There is always a critical point in their careers, when they have to decide what they are going to do next. It is either films, or something substantial for television. In America, TV companies understand much more about what performers need; you only have to look at the way in which American TV creates narrative comedy for stand-up comedians from Bill Cosby right through to Ellen. They create a real strong writing team around them, and they develop a narrative vehicle for these people, and that means that they have years and years of interesting work on TV as sitcom performers.

'But in this country, we are very bad at doing that. What Lenny needs is a very strong narrative comedy to shine in, that enables him to do all the things that he does well and to put him up there with *One Foot in the Grave* and all that. If you look at the younger stand-ups, like Jo Brand and Jack Dee, they are fairly limited in what they do. Lenny does *Chef!* but it isn't a big audience puller even though it's good in various ways, and has a lot going for it. But he can do so much more. Another thing I have always thought he should try at some point is a *Saturday Night Live*-type show. He is so good live on Comic Relief he has got a sense of adventure and occasion and I think something like that would really make a mark.

'But in his position, because he has had so much success, there are not many people around who know more than he does. What he needs are people who understand him and who are prepared to come along and say, "Listen, what about this and why don't you do this?" Instead, he comes up with most of his own ideas at the moment and will decide what he wants to do, and then everybody will fall in with it because he is such a charming man. He is very generous, very helpful, very positive about his work and working with people. Over the years, we have done things which have worked and things which haven't worked, but he has just got this enormous energy and optimism – and those are a big thing to have these days.'

Bob Geldof, whose charity career Lenny's has so paralleled, echoes Fuller's thoughts. 'He thinks a lot about things,' Geldof says of Henry. 'He thinks about his position and what he can do with it. The thing is that he's in a unique position as a black Englishman, but he's broken down that fact. He's managed to get away from it. As a bloke he's a lovely man. Every time he's been in my house he's been a very gentle sort of man. He's also a very modest man, and I've seen him in a lot of intimate situations. As for charity work, that's not something that we particularly talk about. I don't bore people to death with what I do – and neither does he.'

The TV show that grew out of Lenny's Riverside Studio gigs early in 1995 was shown on BBC 1 in 1995. As brilliant as the live show was, Fuller's feeling that Lenny does not always come across on TV was borne out. The show drew downbeat reviews, none more so than that of Matthew Norman, the acerbic *Guardian* diarist, who reviewed it the London *Evening Standard*. It was without doubt the most savage critical mauling Lenny had ever received.

'There is a rule of comedy that I've just made up which states the following: A comedian's capacity to be funny is in inverse proportion to his self-confidence. Let us, by way of tribute to that brilliant but most self-detesting of souls, call it Fry's Law,' Norman wrote.

'What Fry's Law means is that the really funny men (Lenny Bruce, Peter Sellers, pre-therapy John Cleese, Spike Milligan, Stephen Fry himself and so on) are always the ones ravaged by self-doubt and disgust; while the really awful ones tend to exhibit an unshakeable belief in their own ability.

'Take Lenny Henry (and to borrow from Max Miller, please do take Lenny Henry). In the fifteen years or so during which he has appeared regularly on television, Mr Henry has done absolutely nothing to suggest that on the very top of his form and armed with several tons of herrings, he could provoke a smile amongst a troupe of performing dolphins: or indeed a laugh among a pack of hyenas, renowned throughout the hyena world for being incurable gigglers.

'And yet in Mr Henry there appears to be no grain of doubt that he is a very great comedian. His performance on Comic Relief (where he not only took centre stage but the wings, the orchestra pit and the first seven rows of the stalls) illustrated to perfection an old Yiddish phrase which translates, "Of all his mother's children, he loves himself the best."

'The saving grace then was that he was diffused by the company. But in *The Lenny Henry Show*, he was alone – and in his solitude unleashed a torrent of such sustained witlessness that it evoked something close to a longing for Russ Abbott. Psychologists report that there is already enough pain and misery in all our lives, so I will avoid quoting any material directly; suffice it that, with a show like this, there comes to a point when the act of taking notes starts to feel like a written request to be sectioned under the Mental Health Act.

'Wearing a three-piece silver suit in crushed velvet, Mr Henry began with a routine that would, were it delivered by a child in Safeways, be put down by shoppers to an attack of Tourettes' Syndrome – an aimless screeching of apparently random sequence of words revealing, at least, that he still believes an exaggerated Birmingham accent to be an automatic rib cracker.'

Norman concluded by wickedly speculating on whether Dawn French, whom he enormously admires, 'watching this cobblers at home with her husband, was able to do for faked laughter what Meg Ryan did for the faked orgasm. Mind you, given Lenny Henry's awesome self-confidence, he probably wouldn't be able to spot the difference.'

How Lenny, an essentially youthful comedian, but one still approaching forty, dealt with such a going over by a young critic with a growing following can only be guessed at. (His amiable manager, Peter Bennett-Jones, who is known in the comedy world as PBJ, was certainly stung by the piece, regarding it as unduly harsh.) But the Norman review raised several issues that are of equal concern to devoted fans of Lenny, as they are to such close friends and associates. Several of these, like Fuller, say that they feel his career needs to be handled with great care if he is to avoid it gracefully petering out like Geldof's.

Every one of Lenny's career turning points over the past twenty years has been just that; a move on to better and funnier things. He has never had the experience of a crash landing; even the Disney film was part of an upwards learning curve. The odd thing about *True Identity* is that the film totally belies its reputation as a turkey; its failure was an unpredictable oddity. It was actually quite a good film, and Lenny's performance in it was faultless, and acknowledged as such by the notoriously demanding American critics. There is an argument that it is only by fluke that Lenny Henry is not today a big Hollywood star; for Tracey Ullman and Billy Connolly to be the only contemporary British alternative comedians to have made it in America suggests that there is a measure of luck involved in the comedy export market.

Failure is not, anyway, something that daunts Henry, so one bad notice may not necessarily bother him. 'Lenny's not afraid to fail,' says Dawn French. 'He's got a great attitude to his career, which is that he'll try anything, and if he can't do it, he's not ashamed. But he can do a lot of things he hasn't even tried.'

One of the problems is his supremacy in the profession. He is respected – and almost feared – by senior executives in television. This is partly because he is black, which, in an industry keener than most on establishing a racial equality, means nobody is keen to cross him. But on top of that, he is accomplished decades beyond his years, and has an entirely unique range of experience to draw on; a Ben Elton can criticise the old, sexist racist comedy, but Lenny Henry has actually performed it. The result of all these attributes is that Lenny is enormously liked by his professional colleagues, from the far right, in political terms, to the left.

'All I'm trying to do,' Lenny says, 'is to try to better myself as a comedian, to make it more organic, to make it more personal, just by nature of being more honest and more truthful on stage. Audiences like stuff if it rings true. The more I can make things ring true, the better I get.

'I don't think I've ever been entirely happy with any performance I've ever done. There have been things where I've said to myself, "Yeah, that's fine, that's OK," but I'm always slightly disappointed ... I'm looking for something that will give really strong job satisfaction, and for me that would be achieving real truth in acting and true lunacy and madness in comedy. There's still plenty I want to do – many, many things.'

Just as when you listen to his Delbert Wilkins character, you may not agree with everything Lenny says, or like everything he does. But you know what he means.